BECOME PART OF THE LEGEND

Dalton
Model 1873,
.45 LC, 5½"

Hardin
1875 Top-Break,
.45 LC, 7"

OUTLAWS & LAWMEN SERIES

The Outlaws & Lawmen series pays homage to the most legendary names in the Wild West. Each piece in this collection is inspired after revolvers actually carried by famous heroes and villains, undying characters in the riveting drama of American history. Stunning to look at, fantastic to shoot, available in limited quantities through your Uberti USA dealer.

Find us on **f** Facebook
Uberti-USA.com

Uberti USA.
HISTORY REPEATS ITSELF

TAYLOR TUNED

GET TUNED
GET TAYLOR'S

THE PERFORMANCE UPGRADE

Taylor Tuned action is a custom upgrade for shooters wanting a stellar performing revolver or rifle right out-of-the-box. Our skilled in-house gunsmiths fine tune 1873 models by hand polishing internal parts and replacing springs. The result is a light consistent trigger pull and a smooth lever-throw or hammer pull. This work is available on any 1873 single action revolver or 1873 lever action rifle.

@TAYLORSFIREARMS   TAYLORSFIREARMS.COM

Mernickle Custom Holsters
Mernickle Holsters
Veteran and Family Owned. US Made
Helping to Create World Champions Since 1975
Artistry in Leather
13043 County Road C, Pampa, TX 79065
Sales@mernickleholsters.com / 800-497-3166 / www.mernickleholsters.com

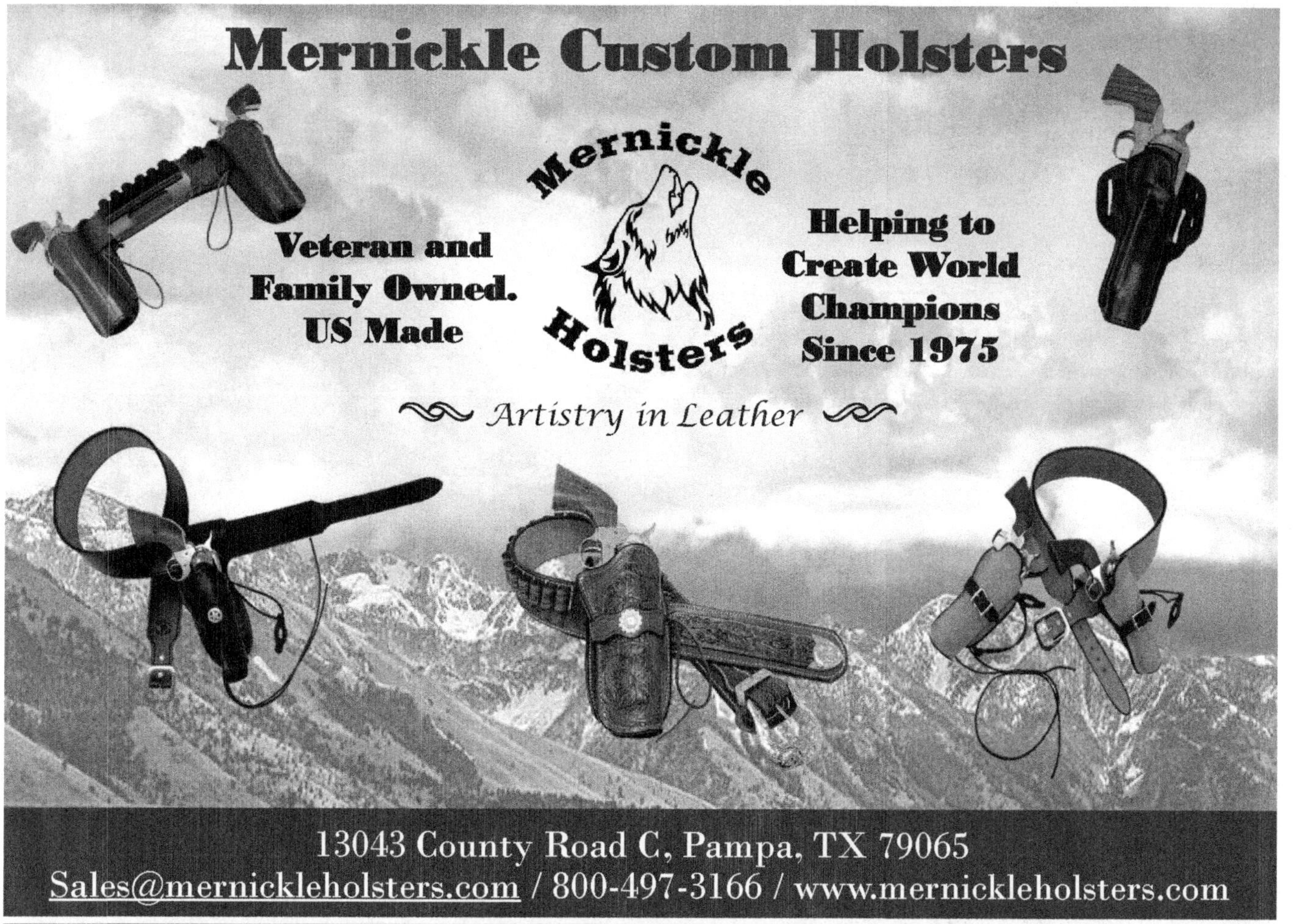

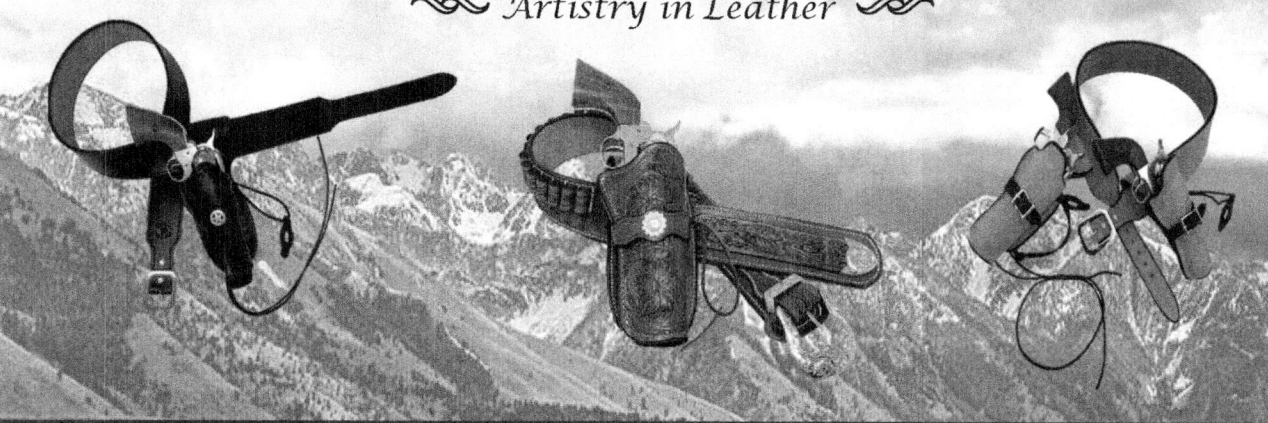

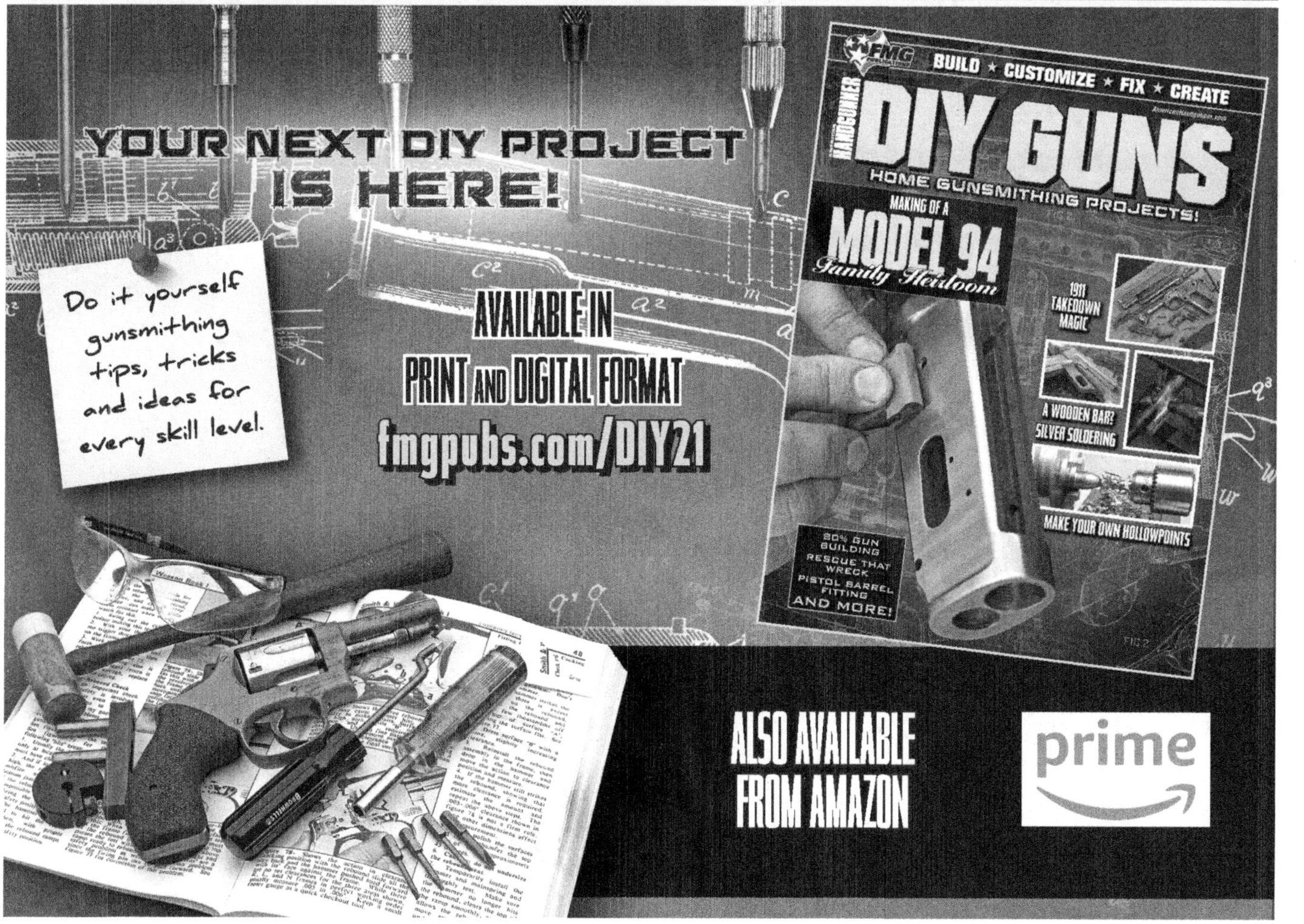
YOUR NEXT DIY PROJECT IS HERE!
Do it yourself gunsmithing tips, tricks and ideas for every skill level.
AVAILABLE IN PRINT AND DIGITAL FORMAT
fmgpubs.com/DIY21
FMG
BUILD ★ CUSTOMIZE ★ FIX ★ CREATE
DIY GUNS
HOME GUNSMITHING PROJECTS!
MAKING OF A MODEL 94 Family Heirloom
1911 TAKEDOWN MAGIC
A WOODEN BAR? SILVER SOLDERING
MAKE YOUR OWN HOLLOWPOINTS
80% GUN BUILDING
RESCUE THAT WRECK
PISTOL BARREL FITTING
AND MORE!
ALSO AVAILABLE FROM AMAZON
prime

GUNS MAGAZINE OLD WEST
HISTORY, GUNS & GEAR
SPECIAL EDITION

FEATURES

8   **BEARS, TEDDY AND FEROCIOUS ...**
THE CURIOUS TALE OF HOLT COLLIER
WILL DABBS, MD

12   **BEST OF THE WEST?**
THE METICULOUS AND OFTEN CUSTOM-ORDERED BULLARD REPEATER
FRANK JARDIM

18   **SLICK ACTIONS**
REAL PISTOL-CALIBER CARBINES HAVE LEVERS!
JOHN TAFFIN

24   **OLD SLABSIDES IN THE WEST**
THE 1911 AS A PEACEMAKER
JEREMY D. CLOUGH

30   **BATTLE FOR SUPREMACY**
THE .44XL AND THE .410 SMALL-BORE SHOTSHELLS
ROGER SMITH

36   **SMOKE, NOISE AND BIG TIME CONCUSSION**
LOADING BLACK POWDER REVOLVER CARTRIDGES
MIKE "DUKE" VENTURINO

40   **JOHN "LIVER-EATING" JOHNSON**
THE CROW-KILLING CANNIBAL
WILL DABBS, MD

44   **HAMMER TIME**
THE SLIP GUN: FAST AND DANGEROUS
FRANK JARDIM

50   **SHOCK, AWE AND LOTS OF SMOKE**
AN INTRODUCTION TO BLACK POWDER SHOOTING
SERENA JUCHNOWSKI

56   **PRICELESS!**
COLT'S LOST SINGLE ACTION ARMYS
GARY PAUL JOHNSTON

60   **RUSTY, PITTED AND PRICELESS**
RESURRECTING A RELIC COLT SINGLE ACTION ARMY
JOHN TAFFIN

64   **A COUNTY HANGING**
WILL MATHIS: CRIME, PUNISHMENT AND A TIDY LOCAL HORROR
WILL DABBS, MD

68   **LOW TECH & FEARSOME**
GERONIMO'S BOW: A FORMIDABLE WEAPON
FRANK JARDIM

72   **POWER THAT SIXGUN**
RELOADING THE .44-40
JOHN TAFFIN

76   **CARBINES, REPEATERS, MUSKETS & REVOLVERS**
GUNS OF THE INDIAN WARS
MIKE "DUKE" VENTURINO

82   **FRONTIER JUSTICE**
THE SECRET VIGILANTES OF MONTANA
ROGER SMITH

86   **HAVE GUN, WILL TRAVEL**
EDWARD "JACK" BRYANT: LIFETIME TEXAS LAWMAN
FRANK JARDIM

92   **DEMYSTIFYING COLT SAA GENERATIONS**
CALIBERS, OPTIONS, SIMILARITIES & DIFFERENCES
MIKE "DUKE" VENTURINO

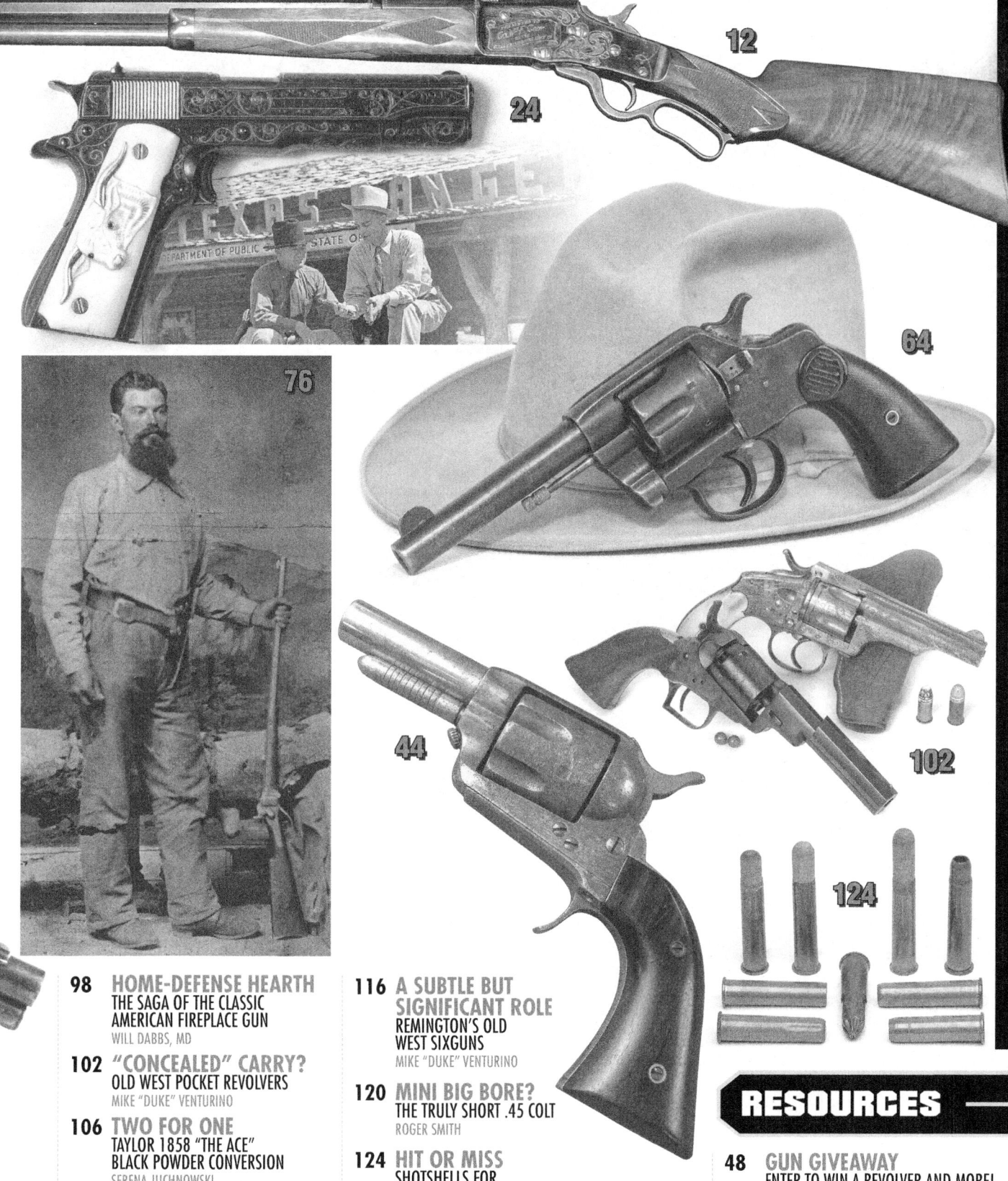

98	**HOME-DEFENSE HEARTH** THE SAGA OF THE CLASSIC AMERICAN FIREPLACE GUN WILL DABBS, MD
102	**"CONCEALED" CARRY?** OLD WEST POCKET REVOLVERS MIKE "DUKE" VENTURINO
106	**TWO FOR ONE** TAYLOR 1858 "THE ACE" BLACK POWDER CONVERSION SERENA JUCHNOWSKI
110	**COMPLICATED OR FUTURISTIC?** STARR MODEL 1858: DOUBLE ACTION FROM ANOTHER PLANET? FRANK JARDIM
116	**A SUBTLE BUT SIGNIFICANT ROLE** REMINGTON'S OLD WEST SIXGUNS MIKE "DUKE" VENTURINO
120	**MINI BIG BORE?** THE TRULY SHORT .45 COLT ROGER SMITH
124	**HIT OR MISS** SHOTSHELLS FOR PISTOLS AND RIFLES ROGER SMITH
128	**FAVORITES** REPLICA SINGLE ACTION SIXGUNS JOHN TAFFIN

RESOURCES

48	**GUN GIVEAWAY** ENTER TO WIN A REVOLVER AND MORE!
90	**NEW PRODUCTS**
127	**ADVERTISER'S INDEX** WHERE TO BUY YOUR MUST-HAVE GEAR

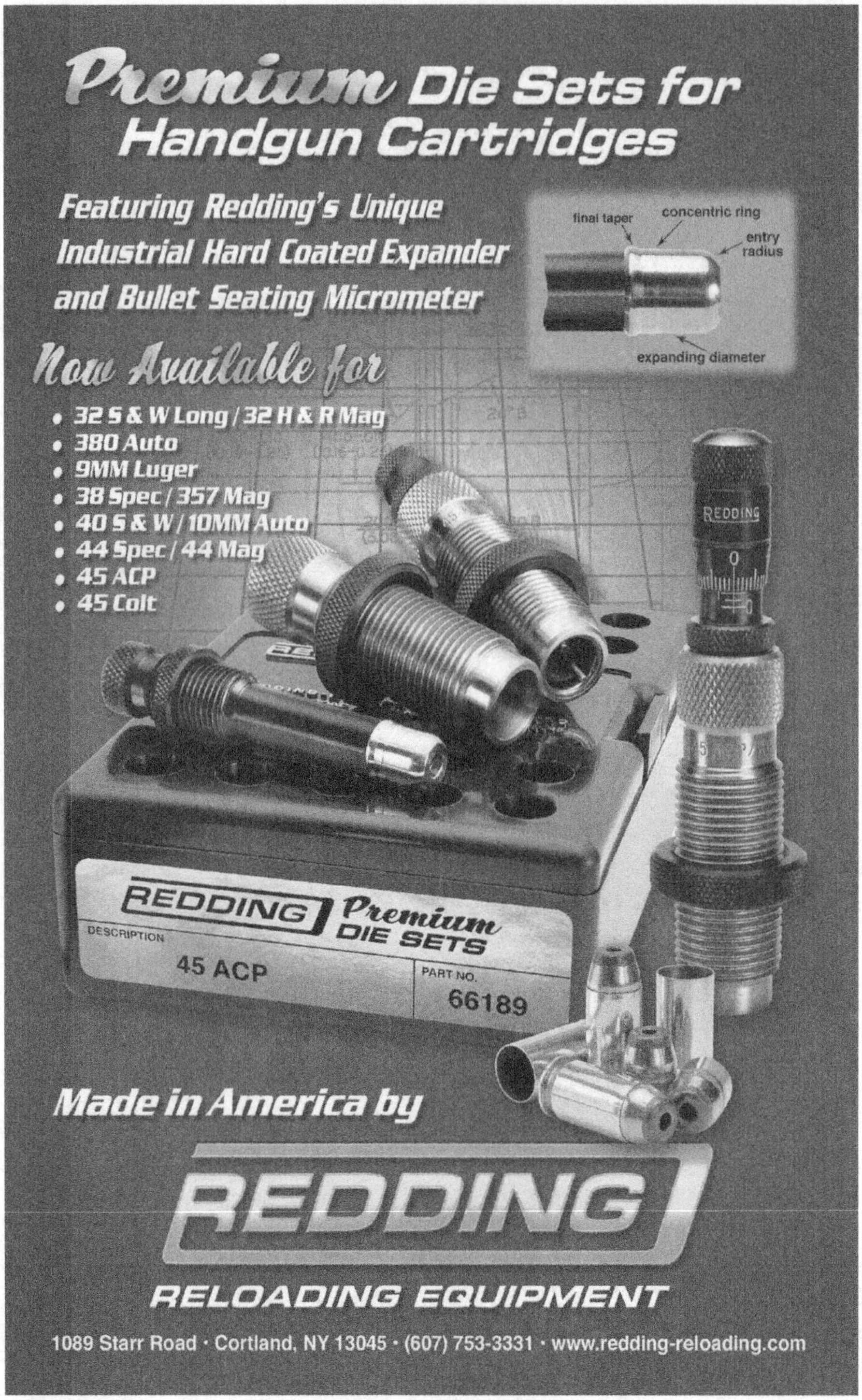

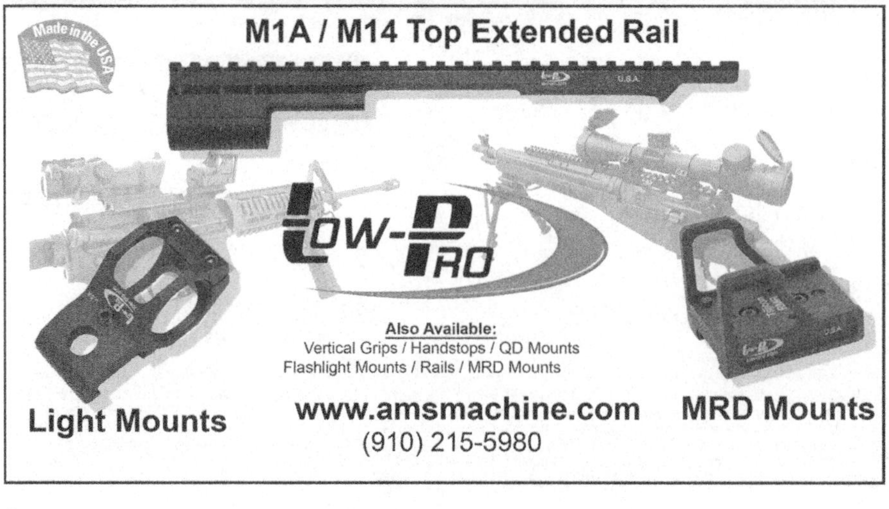

GUNS OLD WEST
HISTORY, GUNS & GEAR

CORPORATE OFFICERS Thomas Hollander, Randy Moldé, Marjorie Young

Editor Tom McHale
Associate Editors Jenna Buckley, Jazz Jimenez
Art Director Jennifer Lewis
Production Manager Jennifer Phillips
Digital Content Editor Serena Juchnowski
Website Manager Lorinda Massey
Staff Photographer Joseph Novelozo
Grammar Guru Gwen Gunn

CONTRIBUTING EDITORS

Will Dabbs, MD • Frank Jardim
John Taffin • Jeremy D. Clough
Roger Smith • Mike "Duke" Venturino
Serena Juchnowski • Gary Paul Johnston

FMG PUBLICATIONS

SPECIAL EDITIONS fmgpublications.com
Editor: Tom McHale

HANDGUNNER americanhandgunner.com
Editor: Tom McHale

GUNS gunsmagazine.com
Editor: Brent Wheat

SHOOTING INDUSTRY shootingindustry.com
Editor: Jade Moldae

AMERICAN COP americancop.com
Editor: Denny Hansen

NATIONAL AD SALES 800.537.3006
NORTH EAST Tom Vorel • tom.vorel@fmghq.com
SOUTH EAST Paula Iwanski • paula.iwanski@fmghq.com
WEST Delano Amaguin • delano.amaguin@fmghq.com
INTERNATIONAL Amy Tanguay • amy.tanguay@pubdev.com

Online Traffic Manager: Kevin Lewis
TEL: 858.842.3941, kevin.lewis@pubdev.com

CUSTOMER SERVICE
gunsmagazine.com

EDITORIAL 858.842.3943
Email: . . . . ed@gunsmagazine.com

PRODUCTION 858.842.3941
Email: . . . . annuals@fmghq.com

PRODUCED IN THE U.S.A.

From The Desk Of Tom McHale, Editor

Nowadays, we think the struggle is real when the internet goes down for 20 minutes. Or perhaps the local coffee house inadvertently spikes one's latte with 2% milk instead of skim. Social media is chock-full of such modern-day tragedies.

Try telling this to John Johnson. After returning to his homestead to find his pregnant wife murdered, he embarked on a new occupation: full-time Crow Indian killer. Revenge is a tough gig, and Johnson eventually found himself a captive of a Blackfoot Indian patrol. Knowing the Crow were slightly agitated by Johnson's killing of their 300 braves, the Blackfoot warriors intended to sell Johnson to the Crow, earning a tidy profit and their eternal gratitude. The Crow were keen on the revenge business, too.

So as not to spoil the rest of the story, let's just say the Indians neglected to relieve Johnson of his flint firestarter when they confiscated his rifle, knife and the two casks of whiskey he was taking to market. Later, after sampling a bit much of the whiskey Johnson had been transporting, the Blackfoot patrol became the target of Johnson's desperation to escape. Knowing the next day likely involves being skinned alive has a tendency to inspire one's motivation and improvised weapon creativity. You'll read the full story in these pages, but for now, here's a hint: Our hero didn't earn the nickname John "Liver-Eating" Johnson for nothing.

Part of the mystique of the Old West is the incredible tales, sometimes embellished, but often entirely true. For example, if you were a ne'er do well in late 19th century Montana, would you think twice about tormenting a town with the markings "3-7-77" on the doors? You should. Better yet, turn around and skedaddle before a shockingly efficient secret society of vigilantes picks up your trail.

There's plenty to learn about the guns and other weapons. You might be surprised at how long various Indian tribes favored the seemingly out-of-date bow and arrow — even after the advent of firearms. And with good reason. While bullets make nice clean holes (relatively speaking), flint arrow tips tend to make a royal mess of things not only going in but also coming out.

We've got some stories for the modern-day cowboys and cowgirls, too. Want to learn the joys of smoke-and-awe-filled black powder shooting? Read on. How about tips to reload classic "Western" calibers like .44-40 and .45 Colt? That's covered also. And much, much more.

I hope you enjoy this edition of *Old West: History, Guns & Gear*. Sit back, read a story or three, and appreciate the comfy life we all enjoy now.

Would you serve your liver to this man? Perhaps involuntarily …

TURNBULL RESTORATION SERVICES
TurnbullRestoration.com/owg

Committed to honoring the earliest gunmakers by returning firearms to their original condition.

TurnbullRestoration.com/owg
(585) 412-2930
Ask for your no-cost restoration quote.

Will Dabbs, MD

BEARS, TEDDY AND FEROCIOUS...

Holt Collier was an enigmatic man whose life and exploits do not fit into any tidy historical narrative. He was likely the most successful bear hunter in human history. Wealthy patrons came from around the world seeking his services.

The Curious Tale of Holt Collier

Collier once refused an offer of $1,000, a king's ransom in the day, for his pack of trained hunting hounds.

Collier's most famous hunt hosted President Theodore Roosevelt. Here, the two men are in the field.

In these days of social justice and such insufferable suffocating wokeness, there have been a few undeniable casualties in the culture wars. Civility has certainly taken a hit, and chivalry was willingly sacrificed on the exalted altar of gender reimagination. However, arguably the greatest loss is simple unfiltered historical accuracy.

History is an untidy thing. The more emotionally charged the narrative, the greater the chances of historical manipulation. In few areas is there greater opportunity for controversy than in the sticky issues of race in the antebellum American South.

The War Between the States was fought for a wide variety of reasons, and slavery was undeniably front and center throughout. The ownership of one human being by another is morally indefensible to the contemporary mind no matter the circumstances. One and a half centuries ago, though, the world was a very different place.

Sometimes reality does not fit into the tidy slots we imagine it might. One particularly striking instance was the curious tale of Holt Collier.

A Most Remarkable Man

Slaves in the antebellum South represented a simply breathtaking investment. A typical enslaved person cost about $23,000 in today's dollars. While there were invariably cruel sadists and psychopaths who owned slaves, in many cases slaves were considered a part of the extended family, albeit involuntarily.

Holt Collier was born in 1846, part of the third generation of African slaves to serve the Hinds family on their Home Hill Plantation in Jefferson County, Miss. At the time of Holt's birth, the plantation master was a man named Howell Hinds. His son Tom was of a roughly similar age as Holt, and the two boys were raised together at another family property called the Plum Ridge Plantation.

Plum Ridge was built by General Thomas Hinds, a hero of the 1815 Battle of New Orleans. Thomas Hinds was politically connected, as are most

The American Civil War was obviously a bit murkier to those who were there than we modern observers might believe. History has since sanitized a great deal of the moral ambiguity.

Some of Holt's earliest duties involved attending the large pack of hunting dogs the Hinds family maintained. He was also responsible for subsistence hunting to help keep the plantation staff fed.

Holt Collier rendered distinguished service as a cavalryman fighting for the Confederacy.

general officers, and played an outsized role during the development of Mississippi in the 19th century. At the behest of President Andrew Jackson, General Hinds conducted one of the earliest formal surveys of central Mississippi. He also chose the location for the state capital of Jackson. Jackson is Mississippi's most populous city and is located in Hinds County, named for this esteemed general.

Some of Holt's earliest duties involved attending the large pack of hunting dogs the Hinds family maintained. He was also responsible for subsistence hunting to help keep the plantation staff fed. He hunted with a muzzleloading 12-gauge shotgun and was purportedly equally facile from either shoulder. *Collier killed his first bear at the age of 10 and acquired an early mastery of fieldcraft.* These skills would later hold him in good stead on the battlefield.

With the onset of the Civil War, Howell and his son Tom left to fight, freeing Holt before they departed. Holt asked to accompany them, but at only 14, was told he was too young for war. However, Holt later stowed away on a riverboat and made his way to Memphis where he sought out the Hinds men in garrison. Holt, Howell and Tom served together at the Battle of Shiloh in 1862. Collier was present at the death of Confederate General Albert Sidney Johnston.

There was a general prohibition against black men serving in uniform for the Confederacy, however, an exception was allowed in Holt's case given his exceptional skills and dedication. He was eventually assigned to Company I of the 9th Texas Cavalry Regiment. *Collier remained with the 9th through the rest of the war, fighting in Tennessee, Alabama and Mississippi, and earning a place as one of Nathan Bedford Forrest's most trusted scouts.* He even successfully served for a time as a Confederate spy.

After the war, Collier returned to Mississippi to work on the Hinds plantation as a freedman. Federal Captain James King apparently attempted to use labor overseen by the Freedmen's Bureau on the Hinds plantation. The Freedmen's Bureau was a Northern enterprise that operated during Reconstruction to help settle, educate and support freed slaves in the post-war

At the completion of the famous Theodore Roosevelt Mississippi bear hunt, the president gave Holt Collier a new Winchester rifle to replace the one he had damaged.

President Roosevelt's Mississippi bear hunt was an expansive social event.

> The president later called Holt "the greatest hunter and guide I have ever known."

South. A disagreement erupted, Capt. King attacked the unarmed and aged Howell Hinds with a knife, and Collier killed King. Holt Collier was tried by a federal military tribunal in Vicksburg but acquitted.

In the immediate aftermath, Mississippi Senator William Alexander Percy recommended Holt leave the state. As is evidenced by the sordid demise of Capt. King, justice then was not the refined thing it is today. *A freed black man having killed a white Union Army officer, even in the convoluted social calculus of the post-war South, could find himself in serious peril.*

Collier had made a great many friends during the war, so he traveled to Texas and took a job as a cowboy on the ranch of Lawrence Sullivan Ross, his former commander with the 9th Texas Cavalry. He remained there about a year until, hearing of the murder of his former master Howell Hinds, he returned to Mississippi where he lived out his days.

Holt Collier — Rugged Individualist

Throughout it all, Holt Collier developed a well-deserved reputation as an accomplished bear hunter. While black bears are extremely scarce in Mississippi today, they were commonplace back then. *Over the course of his life, Collier killed more than 3,000 of the animals. This tally is greater than that of Davy Crockett and Daniel Boone combined.* Collier typically hunted with dogs and finished his bears off with a rifle shot. Wealthy hunters paid handsomely for Collier's peerless guide services.

In 1902, President Theodore Roosevelt traveled to Mississippi in his official capacity as Commander in Chief. A legendary hunter, naturalist and all-around manly man, Roosevelt planned to sample the hunting in the Magnolia State during his visit. Major George Helm was tasked to organize the hunt, so he reached out to the most accomplished bear hunter in the Southeast, 56-year-old Holt Collier.

Holt Collier, shown here among a hunting party he was leading, was in great demand as a professional guide (above). A remarkable man who led a most remarkable life, Holt Collier died of natural causes in 1936 at age 90 (right).

This political cartoon by cartoonist Clifford Berryman ultimately inspired the ubiquitous Teddy Bear.

Collier later had this to say: *"I got things ready; found a beautiful campin' place. I was boss of the hunt. Along came the President with a carload of guards, but he left all but one of 'em in the car. Anyway, he was safer with me than with all the policemen in Washington. The President was a pleasant man; when he was talking he'd stop every little while to ask other people's opinion."*

This presidential hunt was quite the spectacle. In addition to an entourage of reporters, famed big-game hunter John Avery McIlhenny was in attendance. McIlhenny hailed from Louisiana and had served alongside Roosevelt in the Rough Riders during the Spanish-American War. Mississippi Governor Andrew Longino and railroad tycoon Stuyvesant Fish were also present.

In short order, Collier had his dogs in pursuit of a large male black bear. Once cornered, the big animal turned on Jocko, Collier's favorite hunting hound, and killed him. While Collier would have typically dispatched the bear at this point, he rather smacked it over the head with his rifle, bending the barrel and ruining the gun. Eventually he got a rope around the animal's neck and secured it to a willow tree.

When President Roosevelt arrived and saw the bear tied to the tree he refused to shoot it. Another member of his hunting party did eventually dispatch the creature with a knife. The *Washington Post*, along with several other period newspapers, publicized the story emphasizing the rugged president's sense of compassion and fair play.

An editorial cartoonist of the day named Clifford Berryman subsequently penned a political cartoon depicting the event titled, "Drawing the Line in Mississippi." In the cartoon the bear in question was falsely depicted as a cub. The American public was quite enamored with the image.

Inspired by the cartoon, *a New York store owner named Morris Michtom created a stuffed animal and titled it "Teddy's Bear."* This toy turned out to be phenomenally popular and served as the foundation for the Ideal Toy Company. Many's the young child who has since drawn comfort and solace from their stuffed Teddy Bear. In 2002, on the Teddy Bear's centennial anniversary, the Mississippi state legislature named it the official state toy.

President Roosevelt was most taken with Holt Collier's abilities, and he presented the former slave with a Winchester rifle to replace the one damaged during the hunt. Five years later, Roosevelt called upon Collier to serve as tracker for another bear hunt, this time in Louisiana. The president later called Holt "the greatest hunter and guide I have ever known."

The Holt Collier National Wildlife Refuge near Darlove, Miss,, is named in his honor. It is the only American National Wildlife Refuge to be named for an African American.

Ruminations

Holt Collier, freed slave, loyal friend, soldier, cowboy and bear tracker for the president, died peacefully in Greenville, Miss., in 1936. He was 90 years old. *During the course of his long and distinguished hunting career, Collier likely killed more bears than any man in history.*

Modern-day Americans tend to view historical figures through a tainted lens. Flawed figures doing great things are frequently now remembered more for their warts than their accomplishments. Reality is none are truly righteous. Everybody everywhere has their flaws.

However, Holt Collier destroyed paradigms. A freed slave who fought brilliantly for the Confederacy, a black man who wrangled as a cowboy and an inveterate world-class hunter who ultimately inspired a wildlife refuge, Collier really represented the best of us. Holt Collier was a truly great American.

For more info: HoltCollier.com

Frank Jardim

BEST OF THE WEST?

The Meticulous and Often Custom-Ordered Bullard Repeater

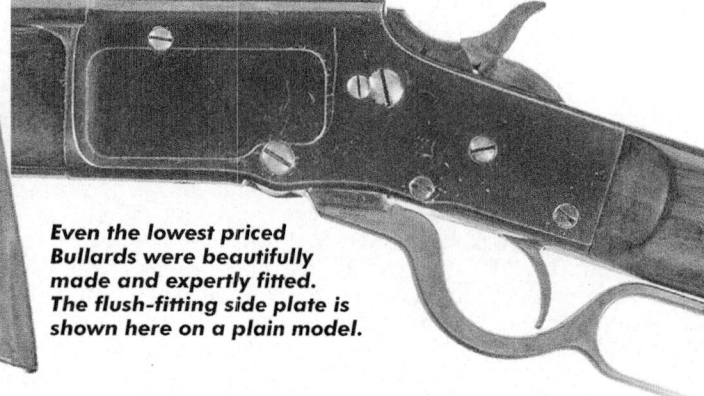

A man of diverse genius, James H. Bullard invented many things. He left the rifle company and started to pursue other interests. It went bankrupt a few years later.

Bullard repeaters came in two frame sizes: large for calibers .40 and up, and a thinner small frame for cartridges under .40 caliber. What varied widely was the level of customization requested by the purchaser.

Even the lowest priced Bullards were beautifully made and expertly fitted. The flush-fitting side plate is shown here on a plain model.

The lever-action repeating rifle is an American icon, and Winchester has long enjoyed the reputation of being its premier manufacturer. However, though Winchester made fine lever-action rifles, they did not make the finest. Many would argue the late 19th century Marlin designs were better, and their side ejection of spent cases made more practical sense than Winchester's manner of throwing them back in the shooter's face. I would argue Marlin can no more lay claim to the accolade "best lever-action repeater" than Winchester. It is true Winchester and Marlin captured the majority of the lever-action rifle market in the 1800s, but neither firm ever offered a gun as fast shooting and smooth cycling as the superbly crafted Bullard.

Today the Bullard repeating rifle is largely forgotten. Like the Betamax video cassette recorder and the 1948 Tucker automobile, the story of the Bullard Repeating Arms Company is one of those ironic business sagas where a clearly superior product simply isn't a commercial success in the marketplace.

Origin Story

The Bullard story begins with the inventor, James H. Bullard. He was born in Vermont in 1842 and made Springfield, Mass., his home. The industrial revolution was transforming the city into a thriving center of manufacturing and James Bullard possessed an inventive genius that made him a man in great demand. From 1877 to 1880 he worked as an engineer for S&W with D.B. Wesson himself. They developed four patents together. During this time

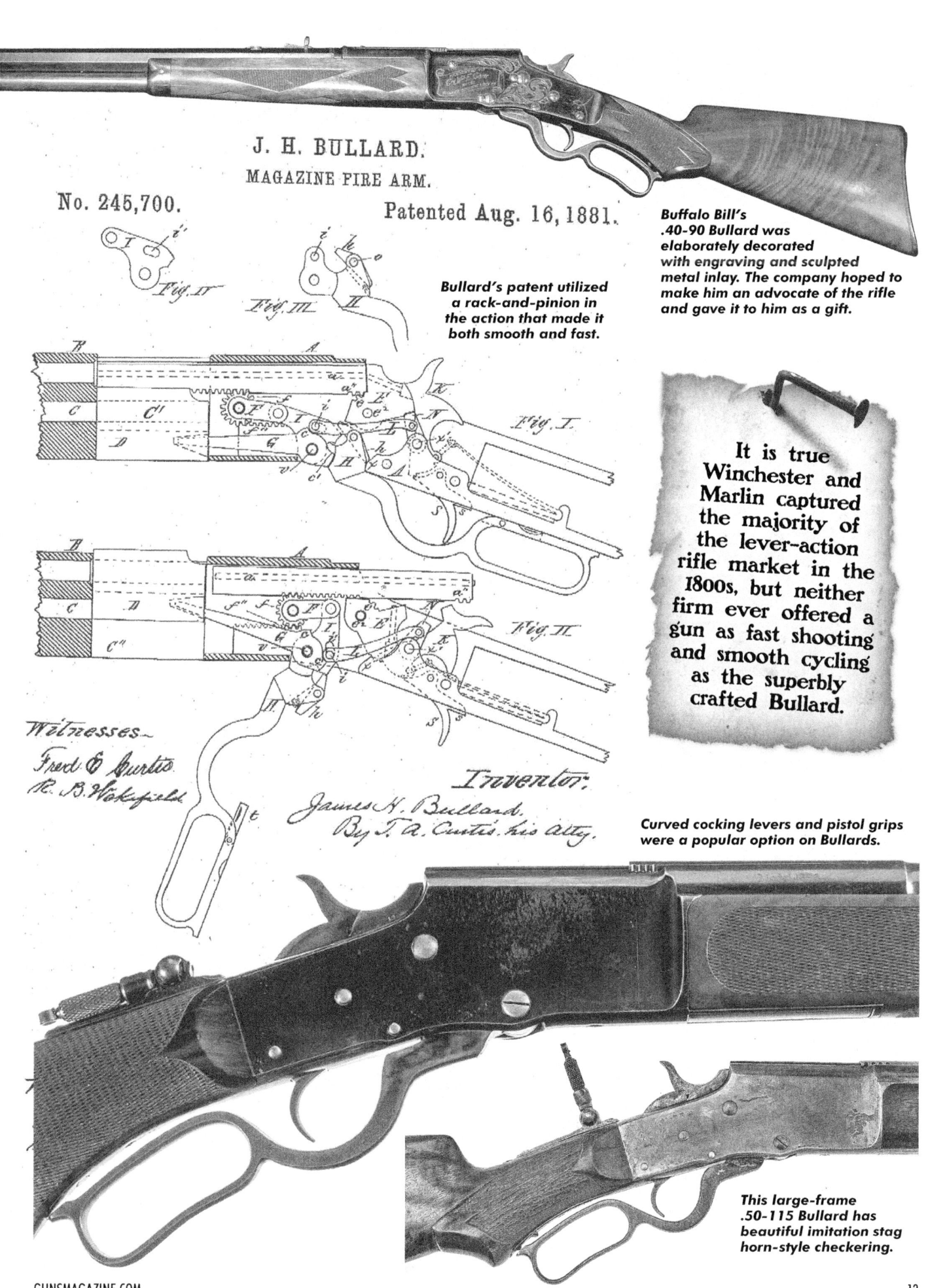

Buffalo Bill's .40-90 Bullard was elaborately decorated with engraving and sculpted metal inlay. The company hoped to make him an advocate of the rifle and gave it to him as a gift.

Bullard's patent utilized a rack-and-pinion in the action that made it both smooth and fast.

It is true Winchester and Marlin captured the majority of the lever-action rifle market in the 1800s, but neither firm ever offered a gun as fast shooting and smooth cycling as the superbly crafted Bullard.

Curved cocking levers and pistol grips were a popular option on Bullards.

This large-frame .50-115 Bullard has beautiful imitation stag horn-style checkering.

GUNSMAGAZINE.COM

Bullard repeaters had exceptionally long throws, but were so smooth and easy to operate the rifle could be cocked with just the pinkie finger. Frank has done it.

While most rifles had full-length magazine tubes, lighter button magazine rifles were made to order. Stock styles, checkering and sights also varied broadly. The tang-mounted Lyman sight was the most popular aperture type and the stepped Winchester style the most common open sight.

The large-frame guns generally used a buttplate featuring an elk and small-frame guns had a turkey motif (above). A few custom models were made with engraved steel trapdoors (left).

The company's lower-cost models had round barrels, straight grips and levers and uncheckered stocks.

period he also submitted patents for his own ideas for lever-action and single-shot rifles, ammunition case manufacture and improvements of the Winchester toggle link design. The latter patent was probably to obstruct improvement of the Winchester 1866, 1873 and 1876 rifles he viewed as the main competitors to his repeating-rifle design.

Bullard's patents for firearms and ammunition were only a small part of his overall achievements. He patented many inventions, from sewing machine needles to a steam-powered car in a career that skipped between various manufacturing firms and self-employment. Rarely did he spend more than a few years at any job. The pattern of his work history suggests a man of immense imagination and curiosity who was more interested in creation than the hum-drum discipline of business management.

When Bullard formed what would later become the Bullard Repeating Arms Company in Springfield, Mass. in 1883, the position he chose for himself wasn't president, or treasurer, but plant manager. He had never run a large business but had experience in factory manufacturing. To what degree his lack of experience or interest in upper management affected the company's success is hard to judge. In mid-1885, Bullard left the company he created to pursue other interests. By January 1891, the Bullard Repeating Arms Company closed and sold off its assets, leaving behind a legacy of might-have-been

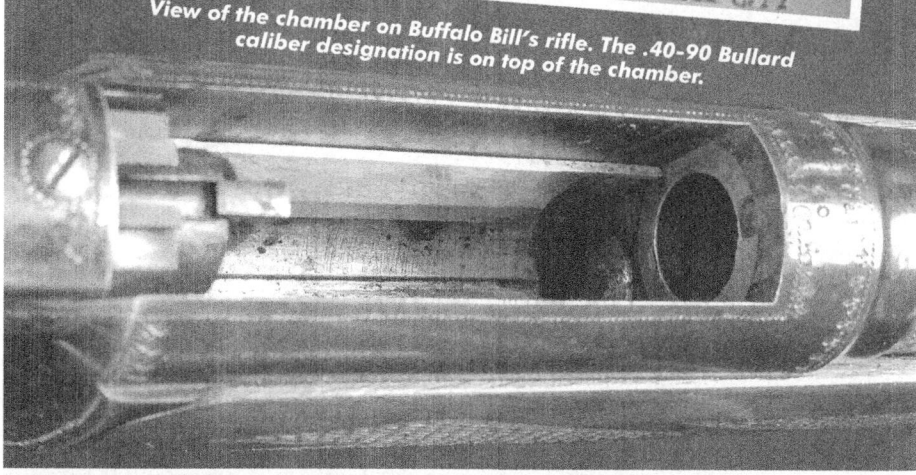

Advertising for the Bullard repeaters showing the wide range of options available.

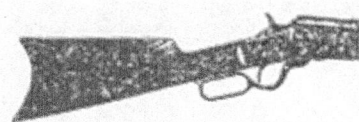

View of the chamber on Buffalo Bill's rifle. The .40-90 Bullard caliber designation is on top of the chamber.

> The question that arises is, "was the Bullard just too good for the marketplace?" It probably was.

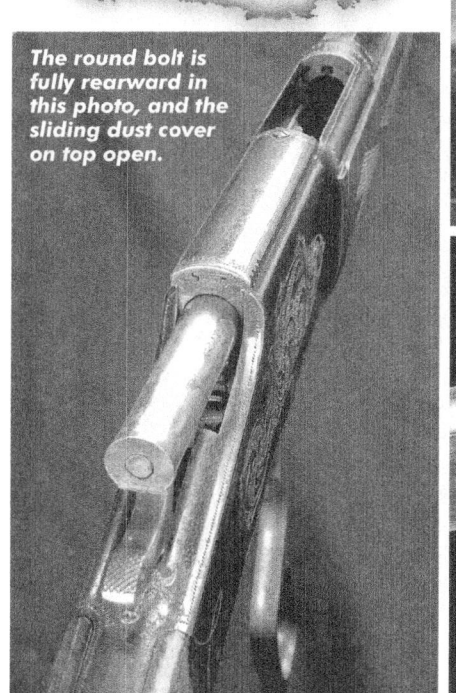

The round bolt is fully rearward in this photo, and the sliding dust cover on top open.

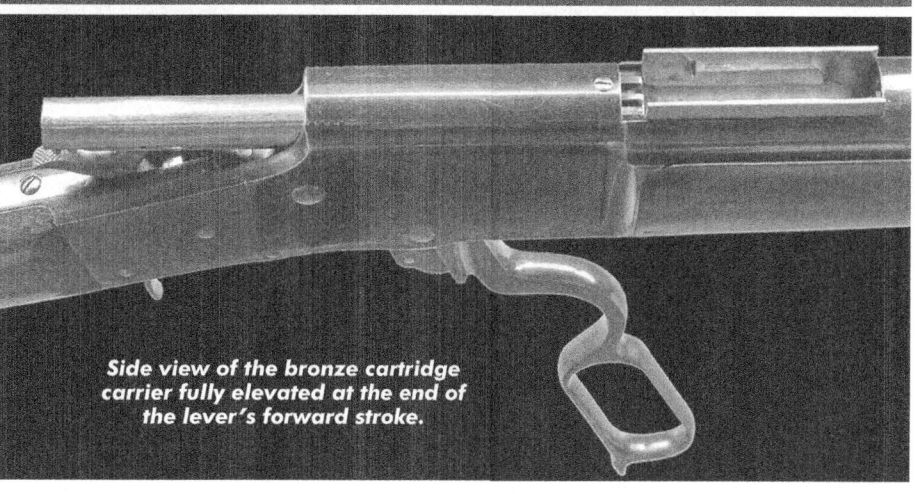

Side view of the bronze cartridge carrier fully elevated at the end of the lever's forward stroke.

Rare studio portrait with a Bullard rifle prominently displayed. If this rifle was a photographer's prop, it was an expensive one. If it belonged to these cowboy brothers, they had very upscale tastes.

Unlike Winchesters and Marlins, the Bullard magazine was loaded from the bottom like a modern pump shotgun.

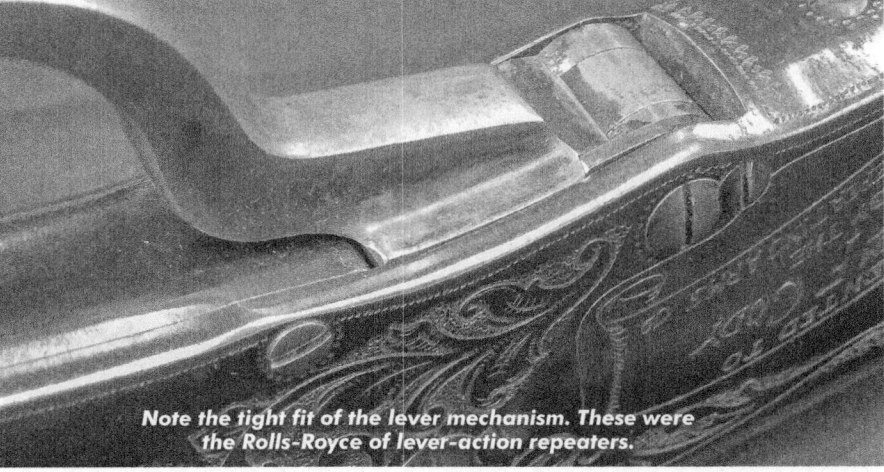

Note the tight fit of the lever mechanism. These were the Rolls-Royce of lever-action repeaters.

Here are four of Bullard's proprietary cartridges. The left two fit the small-frame guns, and the right two the thicker large-frame guns.

greatness in the estimated 2,500 repeating rifles it produced.

Engineering Innovation

Compared to its Winchester and Marlin competition, the Bullard lever action was exceptionally well made but somewhat complicated. Its action was without peer for speed and smoothness because of its patented rack-and-pinion design. It also had great leverage for extraction. The action is so smooth the lever can be worked and the rifle cocked with just the pinkie finger. The round bolt is locked into the receiver before firing in a manner similar to a Remington rolling block, and I see a superficial resemblance to that weapon.

The Bullard had the typical tubular magazine of the day, but it was loaded from underneath the action, much like a modern pump shotgun. It was also easily loaded from the chamber if the shooter wished to fire single shots and hold the full magazine in reserve. Naturally, magazine capacity varied with barrel length and caliber.

Custom Cartridges

There were two frame sizes for the repeaters. The small frame handled cartridges below .40 caliber and the large frame .40 caliber and up. James Bullard developed seven cartridges of his own design for his rifles. They were .32-40 (150-grain bullet), .38-45 (190-grain), .40-70 (232-grain), .40-75 (258-grain), .40-90 (300-grain), .45-85 (290-grain) and the .50-115 (300-grain). The cartridges had their merits, but they probably didn't really help rifle sales. I'll bet finding a box of .40-90 Bullard on the shelf at the general store in 1886 was only slightly more likely than it would be for you to find it today in your local gun shop. In practice, the company chambered the rifles in just about any caliber the customer requested.

Made to Order

It seems the Bullard repeaters were never really mass produced, but rather made to order on customer request. *Collectors have observed no two seem to be alike and repairs to the rifles require replacement parts to be hand fitted.* The company was essentially building customized rifles of the highest quality — a costly proposition.

Winchesters and Marlins were great guns for practical people. By comparison, Bullards seem too beautiful and well made to be practical. It is a case of the perfect being the enemy of the good enough. Bullards even used decorative scalloped end caps on their forends. Where Winchester simply screwed an access plate to the side of their receiver, Bullard designed his to be inlet into the receiver and fit flush with its surface giving the rifle a graceful and clean appearance. It is so finely fitted you could easily fail to notice it.

The question that arises is, "was the Bullard just too good for the marketplace?" It probably was. In 1885, a Bullard rifle's starting price was around $38. An 1876 Winchester rifle cost closer to $25. *With the difference, you could buy a new 1873 Colt pistol.* How effectively potential consumers were made aware of the existence and virtues of the Bullard rifles is subject to debate. Their advertising included printed catalogs, distributors and traveling salesmen who demonstrated the rifles around the country. Ultimately, they sold fewer than 2,500 repeaters so either they failed to attract the upper end of the market from their competitors or the market wasn't really there, perhaps due to the generally depressed state of the American economy at the time.

Because of their rarity, few will ever see a Bullard repeater up close, much less hold or fire one. Still, all of us enjoy a small part of the Bullard repeater's legacy in the form of the solid head brass cartridge cases we fire in our weapons today. Black powder-era balloon-head cartridge cases have always been somewhat weak around the head. James Bullard invented and patented the first solid head cartridge case, which also happened to be semi-rimmed, in the form of the powerful .50-115 Bullard for his rifles.

The Bullard didn't survive long enough to become known as America's premier big-game rifle, but a little bit of it lives on to this day.

John Taffin

SLICK ACTIONS

Real Pistol-Caliber Carbines Have Levers!

Much attention has been given recently to pistol-caliber carbines, especially AR-type rifles and pistols chambered in 9mm. So much attention, in fact, some might think it's a new idea. Not quite. Carbines chambered in pistol-length cartridges go back well over 160 years.

Pistol Origins

The very first attempts, some more successful than others, to come up with a repeating firearm involved pistol-length cartridges. The first successful repeater, the Model 1860 Henry, was chambered in the .44 Rimfire — definitely a cartridge that proved to be suitable for chambering in sixguns. The Spencer arrived about the same time as the Model 1860 Henry, and it also featured a pistol-length cartridge. The Model 1860 Henry was improved to the Model 1866 Winchester and was still chambered in the same .44 Rimfire. Late 1869, S&W came forth with the first successful big-bore cartridge-firing revolver chambered in the .44 S&W American, a centerfire cartridge. It was also chambered in the .44 Rimfire.

1873 saw the arrival of the first Center-Fire Winchester with the Model of 1873 chambered in .44 Winchester Centerfire (.44 WCF), or as it is most commonly called today, the .44-40. The same year, Colt issued its Single Action Army in .45 Colt. Prior to this, Colt cartridge conversions were available in .44 Colt and many believe the first Single Action Army was actually chambered in .44 Rimfire.

I recently read in another magazine the Winchester 1873 was chambered

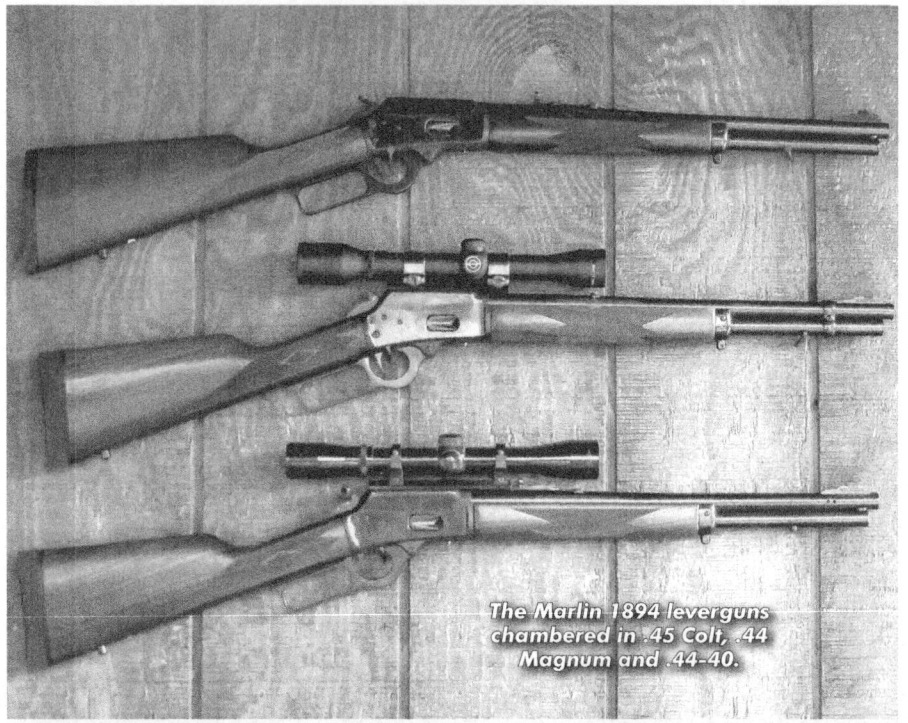

The Marlin 1894 leverguns chambered in .45 Colt, .44 Magnum and .44-40.

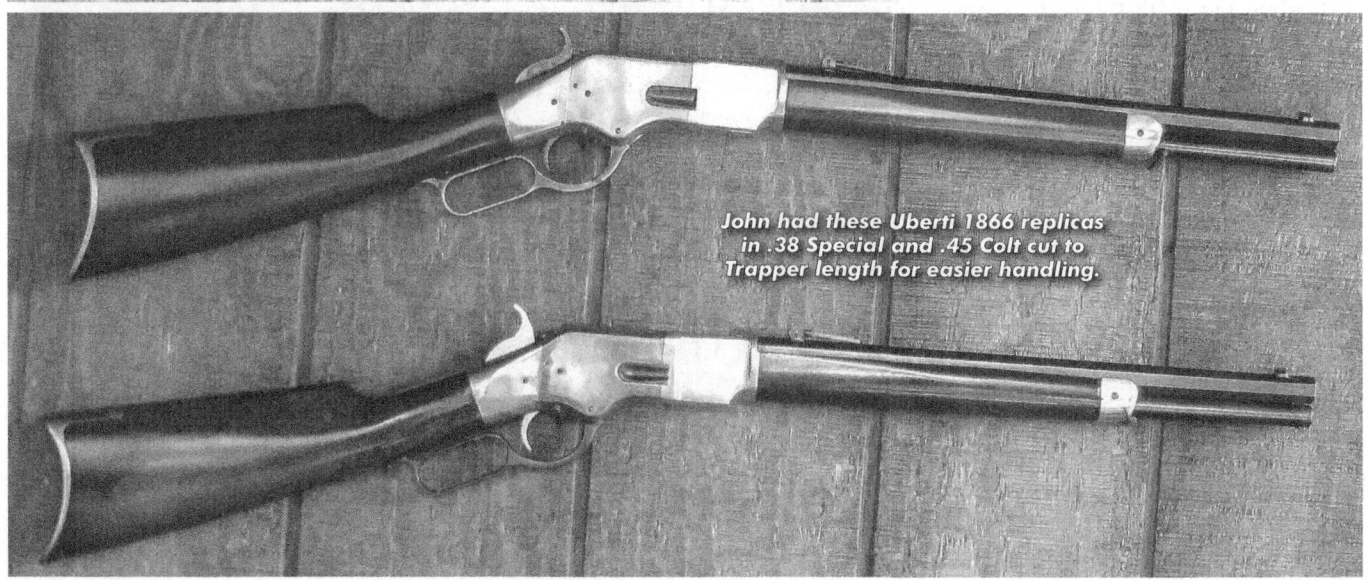

John had these Uberti 1866 replicas in .38 Special and .45 Colt cut to Trapper length for easier handling.

My all-around Perfect Rifle is a PCC levergun chambered in .357 Magnum.

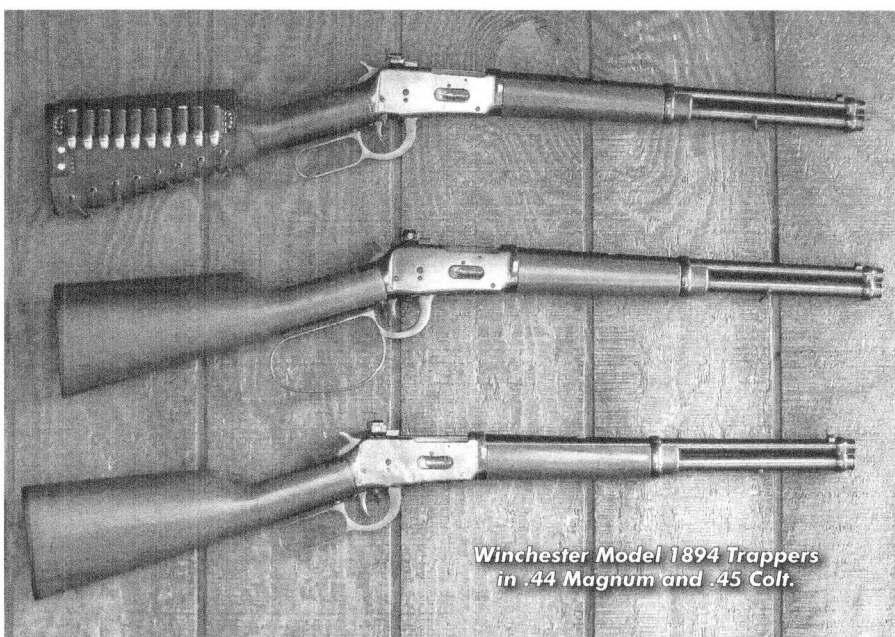

Winchester Model 1894 Trappers in .44 Magnum and .45 Colt.

in vintage revolver rounds. Actually, this is backward! Winchester went on to chamber the 1873 in a necked-down .44-40, the .38 WCF, followed by a small-bore cartridge, the .32 WCF. These are more commonly known today as the .38-40 and .32-20. They were originally rifle cartridges. Colt chambered the Single Action Army in all three of the Winchester Centerfire cartridges, however, they all arrived first in lever-action carbines. Winchester also necked-down the .32-20 to come up with the .25-20, but Colt did not chamber its Single Action Army in this dandy little cartridge.

No .45 Colt?

At the time, Winchester did not chamber their lever-action Model 1873 in .45 Colt for a couple reasons that seem obvious. One problem would be feeding. The .45 Colt is a straight-wall cartridge, while the .44-40, .38-40 and .32-20 are all bottleneck cartridges, making them much easier to feed from the action into the chamber. Another reason relates to the rims. *The original rim was very small, without much area for an extractor to grab.* I recall reading handloaders' complaints in the 1940s-'50s of rims pulling off when cases were re-sized, giving birth to the myth of weak .45 Colt brass. Even today, the .45 Colt cartridge, which has a larger

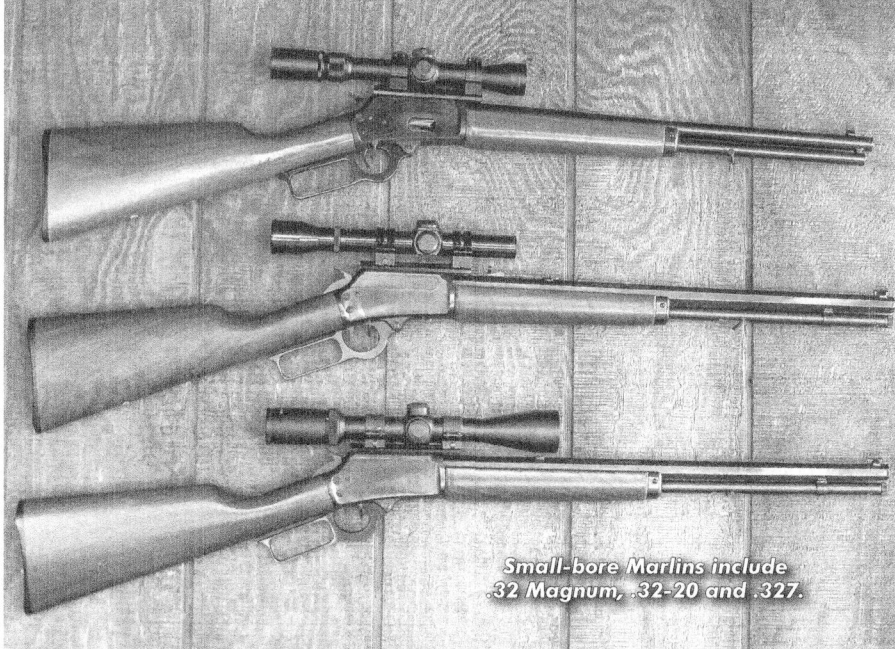

Small-bore Marlins include .32 Magnum, .32-20 and .327.

Modern Marlin .32-20 compared to classic Winchester .32-20 Model 1892.

GUNSMAGAZINE.COM

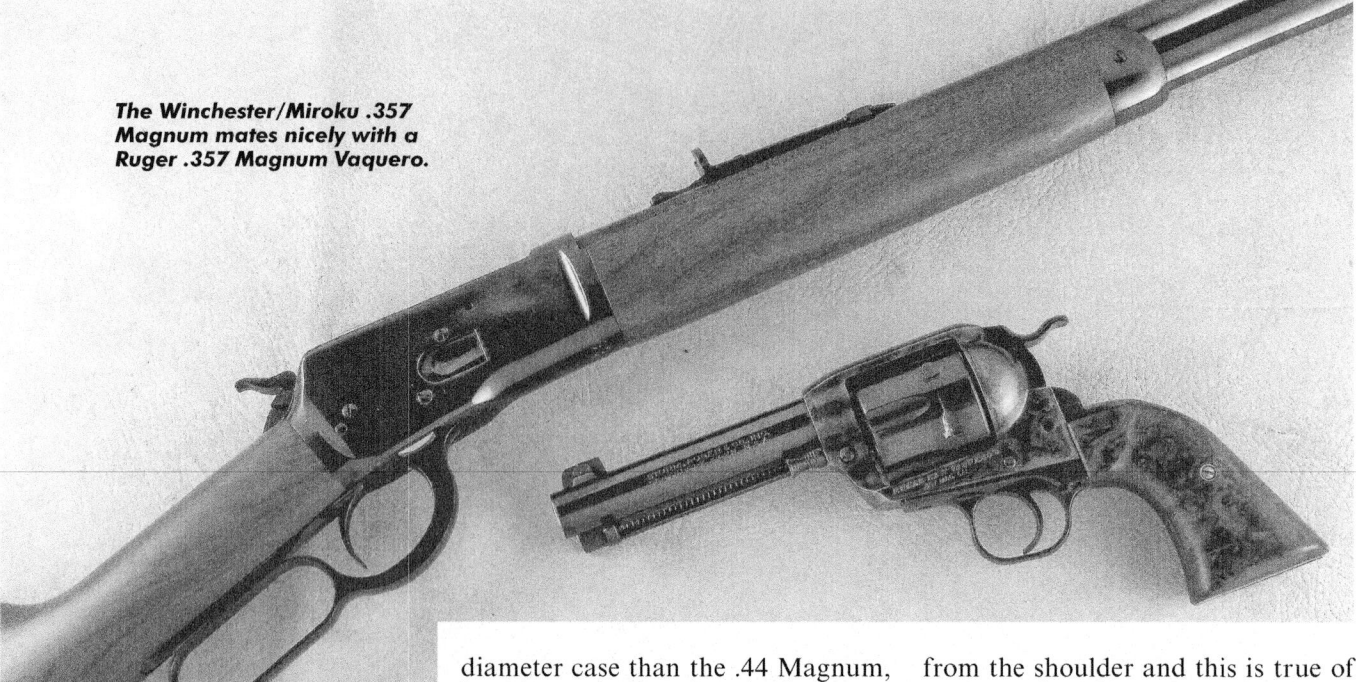

The Winchester/Miroku .357 Magnum mates nicely with a Ruger .357 Magnum Vaquero.

A Marlin Trapper in its natural habitat!

diameter case than the .44 Magnum, has the same size rim. An improvement in modern brass is the channel cut around the base of the cartridge case right in front of the rim which allows a better grasp by the ejector. Even so, I don't believe any lever-action carbines were chambered in .45 Colt until quite a while after both Marlin and Winchester chambered the .44 Magnum in the mid-to-late '60s.

Slick as a ...

One of the great attributes of the 1860s/1866/1873 Winchesters was how smoothly they operated. They are very particular about overall case length, however *with the right ammunition, it is almost a spiritual experience working the lever of one of these great guns.* Today's replicas work exactly the same way. These first leverguns could easily be operated without removing the butt from the shoulder and this is true of most modern leverguns, too. Keep the butt on the shoulder and work the action with authority.

What's Old is New

After the 1873 Winchester, the Models 1876 and 1886 arrived chambered in what we normally think of as rifle cartridges, such as the .45-60 and .45-70. Then in 1892, Winchester went back to their pistol-length roots modernizing the 1873 Winchester into what is basically a miniaturized Model 1886 but chambered in the same cartridges as the Model 1873 Winchester. The Model 1892 proved to be one of the slickest handling and strongest lever-action carbines of all time.

Modern-Era Levers

The real modern era of lever action-style PCCs began in the early

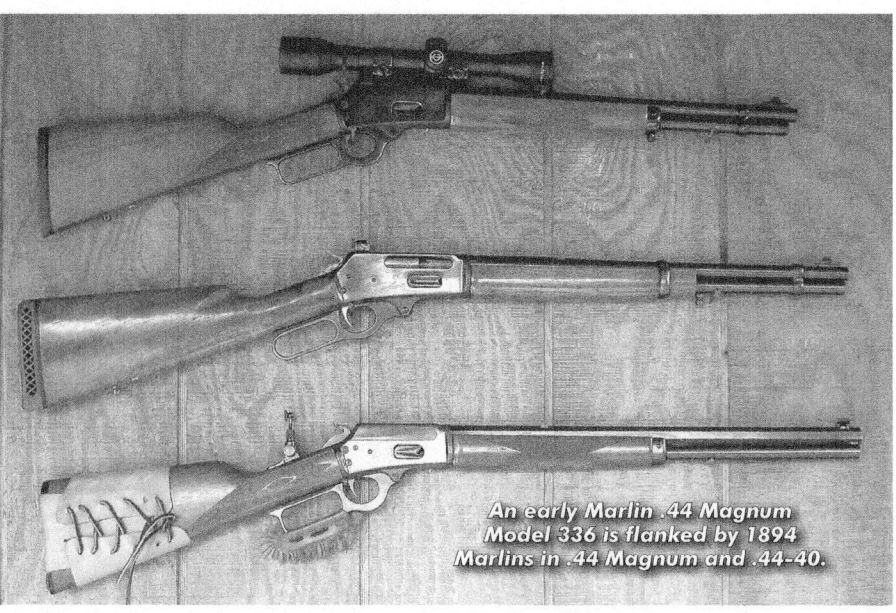

An early Marlin .44 Magnum Model 336 is flanked by 1894 Marlins in .44 Magnum and .44-40.

> With the right ammunition it is almost a spiritual experience working the lever of one of these great guns.

A combination .44 Magnum with Winchester 1894 and Ruger Super Blackhawk.

1950s. Ward Koozer, a gunsmith in Arizona, began converting .32-20 Winchester Model 1892s to .357 Magnum. One of my favorite articles was by Kent Bellah featuring his sixgun/levergun combination consisting of a 3 ½" S&W .357 Magnum and a Koozer-converted Model 1892.

I believe the first lever-action-style Magnum pistol-caliber carbines factory produced were the Winchester 1894 and the Marlin 336 both chambered in .44 Magnum in the late 1960s. In 1969, the old Marlin 1894 was resurrected and offered in .44 Magnum, and then later in .44-40. This action, being shorter, is better suited to sixgun cartridges than the .30-30 length 336 action. Marlin also made a special run of Trapper-style 1894 carbines in .44 Magnum and .45 Colt with a 16 ¼" barrel; full magazine tube that holds seven or eight rounds depending upon the nose length of the bullet; a recoil pad on its straight gripped stock; checkering on forearm and buttstock, and excellent sights.

Winchester would also go on to chamber their Model 1894 in .45 Colt and .357 Magnum offering both in Trapper versions. In the 1970s, Marlin introduced their Model 1894C chambered in .357 Magnum. This is one of the handiest carbines ever offered and our family has four of them currently in use. Marlin also chambered this little carbine in .32 Magnum, .32-20 and .25-20, and since they did not come up with one in .327 Magnum I had my local 'smith convert one of the .32 Magnums to this longer cartridge.

Modern Cowpokes

One of the great benefits of Cowboy Action Shooting is the resurrection of so many classic Winchesters all chambered in pistol-length cartridges by Uberti. All three of the original Winchesters, Models 1860, 1866, and 1873, have been offered in the original three chamberings as well as .45 Colt and .357 Magnum. And now the Model 1873 is even available in .44 Magnum. The .38 Special can also be found, and two of my favorite easy-shooting PCCs are the replica Model 1866 chambered in .38 Special as well as a very rare .44 Special.

In the period between the two World Wars, El Tigre 1892 .44-40 carbines were produced under a license from Winchester in South America. In the 1950s, these could be purchased for $39.95. I waited 50 years too long and had to pay more than 20 times as much to get an excellent example. The bonus is it outshoots my original Winchester 1892. In the 1980s, I believe, the first examples of the excellent Rossi replicas of the Model 1892 began arriving. These have been offered in .44-40, .44 Magnum, .45 Colt and .357 Magnum. I recently purchased a stainless steel version of the latter and had the barrel cut back to 16 ¼". I added a Lyman Model 66A receiver sight and had the stock refinished to make it a weather-beating match to the stainless steel finish. This could easily be *the Perfect PCC*.

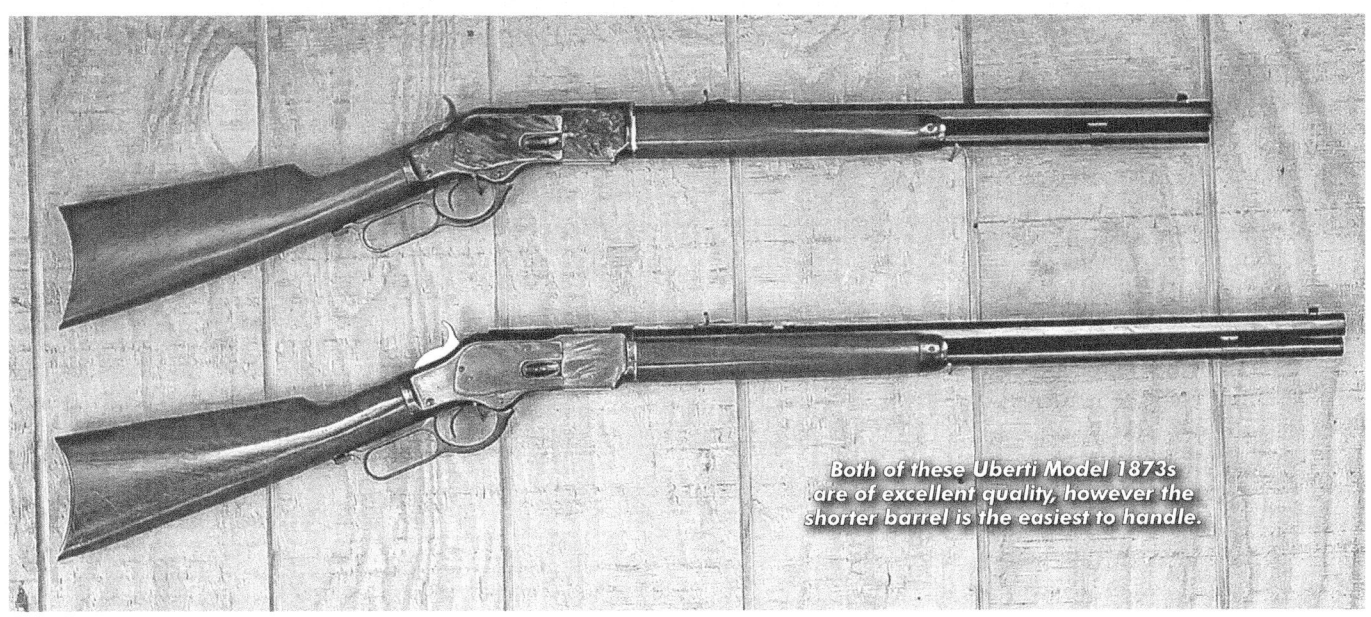

Both of these Uberti Model 1873s are of excellent quality, however the shorter barrel is the easiest to handle.

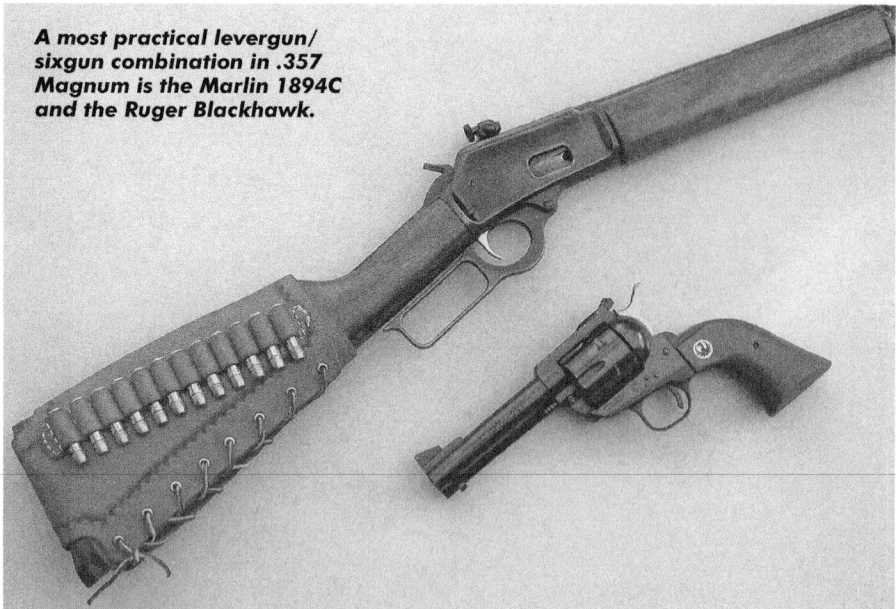

A most practical levergun/sixgun combination in .357 Magnum is the Marlin 1894C and the Ruger Blackhawk.

Henry's .357 Magnum Big Boy performs exceedingly well.

About the same time Rossi was bringing forth their replica 1892s, Browning also offered the Model B92 chambered in .357 Magnum and .44 Magnum. These are beautifully fitted and finished PCCs and worth looking for on the used-gun market. Uberti has also offered a long lineup of Replica Model 1892s in several barrel lengths, including those with octagon barrels and chamberings such as .45 Colt and .44 Magnum. Winchester also now offers their Miroku-produced Model 1892 in most chamberings at various times including .38-40. These are also beautifully fitted and finished, perhaps even better examples than the originals.

Currently, Henry Repeating Arms also offers PCCs chambered in .357 Magnum, .44 Magnum and *is the only manufacturer to offer a .327 Magnum version.* I recently purchased three lever-action .357 Magnum carbines from three different manufacturers. Two of them had very heavy trigger pulls of 7.5–8 lbs., as well as somewhat gritty actions. They were usable as is. However, I had to have both of them smoothed with the trigger pulls reduced to satisfy my levergun-shooting soul. I can do pretty good work with heavy trigger pulls, but it takes a lot more concentration. The Henry .357 Magnum was ready to go right out of the box.

PCC Calibers Galore

I recently took stock of what lever-action-style PCCs I have had extensive experience with and came up with the following chamberings in Marlin, Winchester, Browning, Rossi, Uberti and El Tigre leverguns. In order from smallest to largest those are: .32 Magnum, .32-20, .327 Magnum, .38 Special, .357 Magnum, .38-40, .41 Magnum, .44-40, .44 Special, .44 Magnum and .45 Colt. I was even able to fire the original .454 chambered Winchester 1894 as well as a comparable Marlin. Both actions proved to be inadequate to handle the high pressures of the .454, however Rossi did make it work. None of these .454s can be called pleasant to shoot. Bighorn Armory now offers their lever action in both .500 S&W (not really a pistol-length cartridge) and .475 Linebaugh. At this stage of my life, however I might really like to experience them, this is a case where the spirit is willing, but the flesh is weak.

My favorite rifles are leverguns, and my favorite leverguns are the Trappers with barrel lengths of 16 ¼". Before the government in its infinite wisdom made shorter lengths illegal, factories offered barrel lengths such as 12" and 14" — which would certainly be exceptionally handy. *My all-around Perfect Rifle is a PCC levergun chambered in .357 Magnum* and outfitted as the above-mentioned stainless steel Rossi. Properly loaded, it also makes a very effective home-defense rifle — especially in such a situation I appreciate the fact I'm in control of loading the next cartridge into the chamber.

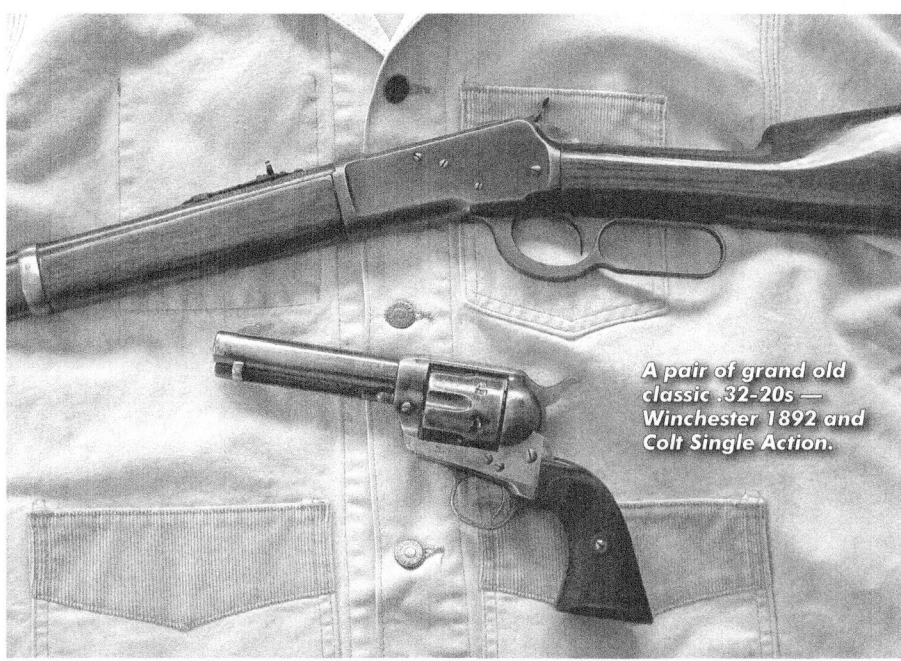

A pair of grand old classic .32-20s — Winchester 1892 and Colt Single Action.

There is nothing I am likely to encounter in my area that cannot be handled with a .357 Mag. levergun such as this, and if I ever wander into a more challenging environment, I can always reach for a Trapper in .44 Magnum or set up for Heavy .45 Colt.

Jeremy D. Clough

OLD SLABSIDES IN THE WEST

The 1911 as a Peacemaker

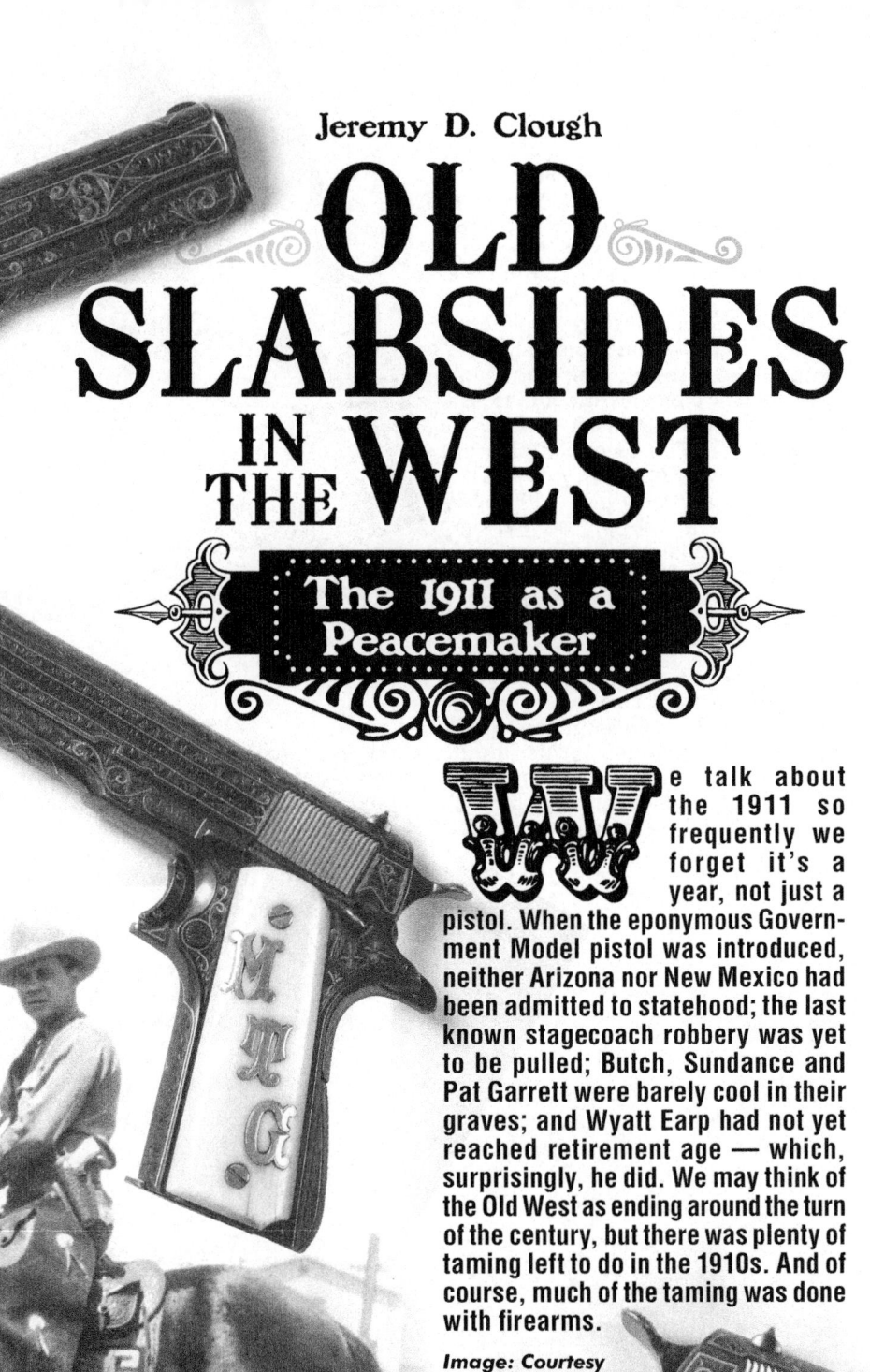

Perhaps the most famous of Western 1911s is the right-hand pistol owned by Texas Ranger M.T. "Lone Wolf" Gonzaullas. The carved and inlaid ivory grips were mirror image on each pistol, with the steerhead side worn on the outside and his initials on the inside. Image: Courtesy of the Texas Ranger Hall of Fame and Museum, Waco, Texas (Loaned by Joyce Green/Catalog #2920.001-002)

The legendary M.T. "Lone Wolf" Gonzaullas, one of the "Christian Rangers," was known to share the gospel with arrestees. He was also known for his highly ornate custom pistols with which he was particularly deadly. Image: Courtesy of the Texas Ranger Hall of Fame and Museum, Waco, Texas

We talk about the 1911 so frequently we forget it's a year, not just a pistol. When the eponymous Government Model pistol was introduced, neither Arizona nor New Mexico had been admitted to statehood; the last known stagecoach robbery was yet to be pulled; Butch, Sundance and Pat Garrett were barely cool in their graves; and Wyatt Earp had not yet reached retirement age — which, surprisingly, he did. We may think of the Old West as ending around the turn of the century, but there was plenty of taming left to do in the 1910s. And of course, much of the taming was done with firearms.

Image: Courtesy of the Texas Ranger Hall of Fame and Museum, Waco, Texas (Loaned by Joyce Green/ Catalog #2920.001-002)

We may think of the Old West as ending around the turn of the century, but there was plenty of taming left to do in the 1910s.

Taken in 1919, this image of a mounted customs inspector is the oldest known photo of a Texas Ranger with a clearly identifiable 1911. His cocked .45 appears to have stag grips, while the gunbelt still has individual cartridge loops on it and the holster resembles a King Ranch version of the Mexican Loop (left).

Dub Naylor and an unidentified Ranger in front of headquarters looking at a pair of 1911s. Naylor's pistol looks engraved, while the other Ranger's 1911 appears to have stag grips and is worn in a Brill-style holster, the definitive Ranger holster of the modern era and the last of the distinctly Western ones (below). Images: Courtesy of the Texas Ranger Hall of Fame and Museum, Waco, Texas

Gonzaullas' left-hand pistol is a match for the other, with the addition of a custom ambidextrous thumb safety lever. Both are engraved above the trigger with "Never draw me without cause, nor shield me with dishonor."

Ranger Up!

It's impossible to talk about law enforcement in the American West without mentioning the Texas Rangers. They weren't the only ones to use .45 Autos from horseback, but with nearly 200 years of history, they loom large and provide a unique timeline of gun use, not least of all because they kept records — incomplete, but still useful. For those who want to know more about Rangers and Ranger firearms, I highly recommend *Firearms of the Texas Rangers* by Doug Dukes. It is well written, shocking, well researched and I relied heavily on it for this article.

Despite their reputation for tradition, *the Texas Rangers are generally early adopters of technology, especially firearms.* The 1911 was a bit of an anomaly, however, and while it was no doubt used earlier, the first known clearly identifiable photo of a Ranger with one dates to 1919. Once accepted, the 1911 was used enthusiastically, and some 80% of the current Ranger force still carry it.

Ironically, the Ranger's delay makes the U.S. Army the first significant user of the 1911 during the 1916 Punitive Expedition into Mexico. Led by General John J. "Black Jack" Pershing, the nearly year-long pursuit of Pancho Villa led deep into Mexico in retaliation for Villa's bloody attack on Columbus, N.M. Notable events included the use of 1911s in a cavalry charge Pershing himself called "a brilliant piece of work," and the killing of two of Villa's men by a young, insistent lieutenant armed with an engraved Colt SAA. This revolver later became world famous, along with its owner, General George S. Patton. *The two notches he carved into the ivory grips that night are generally less known, as they were on the side of the grip normally worn against the body.* But I digress …

Western Fit and Finish

A century later, the modern 1911 generally appears with a standardized suite of changes to the original design so *de rigueur* they're no longer considered modifications. A beavertail grip safety, for example, and extended thumb safety, frontstrap checkering, slotted hammer and an alloy trigger with lightening cuts. It was, of course, not always so. The earliest Western 1911s started as shockingly beautiful, high-polished pistols finished in a deep, lustrous charcoal blue accented by the startling indigo wink of nitre blued small parts — a gun so pretty the military told Colt to tone down its eye-catching polishing game before they got somebody shot. It's hard to think about dragging that glistening gem through the brush and sand on horseback, but into the desert they went.

Like the SAA and the 1851 Navy before it, 1911s were often modified, frequently in ways mirroring what was done on SAAs: engraving, frequently topped with a silver or nickel finish, as well as personalized grips, and the pistols were usually carried two at a time in a double rig. While no doubt attractive, the metal finishes also gave some protection to the gun in *an environment so harsh some Rangers resorted to using saltwater to "rust in" the screws on their SAAs so they wouldn't back out.* While less common, some pistols had modified sights, including at least one Ranger 1911 with the King mirrored front sight usually seen on revolvers — a not-so-subtle reminder these were pretty guns, but still deadly serious tools for a dangerous and bloody business where any edge counted.

Grips

In addition to stag, which adds traction but doesn't rub you raw

Texas Ranger Bob Goss showing off his 1911s. Note they are carried as a pair on the traditional Western second gunbelt, much as a pair of SAAs would be. This photo was taken circa 1930, by which time the 1911 was firmly ensconced in the Ranger world. Image: Courtesy of the Texas Ranger Hall of Fame and Museum, Waco, Texas

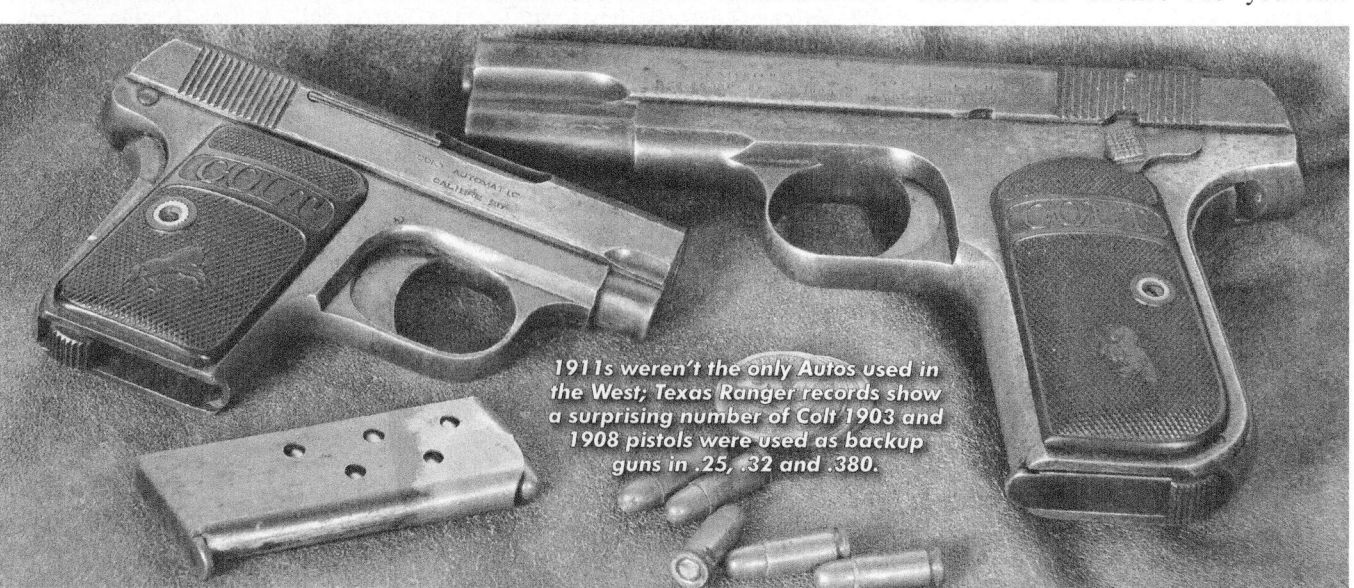

1911s weren't the only Autos used in the West; Texas Ranger records show a surprising number of Colt 1903 and 1908 pistols were used as backup guns in .25, .32 and .380.

The earliest Western 1911s looked like this: High-polished in charcoal and nitre blue, with double-diamond grips and looking way too pretty to be bounced around through the bush. Many were further embellished.

when worn against the skin, custom grips were also made of ivory or pearl. I'm aware of Patton's thoughts on such things, but Ranger Frank Hamer is credited with having killed several of the dozens of men with a pearl-handled sixgun he called "Old Lucky." Patton would have been well-advised to keep his own counsel in the company of such men.

Starting with ivory or pearl, many of the grips were then carved, sometimes with the classic steerhead design seen so often on thumb busters, and usually inlaid with initials or symbols made of precious metals. Mexican eagle-and-snake symbols also showed up, as well as American eagles, Masonic logos or other personally significant iconography.

Others went all the way, adding intricately styled metal grips made completely of gold or silver, carved, engraved, or with precious or semi-precious stones inlaid, a somewhat more tasteful version of the modern narco pistol. These grips were often made across the border in Mexico, such as the pair gifted to famed Ranger Joaquin Jackson who wore them on his Commander.

Of course, prettying a gun up wasn't the only thing done — other more practical modifications included tying the grip safety down with rawhide (apparently the Rangers thought just because the cavalry needed one didn't mean they did), or removing the trigger guard, a modification also found on some SAAs.

"Civilian" Calibers

Proximity to the border also explains one of the caliber choices. The classic 1911 caliber is .45 ACP, which was illegal for Mexican civilians to own as it was considered a military caliber. Not so with the .38 Super; so a lawman (or, you know, whoever) crossing the border was still able to find ammo, as it's what all the civilian-owned 1911s would be chambered for. Some also considered the faster .38 Super to be a better stopper than the big-and-slow .45, and as the Old West faded into the Depression and gangster era, the .38 was prized for its ability to penetrate the primitive body armor of the day or autobody steel.

Christian Rangers

Perhaps the most famous of the Western 1911s is the pair carried by legendary Ranger M.T. "Lone Wolf" Gonzaullas. A fascinating man who was born in Spain and served as a major in the Mexican Army prior to joining the Rangers, Gonzaullas was one of the famous "Christian Rangers," known to share the gospel with men he arrested, and an accomplished lawman whose openness to innovation gifted Texas with a modern crime lab second only to that of the FBI. His pair of blued M1911A1

Engraving and ivory grips were common embellishments. Made in 2011, this pre-A1-style Colt never saw Texas, but many identical ones did.

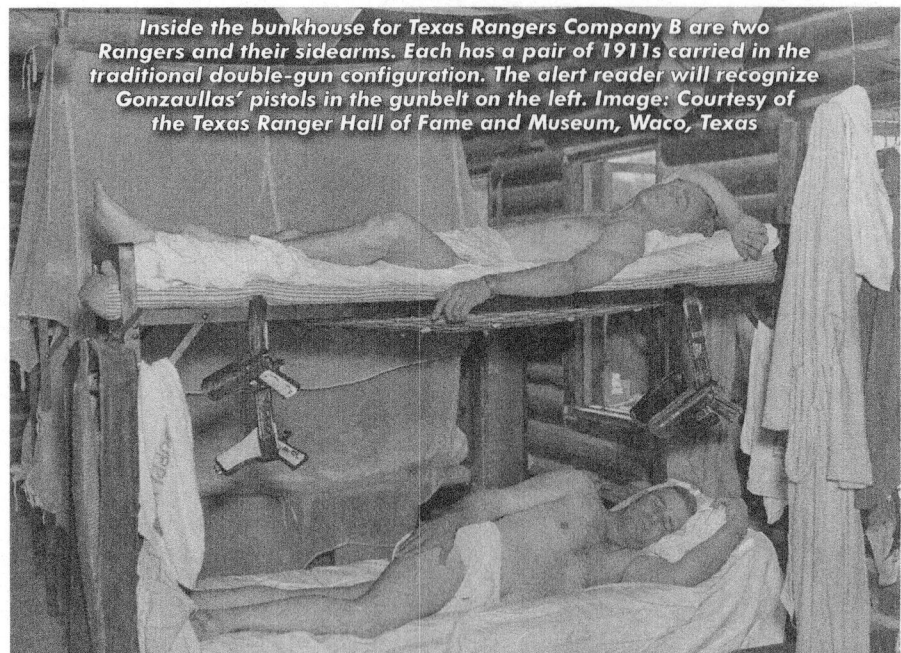

Inside the bunkhouse for Texas Rangers Company B are two Rangers and their sidearms. Each has a pair of 1911s carried in the traditional double-gun configuration. The alert reader will recognize Gonzaullas' pistols in the gunbelt on the left. Image: Courtesy of the Texas Ranger Hall of Fame and Museum, Waco, Texas

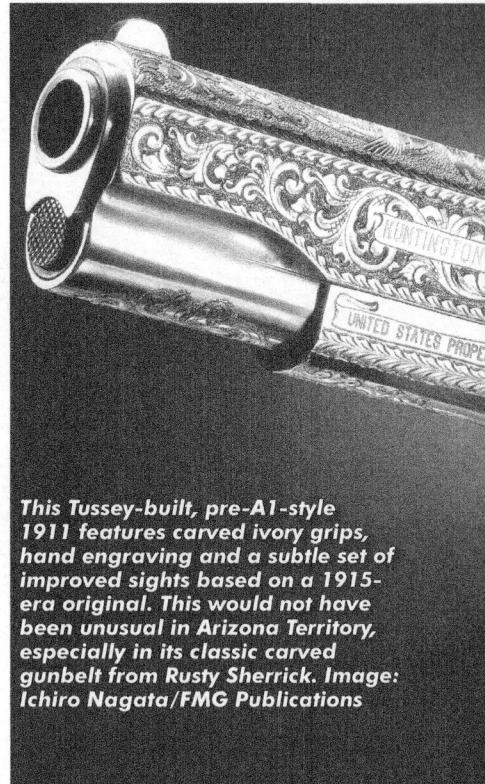

This Tussey-built, pre-A1-style 1911 features carved ivory grips, hand engraving and a subtle set of improved sights based on a 1915-era original. This would not have been unusual in Arizona Territory, especially in its classic carved gunbelt from Rusty Sherrick. Image: Ichiro Nagata/FMG Publications

Texas Ranger Dub Naylor evidently horsing around with his pair of 1911s. Apparently gun-safety rules were a bit different then. Image: Courtesy of the Texas Ranger Hall of Fame and Museum, Waco, Texas

pistols, which are now in the Texas Ranger Hall of Fame and Museum, were factory engraved at Colt and gold inlaid. Among the engraving is the legend, "Never draw me without cause, nor shield me with dishonor."

Clearly a pair, the ivory grips are embellished with his initials inlaid in gold on the side worn closest to the body, while the grip panels facing outward carry a carved steerhead with gold horns and nose ring. If you have trouble figuring out which pistol goes on which side, the left-side pistol has a custom ambidextrous thumb safety, well before the John Bianchi-inspired Swenson ambi safety hit the market.

The addition of pewter grips to this Nighthawk Series 70 Colt takes the gun from retro to Western. The grips have the Rampant Colt on one side and Colt's Armsmear Crest on the other.

Adding elk or stag grips to a 1911A1, à la Walt Longmire, completely changes the look of the gun. These are American Elk grips from Eagle Grips on a minimalist custom Springfield.

And of course, both grip safeties are locked in the downward "fire" position.

Both trigger guards are cut off just forward of the short A1-style triggers, to which wide trigger shoes have been added. This wasn't unique to Lone Wolf, nor was it the only pistol of his from which he had removed the trigger guards. A Fitz-style Colt .38 with a cutaway trigger guard was stolen from his vehicle early in his career, only to be recovered years later in a car used by Bonnie and Clyde, who were killed by Frank Hamer, another Ranger.

Western Simplicity

While most modern interpretations of the Western 1911 omit the cutaway trigger guard, it's relatively easy to customize a 1911 to look Western, since the hallmark of the early guns is simplicity. It's a short step from retro to Western, and simply adding stag or elk grips, à la Longmire, is quite effective — as is the addition of metal grips, though they're much harder to find. An engraved pre-A1-style pistol makes a compelling, though pricey, case. Whatever it is, it should have a spur hammer, not to mention some fine leather.

Hmm … there's an idea. Maybe we'll talk about it a bit more this time next year.

Special thanks to Roy Huntington, FMG Publications' special projects editor, and Christina Stopka of the Texas Ranger Museum and Hall of Fame.

HANDCRAFTED INTO YOUR MASTERPIECE
Precision Handcrafted 1911s

Welcome to Volkmann Precision LLC, where each 1911 is painstakingly handcrafted to the highest standards in the industry. All pistols are built using the best quality raw stock metals and the finest machining processes. Every part is CNC or EDM cut to the tightest tolerances, hand fit and then lapped for a perfect fit. Every pistol is built one masterpiece at a time. These fine works of art are constructed from the best match grade parts and completely combat ready. There are no "assembly lines" at my shop, I am the only craftsman. Your pistol will get the attention to detail it deserves. When you're ready to own the finest 1911 contact me, Luke Volkmann of Volkmann Precision.

www.lukevolkmann.com
www.volkmannprecision.com

303-884-8654
volkmannprecision@yahoo.com

Roger Smith
BATTLE FOR SUPREMACY
The .44XL and the .410 Small-Bore Shotshells

The evolution of .44 and .410 shotshells.
Front row, from left: UMC Wood-saboted .44 CFW, Winchester .44 WCF, American Cartridge paper-saboted .44-40, Western green paper sabot .44XL and Western red paper sabot.
Back row, from left: Eley pinfire similar to this RWS 20-ga., U.S. Cartridge .410-12mm, "410 BEST 12m/m" headstamped REM-UMC, American Cartridge 2" brass .410, recent production CBC 2 ¼" .410 brass shell and early 1960s Dominion .44-40 with #7 ½ shot.

Top: All-American .44 shotguns originally were stamped "44" or "44 CALIBER." **Middle:** Shortly after the .410 made its U.S. debut around 1914–15, new .44 shotguns were chambered to accept it as well, and the barrels were stamped "410-44." **Bottom:** When the .410 was new in the U.S., some companies glamorized it by adding the European 12mm designation.

"**he .44 what?"** Yes, you read that correctly. The .44XL. This is the tale of two shotgun calibers with two totally different origins, one uniquely American and the other originating in the UK, that eventually came together, with the latter overcoming and absorbing the former. And yes, you also read that correctly — the .44XL and the .410 are calibers, not shotgun-gauge sizes.

Small-bore shotguns for pest control and small game go back to the muzzleloading days since they were more efficient than downloading the larger gauges. Users loaded them to whatever level of powder and shot performance desired, from puny pest punishers to the "Good Grief, Gerty!" level of the bigger bores.

.410 Origin Story

When the .410 shotgun first appeared in England in 1847, it used what we for over 100 years have considered a conventional cardboard shell body attached to a brass base. Made by Eley Brothers, the difference was it used the pinfire priming system until about 1874, when they began advertising the modern, reloadable Boxer-primed centerfire 2" .410 cartridges we would easily recognize today. *Firing a mere ³⁄₈ oz. (164 grains) of shot from the get-go, it was considered an expert's round* for wealthy sportsmen's shooting games. It also made an excellent garden gun, an upgrade over the 9mm rimfires with their ¼ oz. of shot, used by the gentlemen's gardeners to keep the vermin

Gunmakers promptly started chambering their .44 shotguns for the .410 instead, stamping the barrels "410-44," since the .44XL and the .44-40 shot cartridges could both be fired in a .410.

26

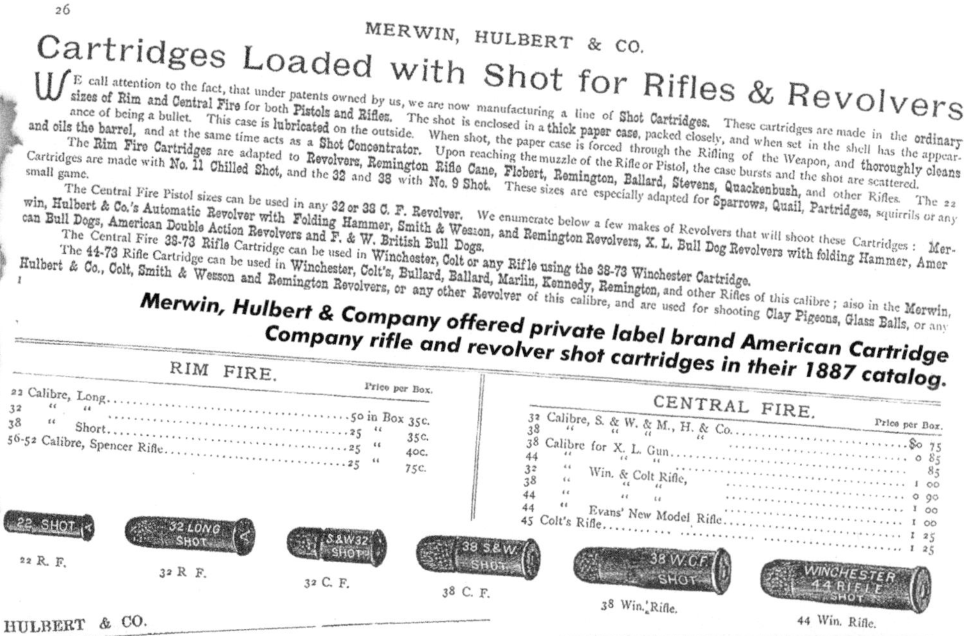

MERWIN, HULBERT & CO.

Cartridges Loaded with Shot for Rifles & Revolvers

WE call attention to the fact, that under patents owned by us, we are now manufacturing a line of Shot Cartridges. These cartridges are made in the ordinary sizes of Rim and Central Fire for both Pistols and Rifles. The shot is enclosed in a thick paper case, packed closely, and when set in the shell has the appearance of being a bullet. This case is lubricated on the outside. When shot, the paper case is forced through the Rifling of the Weapon, and thoroughly cleans and oils the barrel, and at the same time acts as a Shot Concentrator. Upon reaching the muzzle of the Rifle or Pistol, the case bursts and the shot are scattered.

The Rim Fire Cartridges are adapted to Revolvers, Remington Rifle Cane, Flobert, Remington, Ballard, Stevens, Quackenbush, and other Rifles. The 22 Cartridges are made with No. 11 Chilled Shot, and the 32 and 38 with No. 9 Shot. These sizes are especially adapted for Sparrows, Quail, Partridges, squirrils or any small game.

The Central Fire Pistol sizes can be used in any 32 or 38 C. F. Revolver. We enumerate below a few makes of Revolvers that will shoot these Cartridges: Merwin, Hulbert & Co.'s Automatic Revolver with Folding Hammer, Smith & Wesson, and Remington Revolvers, X. L. Bull Dog Revolvers with folding Hammer, American Bull Dogs, American Double Action Revolvers and F. & W. British Bull Dogs.

The Central Fire 38-73 Rifle Cartridge can be used in Winchester, Colt or any Rifle using the 38-73 Winchester Cartridge.

The 44-73 Rifle Cartridge can be used in Winchester, Colt's, Bullard, Ballard, Marlin, Kennedy, Remington, and other Rifles of this calibre; also in the Merwin, Hulbert & Co., Colt, Smith & Wesson and Remington Revolvers, or any other Revolver of this calibre, and are used for shooting Clay Pigeons, Glass Balls, or any

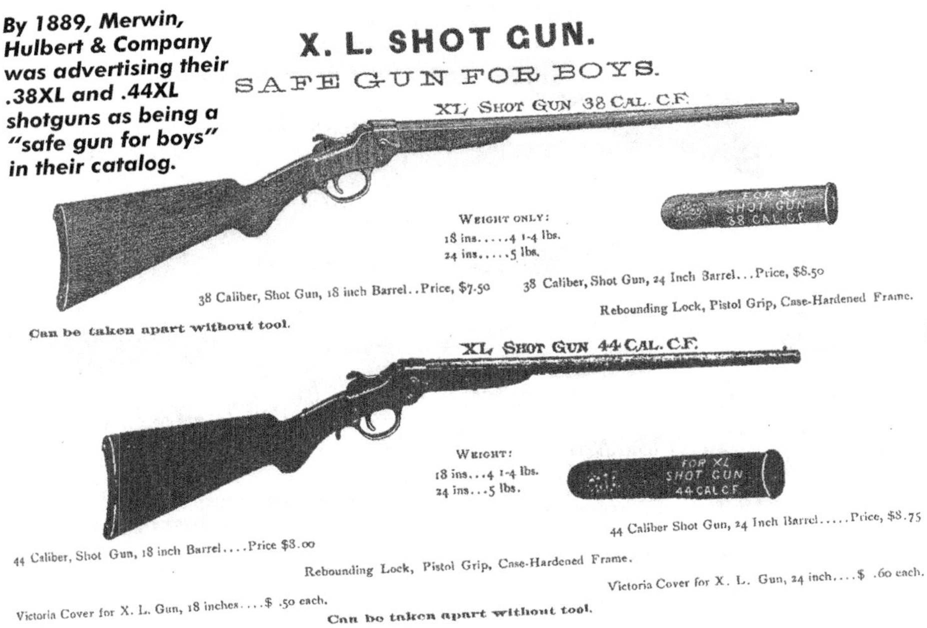

RIM FIRE.

		Price per Box.
22 Calibre, Long		
32 " "	50 in Box	35c.
38 " Short	25 "	35c.
56-52 Calibre, Spencer Rifle	25 "	40c.
	25 "	75c.

CENTRAL FIRE.

	Price per Box.
32 Calibre, S. & W. & M., H. & Co.	
38 " " " "	$0 75
38 Calibre for X. L. Gun	0 85
44 " " "	85
32 " Win. & Colt Rifle,	1 00
38 " " "	0 90
44 " " "	1 00
44 " Evans' New Model Rifle	1 00
45 Colt's Rifle	1 25
	1 25

22 R. F. 32 R F. 32 C. F. 38 C. F. 38 Win. Rifle. 44 Win. Rifle.

MERWIN, HULBERT & CO.

Merwin, Hulbert & Company offered private label brand American Cartridge Company rifle and revolver shot cartridges in their 1887 catalog.

X. L. SHOT GUN.

SAFE GUN FOR BOYS.

XL SHOT GUN 38 CAL. C.F.

WEIGHT ONLY:
18 ins.....4 1-4 lbs.
24 ins.....5 lbs.

38 Caliber, Shot Gun, 18 inch Barrel..Price, $7.50

38 Caliber, Shot Gun, 24 Inch Barrel...Price, $8.50

Rebounding Lock, Pistol Grip, Case-Hardened Frame.

Can be taken apart without tool.

XL SHOT GUN 44 CAL. C.F.

WEIGHT:
18 ins...4 1-4 lbs.
24 ins...5 lbs.

44 Caliber, Shot Gun, 18 inch Barrel....Price $8.00

44 Caliber Shot Gun, 24 Inch Barrel.....Price, $8.75

Rebounding Lock, Pistol Grip, Case-Hardened Frame.

Victoria Cover for X. L. Gun, 24 inch....$ .60 each.

Victoria Cover for X. L. Gun, 18 inches....$ .50 each.

Can be taken apart without tool.

By 1889, Merwin, Hulbert & Company was advertising their .38XL and .44XL shotguns as being a "safe gun for boys" in their catalog.

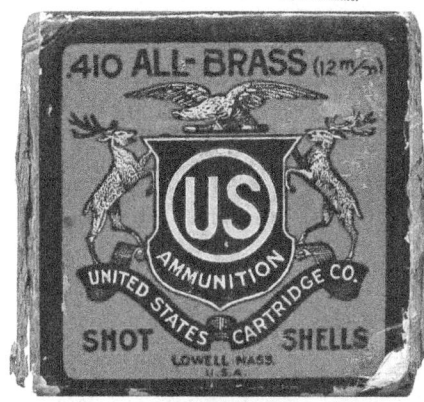

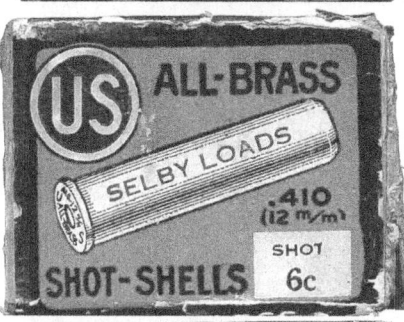

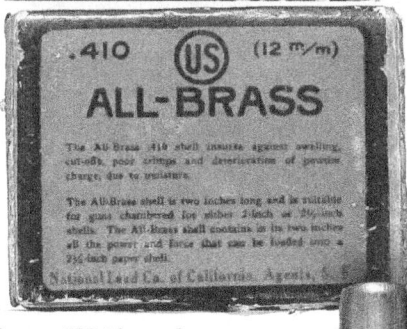

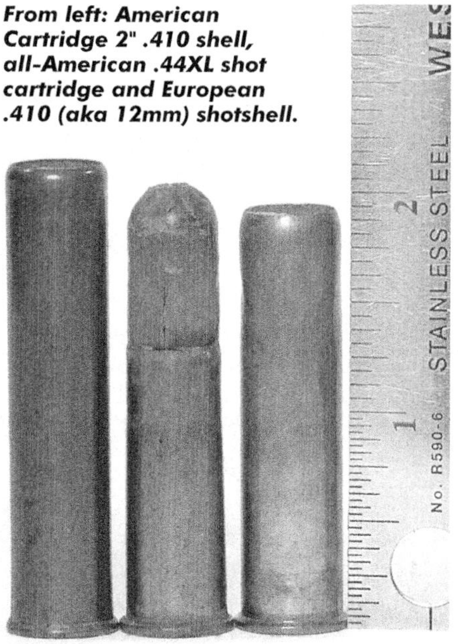

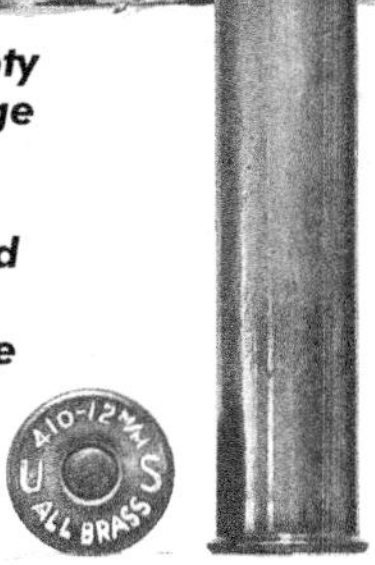

population down. It was unheard of on this side of the pond until 1914. When mention was first made in the pages of the American sporting magazines, it was considered a puny novelty.

Meanwhile, in America ...

Meanwhile, in *Real America*, another small, all-brass shotshell and the shotguns for it had already long been in use by us commoners in and around our gardens and outbuildings. It was simply called the .44.

This original .44 shot cartridge, and the shotguns for it, appeared about five years after Winchester's .44 WCF reloadable cartridge for its new 1873 lever-action rifle. It was the same case, but instead of a bullet, lead shot was contained in a bullet-shaped paper sabot patented by the Phoenix Metallic Cartridge Company in 1879.

From left: American Cartridge 2" .410 shell, all-American .44XL shot cartridge and European .410 (aka 12mm) shotshell.

A pre-1926 box of empty "United States Cartridge Company .410-12m/m All Brass Shot-Shells" to be loaded by the end user (above). View of an empty U.S. Cartridge "410-12m/m" brass shell (right). Images: Guy Hildebrand (OldAmmo.com)

The paper sabots used for the XL shot cartridges were easily damaged. From left, wood sabot by UMC, American Cartridge .44-40 paper sabot, Western green smokeless XL, damaged red REM-UMC XL, Western red XL by Western cartridge and early simple tapered nose Winchester .44 WCF.

Inexpensive single-shot shotguns chambered for the .44-40 quickly appeared, marketed by Forehand & Wadsworth (until 1890), Forehand Arms Company (1890–1902), Hopkins & Allen (until 1916), Merwin & Hulbert and Hulbert Brothers (until 1916), Harrington & Richardson, Iver-Johnson, Savage and Stevens. The last four also reportedly made private-label .44XL shotguns for large wholesale distributors. Several also made side by side double-barrel 44s as well.

Phoenix ran into severe financial trouble, and secretly friendly competitors and co-conspirators (and occasional backdoor partners) Winchester and Union Metallic Cartridge Company were able to purchase Phoenix and its paper sabot patent in 1891 from Merwin, Hulbert & Company. The intent was to keep the patent out of the hands of competitors instead of having to wait for it to expire in 1898 to use it themselves. Under UMC/Winchester ownership, Phoenix was renamed the American Cartridge Company and continued to

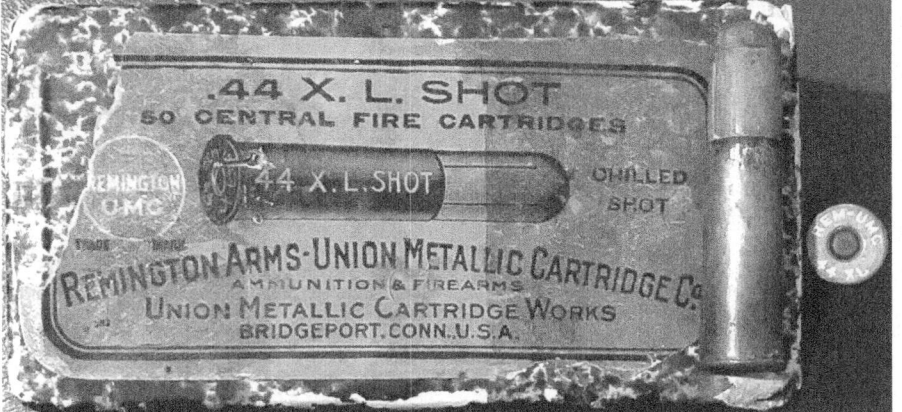

A box of Remington-UMC black powder cartridges dating to the 1913–1916 era. Image: Guy Hildebrand (OldAmmo.com)

Pre-1926 box of United States Cartridge Company .44 WCF shot cartridges, prior to the Winchester takeover. Image: Guy Hildebrand (OldAmmo.com)

A box of empty, primed .44XL shells made by UMC before their 1912 merger with Remington. Image: Guy Hildebrand (OldAmmo.com)

The progression of the .44 WCF (.44-40) shot cartridge crimp style. The four on the left are by Winchester, followed by Peters' bullet-shaped crimp design used by Winchester and a 1960's Dominion, also utilizing the latest Winchester profile.

produce paper-saboted pistol-length shot cartridges. Neither UMC nor Winchester ever did produce paper-saboted shot cartridges with their own name on them, however. Somewhere in the early to mid-1880s, UMC obtained their own patent on a hollow wooden bullet to hold the shot.

The Show Must Go On

The whole shebang really got rolling when *Winchester started making special smooth-bored 1873 lever-action rifles and equally special .44-40 shotshells around 1884 for Buffalo Bill's Wild West exposition.* During their first year they found *shooting lead bullets at aerial targets was too dangerous* and caused too much expensive damage beyond the show grounds.

These special long brass shells were loaded with about 20 grains of black powder (presumably with a thin overpowder card) and ¼ oz. (109 grains) of #7 ½ chilled shot topped with an overshot card. They were then heavily roll crimped with a long taper, bringing them to the same length as a regular .44 WCF (.44-40) round with a bullet. At the usual distance of 15 or so yards they threw a pattern about the same size as the 2 ¼" feather- or flour-filled glass balls thrown into the air for the exhibition shooters. Of course, the cartridge quickly caught on with the shooters employed by the competing wild west shows that soon sprang up.

After 1898, the appearance of the paper-saboted extra-long .44XL version of the cartridge from other companies holding more shot helped boosted the popularity of the .44 shotguns. A full 2" long, the XL is much too long and was never intended for revolvers or repeating rifles. Shot

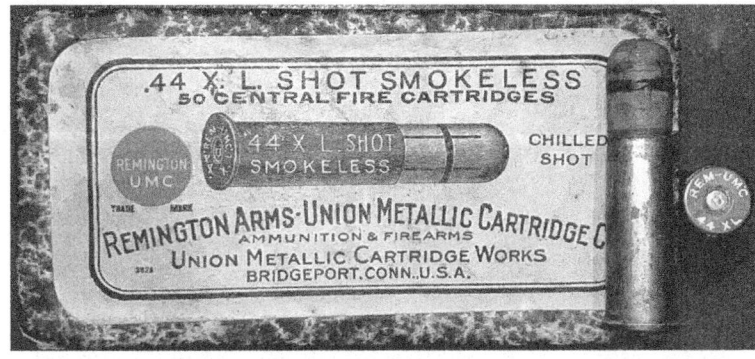

A box of Remington-UMC smokeless cartridges, also from the 1913–1916 era. The black band on the sabot indicates smokeless. Image: Guy Hildebrand (OldAmmo.com)

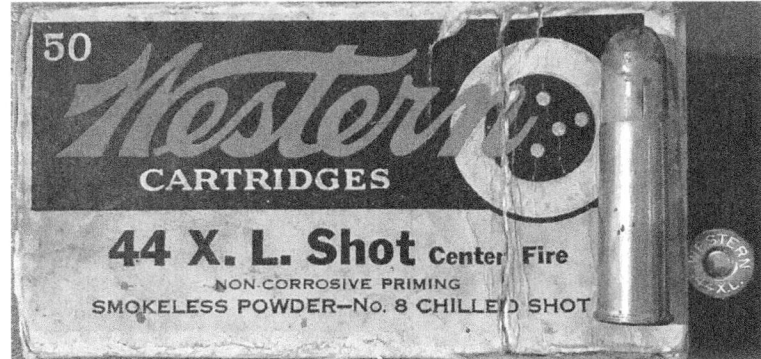

This Western Cartridge Company box (1927–1944) contains smokeless loads with #8 chilled shot and non-corrosive primers. The green sabot apparently means smokeless. Image: Guy Hildebrand (OldAmmo.com)

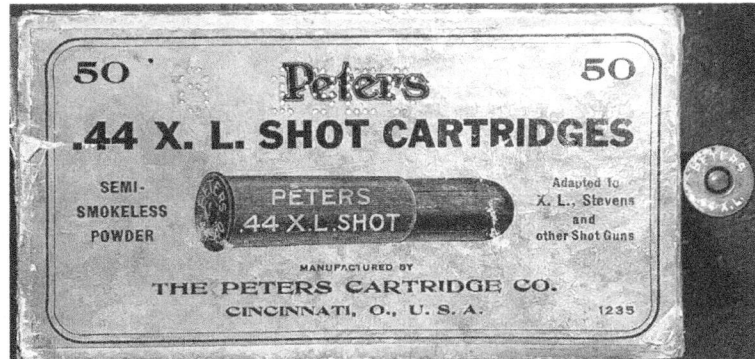

Peters Cartridge Company box, probably from the mid-1920s. "Adapted to X.L. Stevens and other Shot Guns." Semi-smokeless powder was typically a blend of black and smokeless. Image: Guy Hildebrand (OldAmmo.com)

> Small-bore shotguns for pest control and small game go back to the muzzleloading days, since they were more efficient than downloading the larger gauges.

The back of the Western box specifically says, "Adapted to .44-40 single shot rifles, .410 shotguns..." Image: Guy Hildebrand (OldAmmo.com)

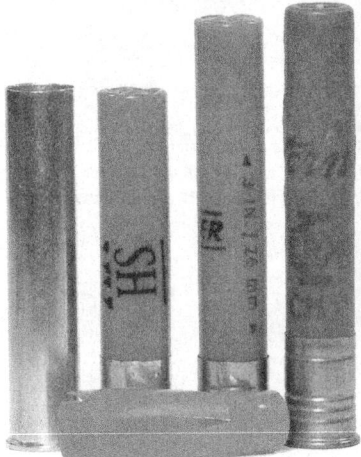
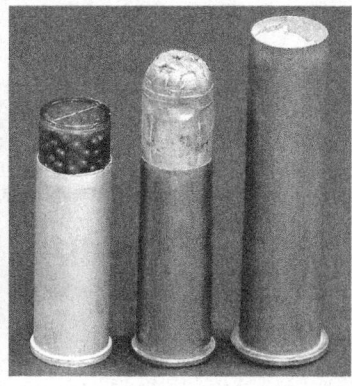

The old smokeless .44XL shotgun cartridge (center) with its approximately 200-grain load of shot didn't give up much to the smokeless .45-70 forager shot shell (right), much less to the modern .45 Colt with its plastic shot capsule holding approximately 146 grains of #9.

Left: A 2½" shot cartridge is really only 2¼" long after crimping, like CBC's current .410 brass shotshell on the left. Winchester introduced the 3" shell (center, right) in 1933, carrying ¾ oz. of shot. Brass goes way back into the 1800s, but paper (far right) was actually first.

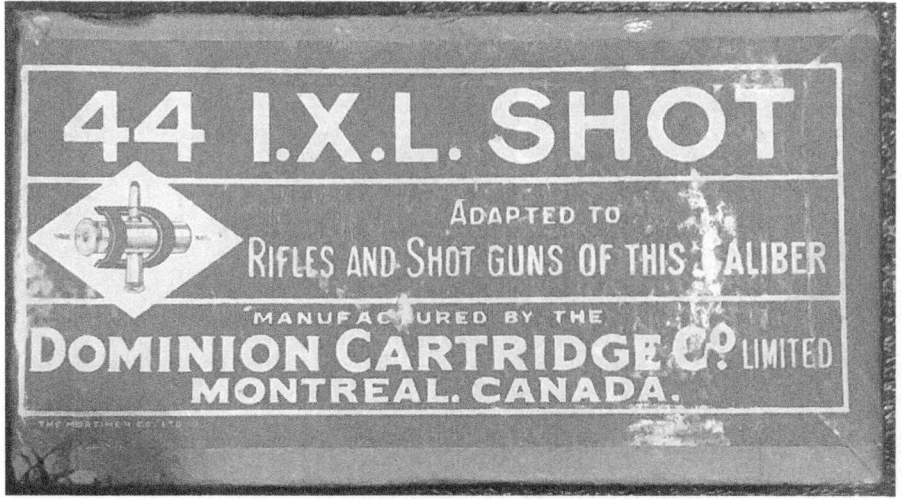

Dominion black powder .44XL cartridge box, 1913–1917. Image: Guy Hildebrand (OldAmmo.com)

sizes were available from #5 to #12, and in even smaller "dust" size. Mice in the house, anyone?

Rise of the .410

The .410 quickly gained a foothold in the U.S. because the full-length shell bodies were much less fragile than the .44XL's thin paper sabot. Gunmakers promptly started chambering their .44 shotguns for the .410 instead, stamping the barrels "410-44," since the .44XL and the .44-40 shot cartridges could both be fired in a .410. Remington offered empty 2" and 2½" .410 paper shells in 1917, all-brass shells in both lengths soon appeared on the market and gunsmiths began rechambering old .44 shotguns for the .410. Peters began selling both empty hulls and loaded .410 shotshells in both lengths in 1925. It doesn't seem to be recorded anywhere just how much the step at the front of the .410 chamber affected the patterning of the old .44 shot cartridges.

There were also early .410 U.S. shotguns stamped .410-12mm, 12mm being the Continental European metric designation for the case outside diameter, while the English decimal .410 is for the bore size. Brass 12mm shells were a few thousandths short of 2" before loading and roll crimping, 1 ⅞" long after. Brass .410s came in nominal 2" and 2½" lengths. My old brass two-inchers measure 2 3/32" long after crimping by the factory.

Winchester introduced the 3" .410 shell in 1933 along with their new high-dollar Model 42 pump shotgun for it. Even in the depths of the Great Depression, it was economically feasible for many of the poorly heeled to have an old single-shot .44 rechambered for the new 3" shell.

The .44XL cartridges were still in Remington-UMC's catalog through 1941 and Western's through 1942. World War II sporting ammunition shortages emptied warehouse shelves of old .44XL inventory along with everything else, and all that were made after the war were the regular-length .44-40 shotshells, mostly marketed for use in the Marble Game Getter. These were still available into the 1960s from Dominion in Canada but eventually disappeared, and the once-popular .44 shotguns became not much more than a footnote in America's firearms history.

I owe special thanks to Guy Hildebrand (OldAmmo.com) and Joe St. Charles (seller oldwestammo on GunBroker.com) for sharing their knowledge and cartridge collections with me. This article would not have been possible without their help.

EXPANDED 2ND EDITION

If You want to Become a Gunsmith You need to read this book!

LEARN HOW YOU CAN BECOME A CERTIFIED GUNSMITH!

Becoming an American Gunsmith shows you a path to follow to become a Certified Professional Gunsmith without having to give up your lifestyle, income, leave home, or spend tens of thousands of dollars attending a campus based school.

Mr. Kelly details how mastering the Design, Function, and Repair (DF&R) training concepts revealed in this book will enable you to maintain, repair, build, and customize firearms as an AGI Certified Gunsmith.

This information will provide you with the ability to follow your passion of working on firearms and ensure your personal freedom and financial security. Included:

- How to set up your shop
- What tools and equipment are *really* necessary
- Numerous suggestions and resources to help you establish a *successful* gunsmithing shop.

Read this book and you will learn how you can be an AGI Certified Gunsmith, protecting and participating in the ongoing history of firearms in America.

2nd Edition Sale - $FREE *Limited Time Offer!*
Just pay $5 shipping and handling.
For complete details and to order go to: (reg $14.95 plus s/h)

1-800-797-0867

www.AmericanGunsmith.com

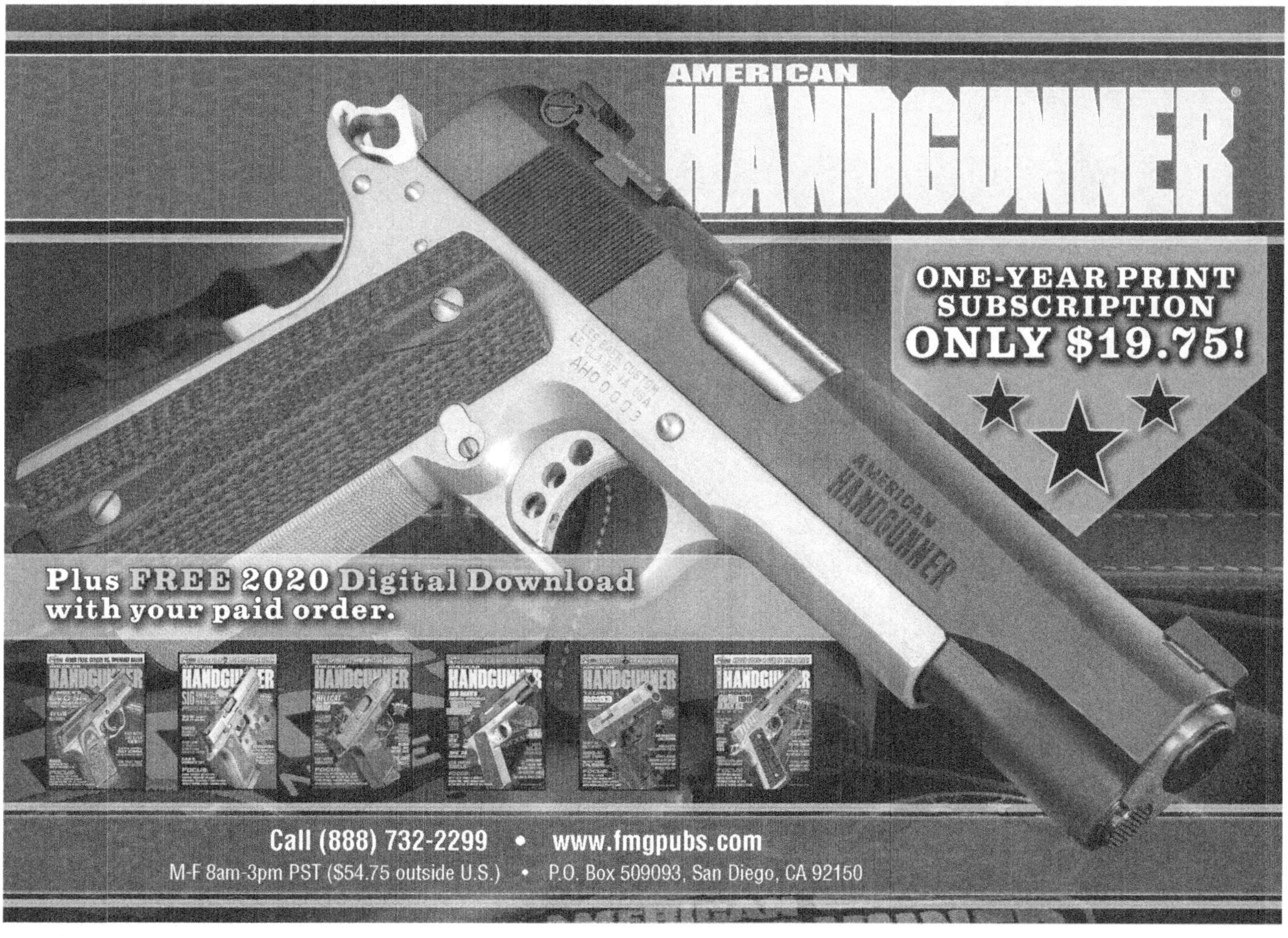

AMERICAN HANDGUNNER

ONE-YEAR PRINT SUBSCRIPTION ONLY $19.75!

Plus FREE 2020 Digital Download with your paid order.

Call (888) 732-2299 • www.fmgpubs.com
M-F 8am-3pm PST ($54.75 outside U.S.) • P.O. Box 509093, San Diego, CA 92150

Mike "Duke" Venturino · Photos: Yvonne Venturino

SMOKE, NOISE AND BIG TIME CONCUSSION

Loading Black Powder Revolver Cartridges

A question often asked of me as a known black powder shooter is, "Why would anyone put black powder through a revolver knowing it's dirty, smelly, hard to clean, weak in power and gives no accuracy worth mentioning." Now get this; in my entire 72 years I've never put anything smoking in my mouth. Nothing! Never! But I've come to adore the smell of black powder smoke!

As to dirty and hard to clean, those points are subjective. Properly loaded black powder revolver rounds are still dirty but guns will clean up easily as we will discuss shortly. I've also learned this over the years: *Nickel-plated revolvers are easier*

All of these types of black powders make fine revolver handloads.

Using 33 to 35 grains of Goex FFFg black powder with 250-grain lead alloy bullets, my Colt SAAs with 7½" barrels break 900 fps.

to clean than blued ones. Fouling is certainly more visible. This may be one reason nickeled sixguns were so popular back in the late 1800s. As for weak in power and inaccurate, both charges are nonsense.

Close up of Duke's baffle box, showing a .45 Colt bullet hit #12 board and .44-40 lodged in #9.

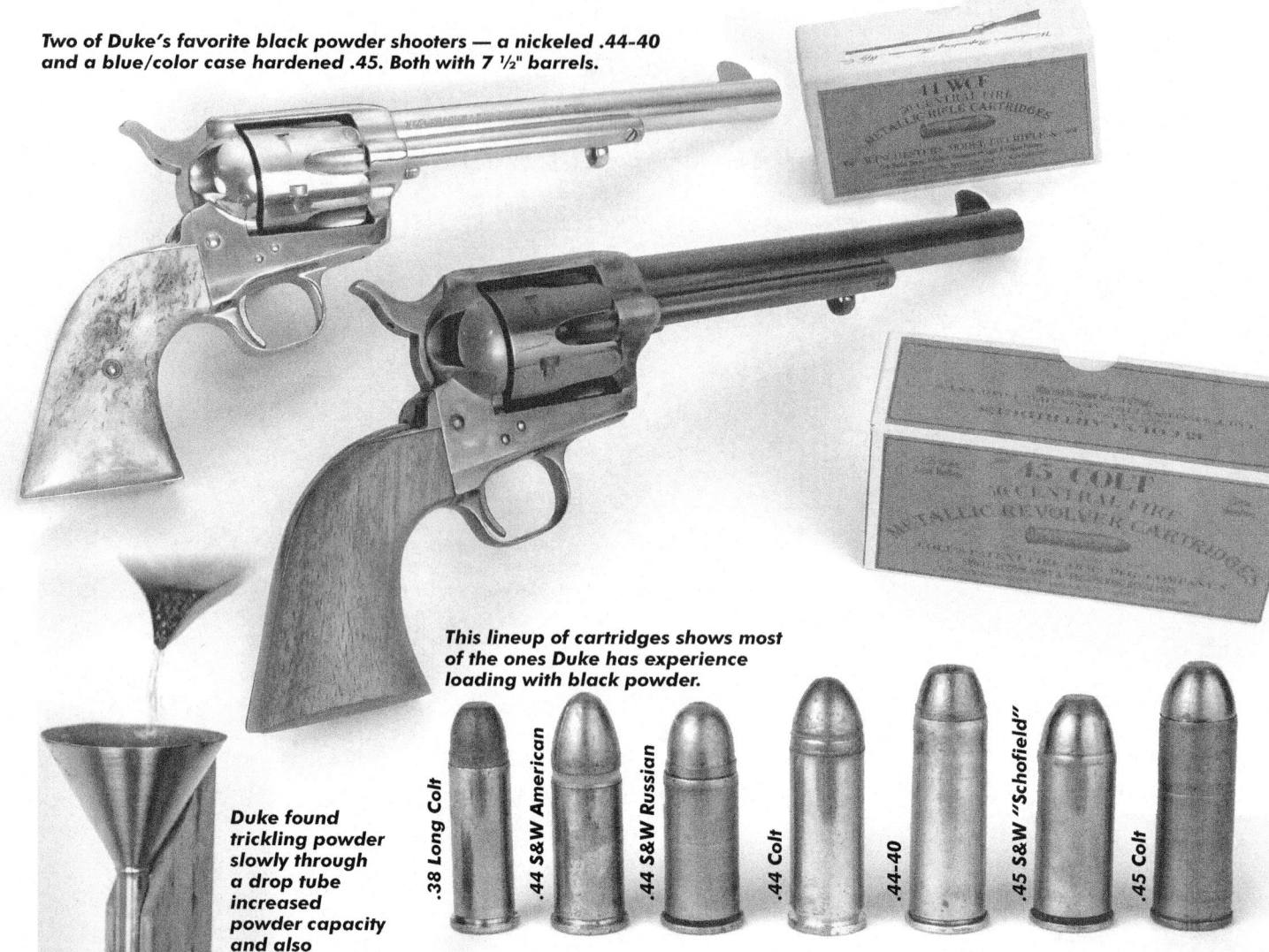

Two of Duke's favorite black powder shooters — a nickeled .44-40 and a blue/color case hardened .45. Both with 7 ½" barrels.

This lineup of cartridges shows most of the ones Duke has experience loading with black powder.

.38 Long Colt | .44 S&W American | .44 S&W Russian | .44 Colt | .44-40 | .45 S&W "Schofield" | .45 Colt

Duke found trickling powder slowly through a drop tube increased powder capacity and also reduced fouling.

Back in the days when reloading black powder was still common, Remington-UMC offered primers specific to it.

Duke says the most important component to black powder cartridge handloading is bullet lubricant. He has used these three.

The Data

Let's consider .45 Colt as an example. In guns of normal strength such as Colt SAAs and all the Italian clones thereof, black powder will give about the same velocities as maximum smokeless loads recommended in current reloading manuals. The *Lyman Cast Bullet Handbook 4th Edition* lists only one smokeless powder load breaking 900 fps with 250-grain cast bullets. The test gun for most of their loads was a 7 ½"-barreled Ruger Blackhawk. Using 33 to 35 grains of Goex FFFg black powder with 250-grain lead alloy bullets, my Colt SAAs with 7 ½" barrels break 900 fps. Once for testing I used a baffle box holding 12 soft pine boards measuring 1" and spaced 1" apart. Fired from about 15' the .45 Colt black powder load mentioned above lodged in the 12th board. A .45 Auto 230-grain FMJ bullet lodged in board number eight. A 200-grain .44-40 bullet with 35 grains Swiss FFFg lodged in board number nine.

As for lack of accuracy, again we must consider how the ammunition was loaded. With this article I've included two photos of groups fired from machine rest using my nickeled Colt Frontier Six Shooter .44-40 with a 7 ½" barrel. One photo is of the first group of 10 rounds fired at 25 yards. The second photo is of the fourth group of 10 rounds fired without cleaning the .44's barrel. Flyers didn't begin until the 40th round.

Reloading Secrets — Volume

As mentioned above, the key in having good black powder revolver ammunition starts at the reloading bench. Let's get one point out of the way first. People often ask me, "How many grains of black powder are suitable?" This answer is short and often causes confused stares, "It doesn't matter!" *The proper amount is however much powder fits in your chosen cases so when the bullet is seated the powder is compressed a bit.* How much is a "bit"? The unscientific answer is about the width of the bullet's grease groove or roughly an eighth of an inch. The exact amount will vary by bullet seating depth and also by case brand. However, here are some hints. About 17 grains fit in .38 Long Colt cases and about 18 in .44 S&W Russian. Perhaps .44-40s and .45 Colts will accept 33 to 35 grains.

In a machine rest test with his .44-40 nickel-plated Colt SAA, Duke fired 40 straight shots with black powder loads. This was the first 10 shot group (left). After firing 30 black powder rounds with no cleaning, this was Duke's fourth 10-shot group. The flyer was shot number 40 (right).

> Once at a Thunder Ranch class I fired some .44-40s in a room of about 16' square while holding a kerosene lantern. Every round's concussion blew out the lantern's flame.

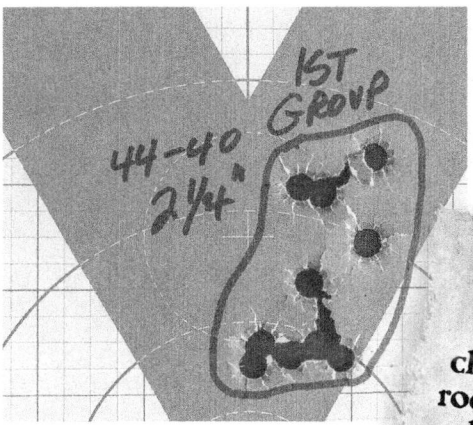

Easy cleaning of black powder mess requires nothing particularly fancy.

Of course, contributing factors are case wall thickness, bullet seating depth and technique.

Powder Compression

A corollary to powder compression is just how the powder charge is dispensed into the cartridge case. Most experienced black powder rifle cartridge handloaders use drop tubes. Such are lengths of copper or aluminum tubes with an aluminum or copper funnel at the top and a flared end at the bottom. One hand holds the case at the bottom while the other hand trickles in powder slowly at the top. My idea is three or four seconds is slow. The powder compacts and allows more to settle in the case than when dropping it straight from scale pan to case. This results in cleaner burning and less fouling. Lyman even offers a black powder measure complete with aluminum powder hopper and drop tube. My home-made copper drop tube is 30" long. Lyman's is 24". I cannot discern a difference in performance between the two.

With my considerable experience with black powder cartridge rifles (BPCRs) I can tell from a rifle's report if the powder was drop tubed or not. *Powder just dropped into the case makes a "boom" sound akin to a shotgun. Drop tubed powders have a sharper "bang" muzzle report.* Upon taking up loading black powder cartridges for revolvers I kept the drop tube as part of my process and credit it with helping with successful results. Black powder revolver loads give tremendous concussion on firing. Once at a Thunder Ranch class I fired some .44-40s in a room of about 16' square while holding a kerosene lantern. Every round's concussion blew out the lantern's flame. Not to mention the concussion also brought all dust and grime from the rafters down on my head.

Lube Matters

I consider drop tubing black powder as the second most important factor in loading black powder revolver loads. The first is bullet lubricant. Unlike with smokeless loads where bullet lube is simply meant for preventing or at least minimizing lead fouling, with black powder our bullet lube has a second job — to keep powder fouling soft. When black powder ignites it leaves hard fouling which will cause accuracy to deteriorate and even tie up revolver functioning. Take note of old drawings or photos of black powder era cast bullet designs. They have wide deep grease grooves. Compare this to modern designed cast bullets. Most have pencil thin grease grooves meant for modern lubes.

Several bullet lubes have been developed with black powder shooters in mind. The three I have first-hand experience with are SPG, DGL and Lyman's Black Powder Gold. I've used SPG (named for its developer Steven Paul Garbe) since 1986. More recently some friends bought the DGL (Damn Good Lube) and I've used it with great results. In between Lyman Black Powder Gold has also been in my lube-sizers. I might add all of these lubes are also great for smokeless powder cast bullets.

Priming

Last but not least are primers. Primers make a great influence on black powder accuracy. This is a strange matter. *Sometimes two different primers will give almost identical ballistics as read by chronographs but vastly different groups on paper.* The key to having the best black powder revolver handloads is to try several primers. Interestingly in the era when black powder was commonly used for reloading but smokeless powders were making inroads, Remington-UMC actually sold different primers specifically labeled for black powder.

Cleaning Secrets

In the beginning I mentioned some comments on cleaning revolvers fired with black powder. The original method was using cotton patches with very hot water. In fact, some literature about Civil War cavalry said after combat units would boil vats of water, remove the revolvers' wood grips, dunk their revolvers in the water on pieces of wire and swish them about a little. When removed from the vats the hot water would quickly evaporate and revolvers were then oiled.

My revolver cleaning area has no easy access to hot water. Instead, I use Windex with vinegar. A spray bottle of it is dumped in a plastic gallon jug which is then filled with water. Cotton patches soaked in that solution eat black powder fouling. Then cylinder, barrel and various angles and crevices are wiped clean. For oil I like Ballistol. Some others have related to me they clean with a mixture of Ballistol and water. So, there are several paths to pursue to cleaning revolvers. But don't put the chore off! Black powder itself isn't corrosive but its fouling draws moisture. Also if your black powder bullet lubricant is doing its job powder fouling will be relatively soft.

Even with my avid enthusiasm for black powder shooting, I don't use it in revolvers all the time. There is such a thing as a lazy afternoon of plinking with mild smokeless loads. However, for special occasions the tremendous muzzleblast and smoke cloud reaching out a dozen feet will impress your shooting buddies.

Will Dabbs, MD
JOHN "LIVER-EATING" JOHNSON
The Crow-Killing Cannibal

I'm currently comfortably ensconced in my favorite writing chair, munching peanut M&M's. From the vantage of my climate-controlled living room it can be difficult to grasp the realities of life on the early American frontier. Anyone unduly concerned with micro aggressions or social justice had long since been beaten up, robbed, killed or eaten. What remained was by necessity of fairly hearty stock. None better exemplified this axiom than John "Liver-Eating" Johnson.

Origin Story

John Johnson was born John Garrison in 1824 in Hunterton County, N.J. He lied about his age to serve aboard a warship during the Mexican-American War. After striking a superior officer, Johnson deserted and fled to the gold fields around Alder Gulch in the Montana Territory. There he supported himself as a "woodhawk," cutting cord wood to fuel steamboats.

At a time when people were markedly smaller than is the case today, John Johnson was an absolute monster. Standing 6' 2" and weighing 260 lbs., Johnson was hard and sinewy. His signature combat move was to lay his opponents low with a single mighty kick to the crotch.

Johnson eventually married a Flathead Indian woman. While he was out running a trapline, a Crow war party raided his homestead and murdered his pregnant wife. When Johnson returned, he then realized his one true calling in life: John Johnson became a

John "Liver-Eating" Johnson was a veritable mountain of a man with an outsized reputation to match. Hard men of the era cultivated some of the most epic whiskers (above). In addition to some rarefied skills as a trapper and woodsman, John Johnson also built a mean log cabin. This example of his work was relocated to the grounds of a Wyoming museum (right). Images: Wikimedia by Acroterion

John Johnson's colorful career spanned the country from coast to coast. Born in New Jersey in 1824, he died in Los Angeles some 75 years later. Image: Montana Historical Society

This memorial in Wyoming commemorates John Johnson's extraordinary exploits. Image: Billy Hathorn via Wikimedia

The tale of "Liver-Eating" Johnson has attained a legendary status through the years.

Johnson's Hawken rifle was typical of the genre. Image: Buffalo Bill Center of the West

"LIVER EATING" JOHNSON
JOHN GARRISON, LATER KNOWN AS JOHN JOHNSTON, BORN HERE C1830. KILLED MANY OF THE CROW TRIBE, SLAYERS OF HIS INDIAN WIFE. ROBERT REDFORD MOVIE "JEREMIAH JOHNSON" POPULARIZED HIS LIFE.

full-time professional killer of Crow Indians.

Liver and Onions?

How much of this tale is real and how much apocryphal matters little to me. It makes for a simply fantastic story. Over the next few years, Johnson traveled about collecting Crow scalps. The Crow believed the liver was the repository of the soul and therefore a critical component of a successful transition to the afterlife. Once John had his victims dispatched, he would excise the liver and eat it. Word of this soon got around. While he was supposedly also known as "Long Toes Johnson" and "Pear-Loving Johnson," it was the *nom de guerre* "Liver-Eating Johnson" that has stood the test of time.

Captured!

When not actively killing Crow warriors, Johnson supported himself predominantly as a trapper. One cold Wyoming winter, Johnson struck out from the trapper cabin he shared with another mountain man named Del Gue with a pair of packhorses and two 20-gallon kegs of whiskey. Johnson felt he could supplement his income by trading the booze to his former in-laws, the Flatheads.

While en route, Johnson was ambushed by a Blackfoot patrol. The Indians overwhelmed him and seized his prized Hawken rifle. In short order Johnson was shirtless and unarmed under guard in a teepee, his hands secured at his front via raw sinew.

Johnson's sole guard was young, with more bile than sense. The Blackfoot warriors had relieved Johnson of his pistol and knife when they took his shirt and jacket, but they had overlooked the flint and steel fire starter he kept tucked into his belt. Finding themselves in a celebratory mood, they began sampling Johnson's whiskey. The tribe members realized they could trade the infamous "Liver-Eating" Johnson to the nearby Crow nation and turn a tidy profit. It was indeed a time for revelry.

> At a time when people were markedly smaller than is the case today, John Johnson was an absolute monster.

A squaw brought the young guard a bowl of rotgut, and with it the kid grew ever more animated. Whenever he would turn his back, however, Johnson would gnaw furiously at his bindings. Eventually the Blackfoot guard became drunk, and John Johnson chewed his way to freedom. A powerful kick to the gonads dropped the poor Indian like a bag of rocks.

Armed with a Leg

Johnson knew he had very little time. He retrieved the young brave's knife and scalped him, apparently just for giggles. He then split the kid's

GUNSMAGAZINE.COM 41

The Hawken plains rifle was a prized staple of mountain men plying the early American frontier.

The accouterments on the original Hawken rifles were formed from iron. Most modern versions are brass (above). Original Hawken rifles were flintlocks. This caplock reproduction from Thompson Center is much more reliable (left).

Johnson's ample knife was befitting a man of such exceptional stature. Image: Buffalo Bill Center of the West

John Johnson's original Hawken rifle and hunting knife are on display at the Buffalo Bill Center of the West.

buckskin trousers, circumscribed the upper thigh with the knife and disarticulated the hip joint. A quick snap to the knee separated the leg cleanly. Despite the crude state of medical affairs, the kid purportedly survived this ordeal, albeit perhaps now with a bit of a limp.

With many Blackfoot now three sheets to the wind, Johnson struck out into the Wyoming winter, shirtless, on foot and equipped with nothing more than flint, an Indian knife and a severed human leg. The tribe eventually sobered up and gave chase. Johnson was worth a fortune to the Crow, and they were determined not to let this opportunity escape.

What followed is a simply epic tale of survival. The winter weather froze the leg in fairly short order, helping keep it fresh and tasty. Johnson moved only 10 miles in the first three days, but later picked up his pace. Once separated from the Blackfoot camp, he made fires to thaw himself in the evenings and cook his unconventional foodstuff.

At one point Johnson found himself in an ample cave that provided protection from a howling winter storm. He crafted a generous fire, consumed a proper chunk of human flesh and fell into a deep sleep. He was awakened by a tugging sensation.

Through bleary eyes by the light of his dying fire, Johnson spotted a massive mountain lion making off with his own personal disarticulated Indian leg. A fearsome tug-o-war ensued. Johnson got the better of the big cat and smacked it over the head with the leg, putting it to flight. How-

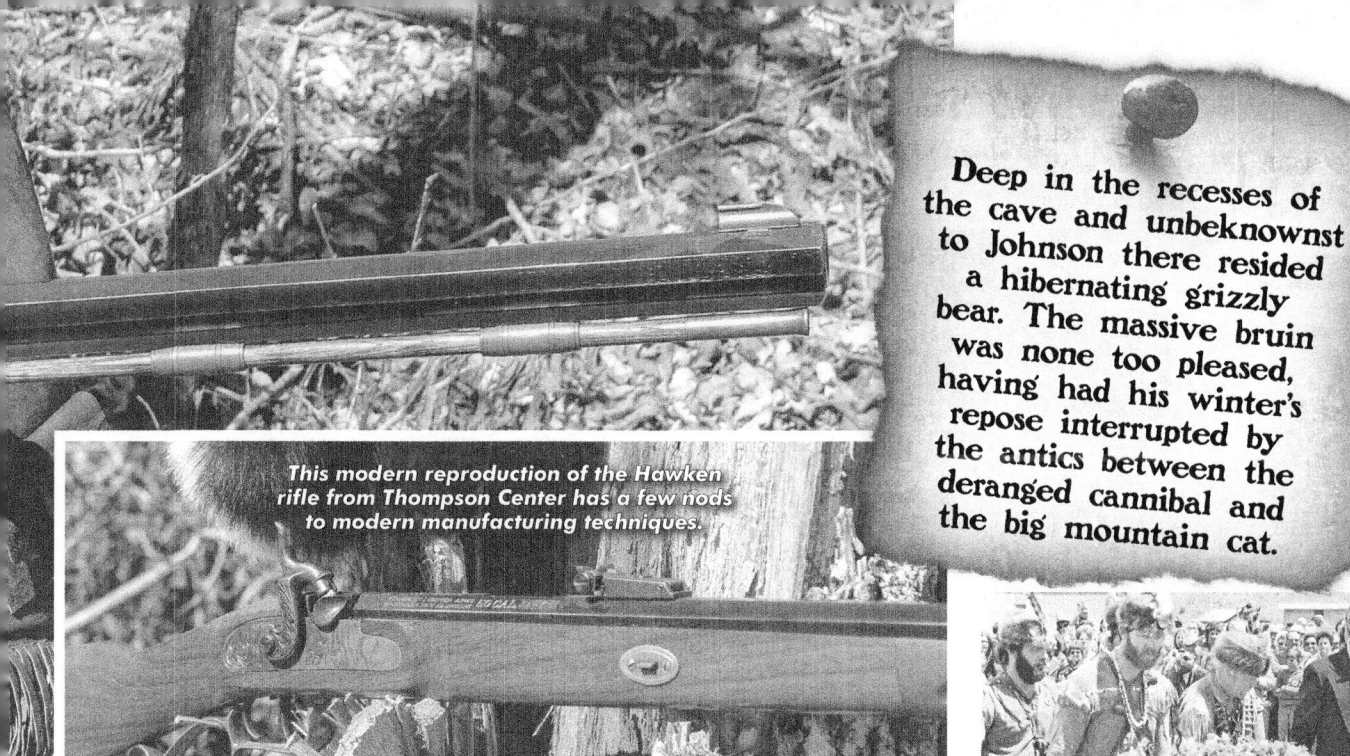

This modern reproduction of the Hawken rifle from Thompson Center has a few nods to modern manufacturing techniques.

> Deep in the recesses of the cave and unbeknownst to Johnson there resided a hibernating grizzly bear. The massive bruin was none too pleased, having had his winter's repose interrupted by the antics between the deranged cannibal and the big mountain cat.

The American actor Robert Redford served as a pallbearer when John Johnson was finally laid to rest in 1974. Image: Dave Shors

ever, in all the chaos, things suddenly got way worse.

Deep in the recesses of the cave and unbeknownst to Johnson, there resided a hibernating grizzly bear. The massive bruin was none too pleased, having had his winter's repose interrupted by the antics between the deranged cannibal and the big mountain cat. A subsequent pugilism ensued between Johnson and the bear, wherein the man wielded the leg yet again as an ample club. Johnson eventually reached the mouth of the cave and beat a hasty retreat before the big bear could press home his attack.

Along the way, Johnson broke his pilfered knife while trying to chip breakfast out of the frozen extremity. Despite these and countless other setbacks, Johnson eventually trekked some 200 miles in this ghastly state until he reached his old trapper's cabin. Now gaunt and rangy he burst in on his trapping partner, tossed the half-eaten human leg on the floor and announced, "How air ye fixed for meat, Del?"

John Johnson's Rifle

At this time and at this place, a man's firearm was his life. For mountain men of this era, the top of the line was the Hawken rifle. The Hawken developed an outsized reputation as the finest mountain man gun extant.

Developed in the 1820s in St. Louis, Mo., by the Hawken brothers Samuel and Jacob, their eponymous smoke pole was also known as the plains rifle or buffalo gun. The Hawken family operated their shop from 1815 until 1858, selling the first Hawken rifle to one William Henry Ashley in 1823. The original Hawken was never a mass-produced contrivance. Each gun was crafted meticulously by hand.

The Hawken rifle was somewhat shorter than the previous Kentucky long rifle and typically fired a heavier ball. Most Hawken guns featured a characteristic half stock that ended midway down the barrel. The Hawken was designed to be accurate, portable, reliable and potent. Most Hawken rifles were .50 or .53 caliber, though some were as large as .68.

Barrels typically ranged from 33" to 36", and the guns weighed between 10.5 and 15 lbs. The octagonal barrels were cut from soft iron to reduce fouling. Stocks were formed from walnut or maple and sported a curved cheek rest described as a beaver's tail. Unlike most modern reproductions, the buttplate and associated trim on the original guns were formed from iron rather than brass.

Most Hawkens featured double-set triggers. To fire the gun, you would pull the rear trigger to "set" the front trigger. Once primed, the front trigger required only the lightest touch for ignition. Sights were a simple front blade and rear notch.

The Rest of the Story

"Liver-Eating" Johnson continued killing Crow Indians until he grew weary of it. Revenge is an arduous career, and it doesn't pay terribly well. Before the dust settled, it was estimated Johnson had killed some 300 Crow braves.

John Johnson sustained himself as a sailor, trapper, trader, gold seeker, constable, purveyor of spirits, deputy, peddler and homebuilder. His capacity to craft a proper log cabin turned out to be a marketable skill on more than a couple of occasions. He served with Company H, 2nd Colorado Cavalry of the Union Army during the Civil War and by all accounts acquitted himself honorably.

Eventually the rigors of frontier life and his unconventional diet caught up to "Liver-Eating" Johnson. He reported to the veteran's home in Santa Monica, Calif., December 1899 and died a month later. He was interred in the Los Angeles Veteran's cemetery.

John Johnson's trail doesn't end there, however. A concerted campaign led by 25 Wyoming seventh graders ultimately led to his disinterment. John "Liver-Eating" Johnson was eventually laid to rest in Cody, Wyo., the land of his most remarkable exploits, June 1974.

In 1972, Robert Redford starred in *Jeremiah Johnson*, a film based loosely upon John Johnson's remarkable life. The movie inexplicably glossed over some of the most fascinating bits. When Johnson was finally laid to rest in 1974, Redford served as a pallbearer.

The book *Crow Killer: The Saga of Liver-Eating Johnson* by Raymond Thorp and Robert Bunker is an epic read.

Baz Outlaw used this custom slip gun when he needed to be discreet about being armed. His slip gun was highly modified for concealment, extreme speed and sure handling in a close-range gunfight.

Frank Jardim

HAMMER TIME

A slip gun is made by removing the trigger so the revolver is fired by only cocking and releasing the hammer. It's crazy-fast but dangerous to handle!

The Slip Gun: Fast and Dangerous

On the last day of his life, April 4, 1894, prior to making his customary rounds of El Paso's saloons and brothels for recreational purposes, a particularly disgruntled Deputy U.S. Marshal named Bazzell "Baz" Lamar Outlaw left his full-sized Colt and gun belt in his room. He would not go unarmed, of course. In case there was trouble, he had a more concealable pistol tucked inside his waistband, a .44-40 1873 Colt customized into a slip gun.

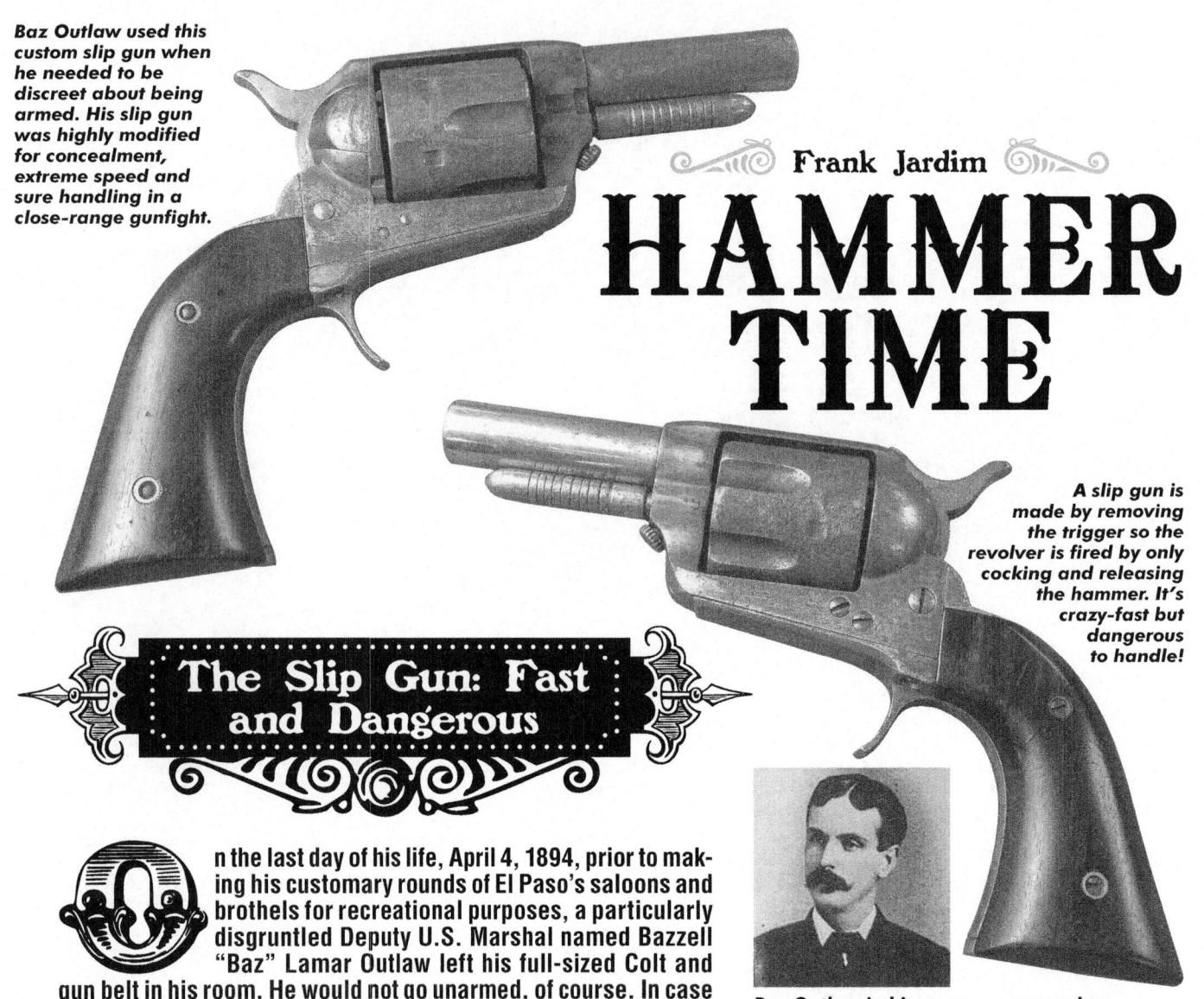

Baz Outlaw in his younger, more sober days, when the ladies regarded him as an intelligent, charming Southern gentleman.

Unfortunately, the combination of liquor and Baz Outlaw was the scientific formula for trouble. By the time he got to Tillie Howard's sporting house to visit his favorite whore, he was very drunk and became angry when she was not available. Somehow his pistol discharged, perhaps accidentally, and the madam began blowing her police whistle for help.

Blue on Blue ... Sort of

Outlaw went into the yard where he encountered Texas Ranger Joe McKidrict who had come running to investigate; he asked Outlaw why he had shot. His answer was to draw his belly gun and fire, instantly killing the young Ranger with a shot to the head and shooting him again in the back as he fell.

When El Paso Constable John Selman arrived on the scene a moment later, Outlaw thumbed off another round, narrowly missing Selman's head. They were so close the muzzleblast burned Selman's eyes, but the 56-year-old gunfighter drew and fired a single round from his own 1873 Colt .45 through Outlaw's right lung, mortally wounding him. Outlaw fired twice more, hitting Selman in the thigh and hip before withdrawing from the fracas by jumping the backyard fence. He collapsed into the arms of Ranger Frank McMahon and surrendered.

I've often wondered if Outlaw surrendered because he was out of bullets, or because he realized his heinous deed murdering Joe McKidrict. Selman was no angel, and shooting him on sight might have been a justifiable act of self-defense in light of Selman's reputation as a killer. Outlaw took the answer to his grave within hours. Selman lived but walked with a cane for the rest of his life, which wasn't very long either. He would die two years later in a gunfight with another U.S. Deputy Marshal named George Scarborough.

The tragedy of Baz Outlaw is he might have gone down in history as one of the Old West's greatest and bravest lawmen, *but his weakness for liquor was his undoing.* Author Bob Alexander, in his well researched and lively book *Whisky River: The Old West Life of Baz Outlaw* tells the story in a broadly illuminating way and I heartily recommend it.

Baz's Slip Gun

For my part, I'll focus on the gun Outlaw used that fatal day because I had a chance to personally examine it many years ago. Unlike many Wild West guns of dubious provenance, Outlaw's slip gun is well documented. May 8, 1894, the County Court of El Paso ordered his weapons turned over to the undertaker, who prepared his body for burial as payment for his services. The order listed the guns specifically by serial number.

44 GUNS MAGAZINE OLD WEST • SPECIAL EDITION

This period photo shows Texas Ranger Baz Outlaw was not a physically imposing man in stature, but he was said to be worth several men in a tight spot. However, when drunk, he could — and did — become a wild man even his fellow Texas Rangers feared.

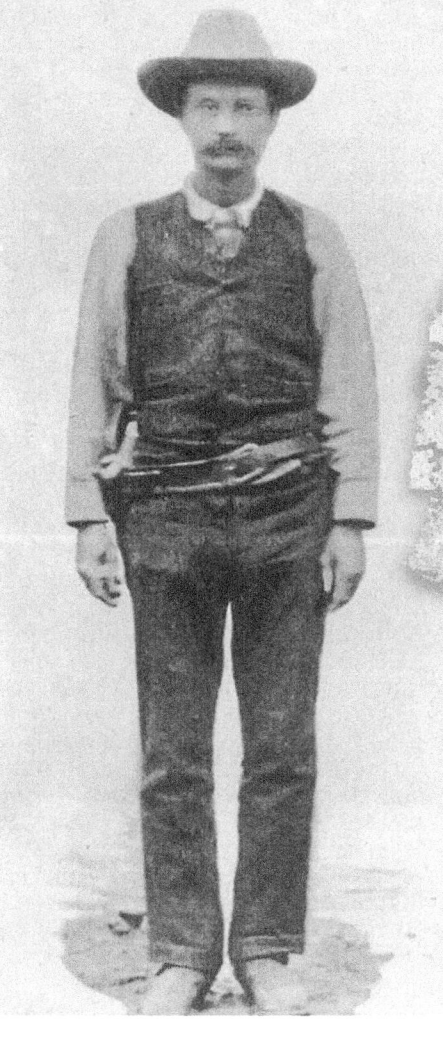

> Somehow his pistol discharged, perhaps accidentally, and the madam began blowing her police whistle for help.

For better control in recoil, the larger grip frame from an 1872 Colt was substituted for the original, smaller 1873 grip frame. Note how the back of the trigger guard was left in place to help with aim and control.

The Colt customized as a slip gun first left the Hartford factory in 1878. It was serial number 42870. Baz Outlaw's initials "BO" are stamped on the trigger guard, and "B.L. Outlaw" on the right side of the frame. There's no way to know if Outlaw had it customized or just acquired it this way. Regardless, it fits the mold of a man who was accustomed to facing danger at close range. *Notches carved into the front of the frame suggest it was used to kill four people before the fateful encounter with Selman.* Outlaw is known to have killed six men, but half of those fell under his carbine's sights. Perhaps there were more.

In case you are wondering, *a slip gun, as it was known in Outlaw's time, is a single action with the trigger removed allowing it to be fired simply by working the hammer.* This is as fast as a single action can get. It's also pretty dangerous, though perhaps no more so than being in a close-range gunfight.

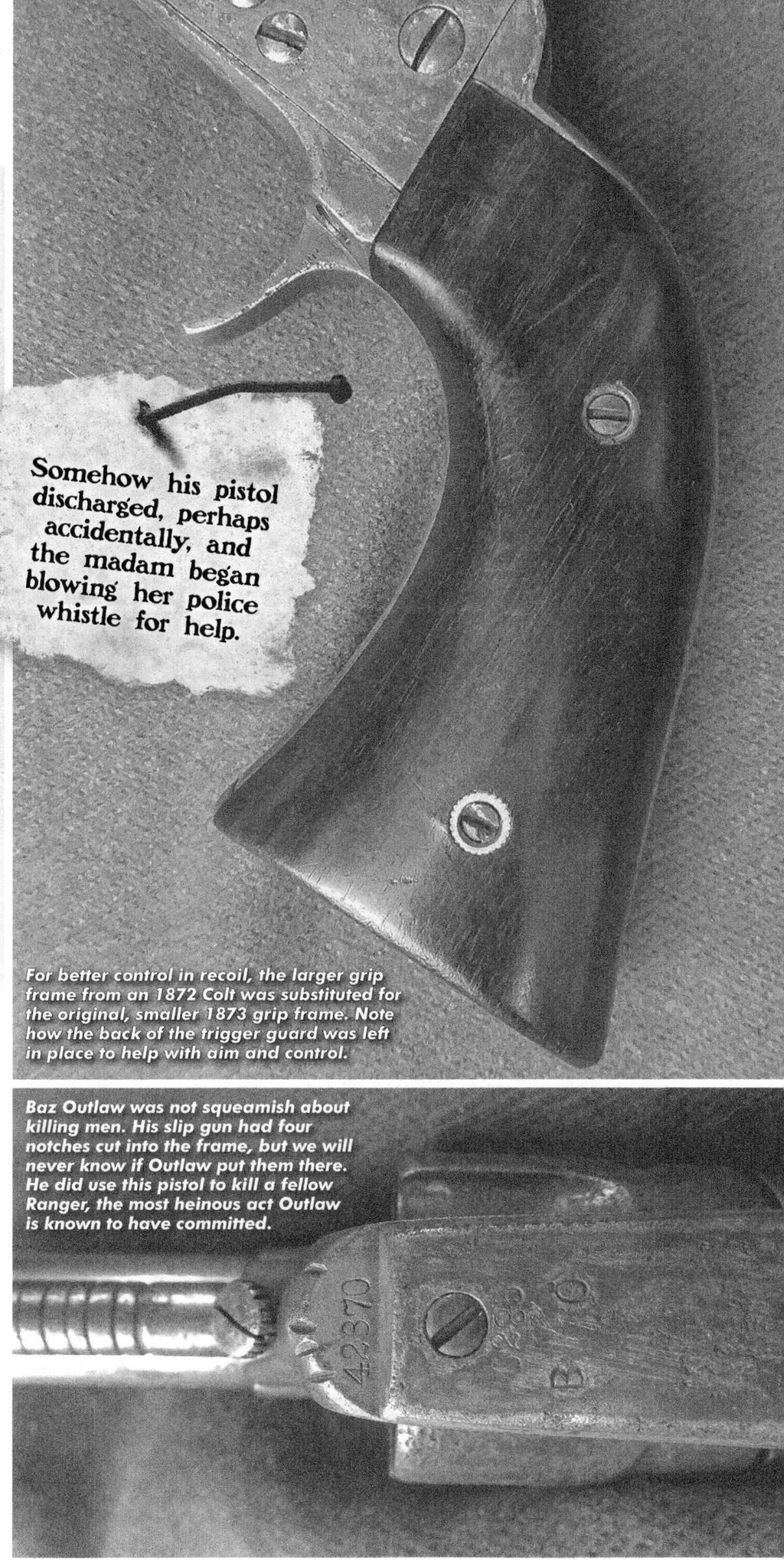

Baz Outlaw was not squeamish about killing men. His slip gun had four notches cut into the frame, but we will never know if Outlaw put them there. He did use this pistol to kill a fellow Ranger, the most heinous act Outlaw is known to have committed.

In this photo of some Company D Texas rangers, Outlaw is in the back row, second from the left, with an 1873 Winchester carbine. He owned one at the time of his death that was also nickel plated and stamped with his name like his slip gun.

The initials "BO" for Baz Outlaw are handstamped on the trigger guard (below).

El Paso, Texas constable and notorious killer John Selman fatally shot Outlaw, but not before Outlaw crippled him with his slip gun.

Notches carved into the front of the frame suggest it was used to kill four people before the fateful encounter with Selman.

The extra-large cylinder pin was intended for use in ejecting the spent cases. Its quick removal was facilitated by the knurled thumb screw.

Notice the part of the frame that supported the ejector housing was carefully removed, perhaps to lighten the pistol.

About that Trigger …

Rarely seen on Old West belly guns, but quite common in the double-action era, is the removal of the front of the trigger guard. The front of the trigger guard is just something else to get in the way of your finger finding the trigger and removing it simplifies and speeds up the all-important first shot. However, Outlaw's gun doesn't have a trigger.

What's really interesting is how his pistol retains the abbreviated rear portion of the trigger guard to help stabilize and point the pistol. It's also fitted with the larger grip frame of an 1872 Colt revolver, presumably for the same reason. This makes good sense since a snub nosed .44-40 is a handful to hang onto under recoil. As a matter of finishing, the hole in the trigger guard for the trigger was filled with a soldered plug and the whole gun was nickel-plated. *Holding it in my hand, it was apparent it was thoughtfully and skillfully crafted for a man in the business of gunfighting.*

Outlaw's slip gun has the usual shortened barrel with no front sight, 3" in this case, for easy concealment and fast draw. The ejector mechanism was useless on such a short barrel so the entire assembly was removed. This lightens the pistol slightly and further reduces the chance of snagging on the draw. On Outlaw's pistol, the gunsmith went a step further to save weight and also removed the portion of the frame on the right side that supported the ejector shroud. He fitted the pistol with an extra-long cylinder pin with an enlarged knurled gripping surface that could be used to knock the empty cases from the cylinder. The gunsmith replaced the tiny cylinder pin locking screw typical of first generation 1873 Colts with a larger thumb screw that could be manipulated easily without tools.

A Modern Trial

I removed the trigger from one of my own single actions to explore

46   GUNS MAGAZINE OLD WEST • SPECIAL EDITION

Sights were of no use on a slip gun. Frank found accurate shooting beyond a card table is nigh impossible.

Frank with Outlaw's historic slip gun.

"B. L. OUTLAW" is inexpertly stamped on the frame.

the implication of the slip-gun modification. Take away the trigger and the 1873 Colt loses its half- and full-cock notches. To load and unload, you have to hold the hammer back while you align the cylinder chambers with the loading gate. You have to hold the cylinder in alignment too, or else it will turn. It can be discharged shockingly fast. For reflexive shooting at point-blank range, Outlaw's slip gun would have given him a split-second edge.

In closing *I want to reiterate the dangers of a slip gun.* I noticed if the hammer was released before it was drawn back through the full range of movement needed to completely rotate the cylinder, the cylinder wouldn't rotate all the way around and the hammer would fall on the side of the primer. At best, this is a formula for a misfire. At worst, you might find a 255-grain bullet missing the forcing cone and crashing with full force into the junction of barrel and frame. This might lead to a blown-up gun and injury to the shooter or bystanders.

In the dangerous world of Baz Outlaw, the slip gun made sense. *To modify a pistol like this today is just plain crazy so don't do it.* I will never do this experiment again. Historic curiosity is not worth a bullet wound.

ENTER TO WIN!

UBERTI SHORT STROKE SASS PRO GIVEAWAY

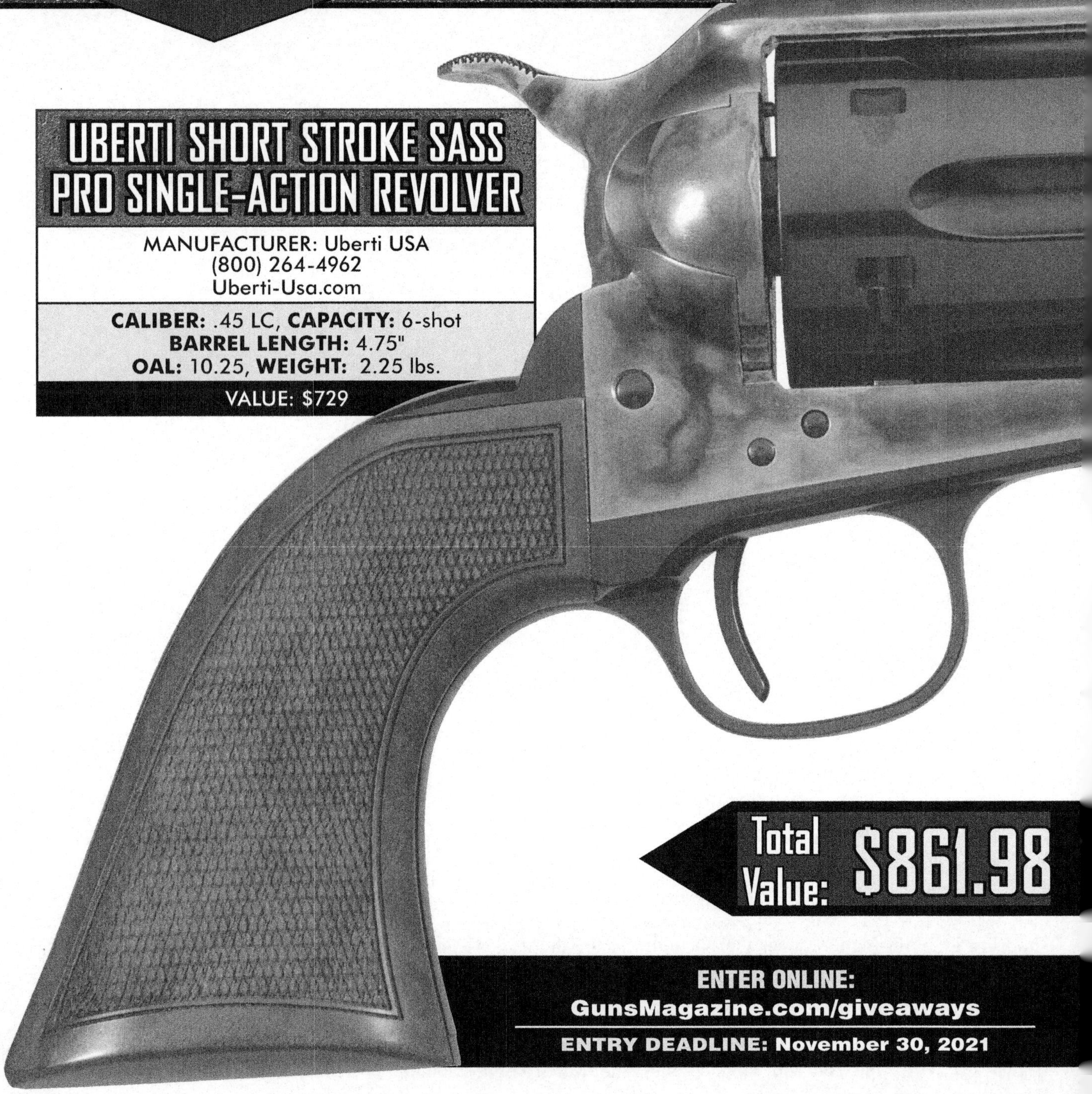

UBERTI SHORT STROKE SASS PRO SINGLE-ACTION REVOLVER

MANUFACTURER: Uberti USA
(800) 264-4962
Uberti-Usa.com

CALIBER: .45 LC, **CAPACITY:** 6-shot
BARREL LENGTH: 4.75"
OAL: 10.25, **WEIGHT:** 2.25 lbs.

VALUE: $729

Total Value: $861.98

ENTER ONLINE:
GunsMagazine.com/giveaways

ENTRY DEADLINE: November 30, 2021

The *Uberti Short Stroke SASS Pro* single-action revolver is designed with one purpose: saving time in competition. This is achieved through a short-stroke hammer with 20% less travel than on a regular SAA revolver. The hammer is extra wide and low profile, offering positive cocking and an uninterrupted view of the sight picture. The custom-grade mainspring encased in the checkered grip ensures a smooth operation and a crisp trigger pull. The gun we're giving away is in .45 LC with a 4.75" barrel, but the SASS Pro single-action revolver also comes in .357 Mag with a 5.5" barrel.

The Wild Hog field and range holster from DeSantis can be worn cross draw or with a forward cant. The ambidextrous holster is made from premium top grain and center cut steer hide and features an adjustable tension device. Available for most SAA revolvers and large-frame revolvers, including the Uberti Short Stroke SASS Pro.

Dependable. This describes CRKT's *Shenanigan*, designed by renowned knife designer Ken Onion. This folder features Ken's assisted-opening innovation and IKBS ball bearing pivot system. It opens smoothly, deploying its 3.35" drop-point blade between maroon, glass-reinforced nylon handles.

Imagine owning the Uberti revolver, DeSantis holster and CRKT knife. But why just imagine? Make it a reality by entering GunsMagazine.com/giveaways or sending a postcard. —Jazz Jimenez

We've heard it's difficult to find postcards these days so here's a tip — use index cards, the back of greeting cards or even cereal boxes or purchase one from your local post office!

THE WILD HOG
Manufacturer: DeSantis Gunhide Holsters
(631) 841-6300
DeSantisHolster.com
Value: $52.99

SHENANIGAN
Manufacturer: CRKT
(800) 891-3100
CRKT.com
Value: $79.99

WINNERS CHOSEN BY RANDOM DRAWING. To protect the privacy and security of winners, their names will NOT be made public. Contest void where prohibited by law. Winners may undergo a background check and comply with all other federal, state and local laws. Taxes and fees will be the responsibility of the winner. Contest open to U.S. residents only. Employees and agents of Publishers' Development Corp. are not eligible. No purchase necessary. Winners will be notified by certified mail on official letterhead. Attention deployed military: Use stateside address! Giveaway guns and accessories may have evidence of being test fired or exhibit minor handling marks. Factory warranties may apply in some cases. The Special Edition giveaway package is awarded only to the entrant drawn and will not be awarded if the firearm presented is illegal in the jurisdiction of the winner. An alternate, authorized winner will be selected. No substitutions or transfers to a third party are allowed.

If you are unable to enter online, mail a postcard with your name and address (no envelopes, please) to GUNS Magazine, Old West Vol. 88, P.O. Box 502795, San Diego, CA, 92150-2795. Entries must be received by November 30, 2021. Limit one entry per household.

Serena Juchnowski

SHOCK, AWE AND LOTS OF SMOKE

An Introduction to Black Powder Shooting

Left to right: an inline muzzleloader, percussion cap rifle, custom made black powder pistol, and cap-and-ball revolver. Sounds like a fun range outing.

Powder, patch and ball, or it won't shoot at all! Black powder ignites more readily than substitutes.

Powder, patch and ball — or it won't shoot at all! The rectangular sticker clung to the inside lid of a utility box. I remember this vividly from my first experiences with black powder. It may sound like a silly phrase, but it's an effective one.

At first it seems complicated. Rather than bring a gun and box of ammunition to the range, you're toting a box of materials and cleaning supplies. The process itself is simple. Determine the correct amount of powder and pour it into the barrel. Next add a patch. Center a lead round ball in the center of the patch, and push both down with a ball starter, then finish with the ramrod. Add a percussion cap and you're good to go. Not all black power guns are loaded this way, different types vary a bit, but the idea's the same.

Types

Just as there are various types of shotguns, pistols and rifles, there are various types of black powder firearms. Many people appreciate black powder for historic reasons and may choose a flintlock rifle. This uses no percussion cap, but the traditional powder, patch

Simple tools like this loading stand create an "extra pair of hands" — often helpful for loading black powder handguns.

and ball. A piece of flint hits a metal piece called a frizzen, producing a spark that ignites powder in the pan. This produces pressure that sends the round ball out of the barrel. Caplock firearms use a percussion cap to ignite powder inside the barrel and were a huge step forward in muzzleloading technology. Caplock firearms are still incredibly popular. Inlines are the modern innovation of the muzzleloading world. They use a 209 shotshell primer. The spark from this primer travels in a straight line to the powder, rather than from an angle outside the gun. This increases the rifle's dependability. They also have removable breech plugs for easier cleaning.

Powder

Modern firearms fire a cartridge. These cartridges or rounds can be purchased ready to use from the store, or you can reload them yourself. Muzzleloading is a more rudimentary version of reloading ammunition, on a shot-by-shot basis. You cannot prep it fully ahead of time. Instead of loading a case, you are using the chamber of your firearm to "assemble" a "cartridge."

Be aware modern firearms use smokeless powder. Most muzzleloaders use black powder. There are a few muzzleloaders that shoot smokeless powder. Never mix smokeless and black powder! Also, never use smokeless powder in a firearm designed for black powder. The two are not interchangeable. Not all powder is created equal either.

Consult load charts from powder manufacturers to ensure the proper granulation (signified by FF, FFF, etc.) and recommended load. It's important to not overcharge your firearm. Though it is possible to overcharge centerfire cartridges, it's more difficult to do with black powder when using cartridges.

Powder, patch and ball — or it won't shoot at all!

A double charge, for example, often won't fit in the case. A muzzleloading rifle, however, can hold a significant amount of powder, though only a few dozen grains are traditionally needed.

More "Fs" in a grade of black powder correspond with smaller grain size. Finer grain powder is easier to ignite and burns faster. FFFg and FFg are most common. FFFg is well-suited for black powder rifles and pistols smaller than .45 caliber while FFg is better for black powder rifles and shotguns .45 caliber and larger.

Black powder is relatively inexpensive compared to smokeless, but it does make a mess, so be sure to have extra cleaning patches on hand. Some prefer black powder alternatives that produce less fouling and lack the traditional sulfur smell. Pyrodex is the most popular brand, and such substitutes are available in pellet form, which makes for easier loading, especially in the field. These smoke-

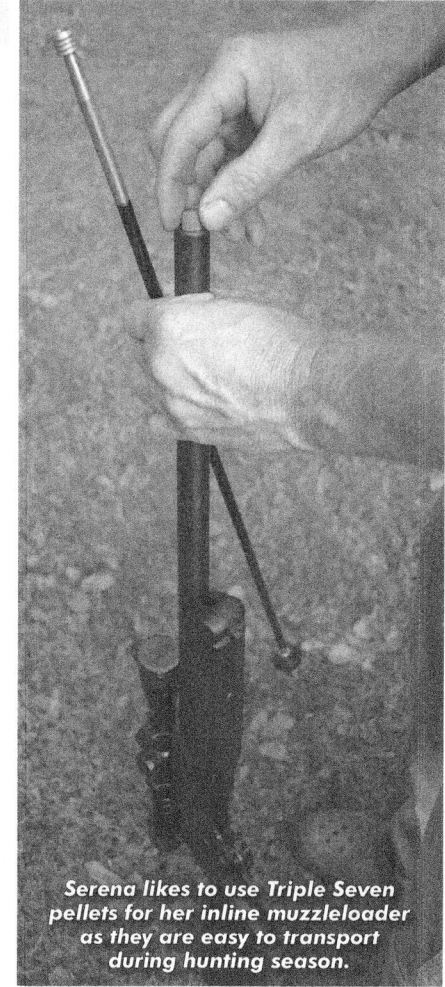

Serena likes to use Triple Seven pellets for her inline muzzleloader as they are easy to transport during hunting season.

Image: Dave Juchnowski

Pyrodex pellets make loading easier as they're pre-packaged and pre-measured.

less propellants are generally slightly more powerful than black powder (much of which doesn't actually burn but gets blown out the muzzle as smoke). The disadvantage — they are much harder to ignite than black powder. Hodgdon's Triple Seven is also growing in popularity as a substitute as it is a little more consistent, powerful and cleaner than both black powder and Pyrodex. It is harder to ignite than both, especially in pellet form. Most people have zero issues with ignition in inline muzzleloaders, though black powder is preferable for sidelock muzzleloaders.

Supplies

Though you can get by with just a few items, tricks and accessories make the process much easier. Black powder is messy. Not only does it foul the barrel but its fine granulation makes spills common. This isn't a big deal, but black powder is also very flammable. It's important to close all open powder containers and step away from the loading station before you shoot.

I bought a new lid with a pour spout for my canister of Goex black powder. Well worth the $5 I spent on it, I went from granules of powder covering my loading table to no spillage. There are various types of powder measures. Like anything, some are of better quality than others. There are several designs, but my favorite has a small funnel you place over the top of the barrel to ensure powder makes it in. Accessories may also depend on your desired application. Many people have turned to blackpowder firearms to extend their hunting season. In this case, I prefer CVA's hunter powder measure with a spot for a lanyard for easy carry and access if not using pellets.

Patches — you need two different types — for shooting and cleaning. Shooting patches need to be lubricated. You can buy them pre-lubed

> I shot a reproduction .36-caliber Kentucky long rifle, nearly as tall as me. Attempting to load and clean it was tricky to say the least, as the ramrod extended above my head.

in different thicknesses or make your own. The first I ever used were strips of pillow-ticking soaked in olive oil. I had to cut each patch around the ball, which adds an extra step to the process. This way may be cheaper, but it really depends on your preferences and how often you plan to shoot. The thicker the patch, the tighter the load will be in the barrel, the more accurate the shot will be — generally speaking. Blackpowder revolvers do not use a patch, but a wad or lube. The wad can sit between the powder and round ball or above it. The lube goes above the ball. Both of these measures are intended to prevent chain firing, and the lube is important for keeping powder fouling soft (and easier to clean!) in the bore.

Most people shoot traditional round balls. These can be cast or purchased from a manufacturer like Hornady. Cast round balls have a flat side called a sprue, which should be facing up when loaded. While round balls are great for target shooting, I prefer Powerbelt bullets for hunting with an inline. These conical projectiles do not require a patch or a sabot. It's important to use a starter with these types of bullets that will not damage the bullet tip during loading to maximize accuracy. Powerbelts are not the only option — other conical bullets exist for all different calibers ideal for hunting. Some require sabots.

A ball starter and ramrod are also necessary. After pouring the powder into the barrel, place a patch over the top of the opening and a ball on top. You can use a ball starter to push the patch and ball into the barrel, then use the ramrod to finish setting it all the way. I actually use a CNC-machined starter and a small mallet to push the ball and patch in just far enough so they are even with the top of the barrel. Next I use the starter and follow with the ramrod. It's important to make sure the load is properly and fully seated. An easy way to do this is to make an

Serena's first blackpowder rifle is nearly as tall as she is.
Image: Dave Juchnowski

Though Serena has never competed in the pistol matches at Canal Fulton Ramrod Club, a dear friend built her a .45-caliber pistol to do so. It is perhaps the most comfortable pistol she's used. Image: Tina Juchnowski

Inline muzzleloaders use a 209 primer rather than a percussion cap.

indicator mark, a line on your ramrod to align with the top of the muzzle when the firearm is properly loaded. This mark will not line up if you use a different load (more or less powder) or a longer or shorter jag.

Cleaning

The ramrod also serves as a cleaning rod. Though you can go several shots without cleaning, many people clean their muzzleloader between shots for improved accuracy. Black powder is water soluble and various solvents exist for these purposes. While you might let your AR sit after a day at the range until you have time to clean it, black powder guns should be cleaned right away. Initially and between shots a series of wet and dry patches run with the ramrod from the muzzle and back

Serena uses a CVA Wolf for deer muzzleloading season. Image: Dave Juchnowski

out again will suffice. Inline muzzleloaders have a removable breech plug for easier cleaning, though it's important to grease it afterward. I am especially impressed with the method for cleaning more traditional firearms. Remove the nipple and attach a cleaning tube. Thread one end of the tube into a small bottle of hot water and dish soap. Use a swab threaded on the ramrod and push the ramrod down and up in the barrel, just as you would with a patch. The pressure cycles the water through the barrel and back into the bottle. Empty the bottle and repeat until the water is clean and finish with plain hot water. An air compressor works well to ensure the barrel is dry. Finish with a rust preventative.

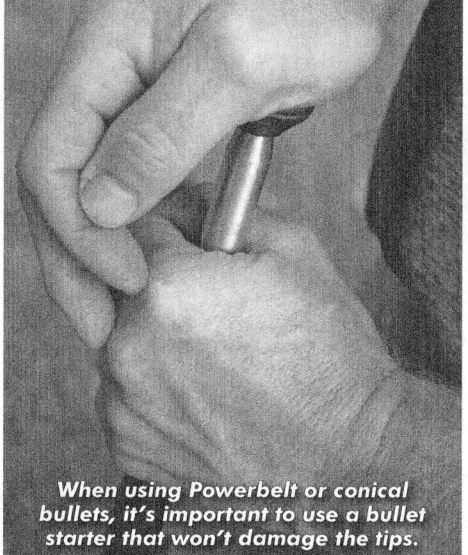

The Experience

My first shots were with a .22, but I was introduced to black powder shortly after. Before, in fact, I ever fired an AR or many modern firearms. Shooting indoors at weekend muzzleloader grocery shoots, competing for cartons of eggs and bacon, I learned proper-fitting hearing protection is a must for an enjoyable experience. I shot a reproduction .36-caliber Kentucky long rifle, nearly as tall as me. Attempting to load and clean it was tricky, to say the least as the ramrod extended above my head. At the Canal Fulton Ramrod Club, notches in the ceiling helped me to extract a stuck ramrod. This facility has a rich history of its own — an unassuming building tucked between houses — the club's origin dates back to the early 1800s when settlers would have matches with local natives.

Black powder is fun. It can certainly be tedious, but nothing compares to the smell and smoke of true black powder. It's a much different feeling, even the loading process, than firing a modern centerfire, and gives you a greater appreciation for the early Americans who fought for our freedom.

When using Powerbelt or conical bullets, it's important to use a bullet starter that won't damage the tips.

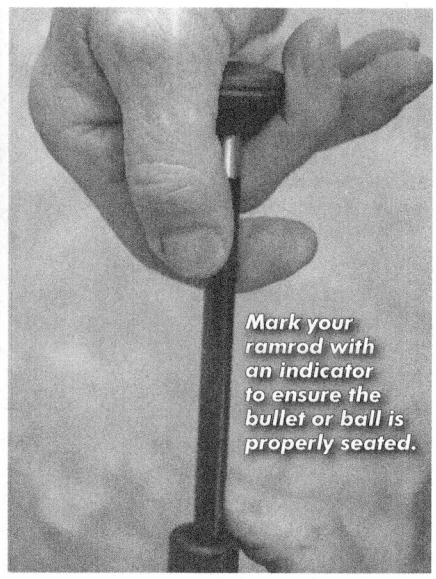

Mark your ramrod with an indicator to ensure the bullet or ball is properly seated.

DIXIE
Gun Works, Inc.

Where "Hard-to-Find" becomes easy.

For generations, re-enactors, modern hunters and competitive shooters have looked to the DIXIE GUN WORKS' catalog for the hardest to find blackpowder items. Our all new 2021 catalog continues the tradition with the world's largest selection of blackpowder replica arms, accessories, antique parts, muzzleloader hunting and sport shooting equipment.

PROFESSIONAL SERVICE AND EXPERTISE GUARANTEED

ORDER TODAY!
STILL ONLY $5.00

VIEW ITEMS AND ORDER ONLINE!
www.dixiegunworks.com
Major credit cards accepted

FOR ORDERS ONLY (800) 238-6785

DIXIE GUN WORKS, INC.

INFO PHONE: 731-885-0700
FAX: 731-885-0440
EMAIL: info@dixiegunworks.com

1412 W. Reelfoot Ave.
PO Box 130
Union City, TN 38281

Made in 1874, Colt's first 6 ½" barrel SAA revolver, #11846, was in .45 Colt caliber and was ordered by the Army for pendulum testing at Springfield Armory. Image: Mr. Nelson Dean, Museum of Connecticut History

Gary Paul Johnston

PRICELESS!
Colt's Lost Single Action Armys

Virtually unknown for a century, three rare SAAs come to light!

When Colt presented William Mason's new single-action revolver to the U.S. Army in 1873, it was a revolutionary new pistol with an equally impressive new cartridge, the .45 Colt. In keeping with the tradition of Colt's U.S. military revolvers, the gun also had a long barrel of 7 ½". The new Colt was adopted as the Model 1873 Single Action Army (SAA) revolver, a name that would remain with the gun in all variations.

Offering the exact U.S. Army style 1873 to the civilian market immediately after it was adopted for the U.S. Cavalry, Colt would introduce a 5 ½" barrel version in late 1875, after sending the first one to the Army for testing earlier that year. As standard production guns, Colt followed up with a 4 ¾" SAA, a 3" "Sheriff's Model" and the longer barrel SAAs for which shoulder stocks were offered. All but lost to antiquity, however, were three Colt Single Action Army revolvers that came with barrels of 6 ½" in length.

A Navy Rarity

The story of one of these Colts first intrigued me some 45 years ago when I saw a photograph of it in an antique-gun periodical. Of particular interest was it was made for the United States Navy, but it's all I could recall in 2009. That was when my longtime friend, well known firearms authority Wiley Clapp told me of the special limited-edition 6 ½" barrel .44 Special Colt he had designed for Colt to make and for TALO to distribute. When I mentioned the "Navy" 6 ½" Colt Single Action, Wiley had never heard of it, but neither had anyone else I had ever told about it.

In contacting noted Colt expert, John A. Kopek, he informed me the gun in question was last known to be in a private collection but was pictured in detail in C. Kenneth Moore's long out of print book, *Colt Revolvers and the U.S. Navy, 1865–1889*. After finding the book on Amazon, I received it to find a lengthy study about the 6 ½" "Navy" SAA beginning on page 38, including profuse illustrations of this ultra-rare, near new Colt.

Navy Caliber

The only color photograph in Moore's book shows this one-of-a-kind Colt, serial #16737, with six original rounds of ammunition, however they are not .45 Colt caliber, but instead, .38 Colt. Colt made this SAA for U.S. Navy evaluation in 1874 when it was still issuing Richards-Mason conversions of the Colt Model 1851 Navy revolver in .38 Colt caliber. Since the U.S. Army had already adopted the Colt Model 1873 in .45 Colt caliber, it made sense to Colt the Navy would follow suit with a new pistol in the caliber they were already using.

Documentation

Although neither Colt's Mfg. Company nor Colt Archives LLC has any record of this gun, it is documented to have been shipped from Colt on July 7, 1875, to the "Bureau of Ordnance, Navy" for testing. Located at the National Archives in Record Group 74 is a letter from Colt Agent, General William B. Franklin to Capt. William N. Jeffers, Chief of the Bureau of Ordnance, Navy, regarding the gun in detail. General Franklin had been trying to sell the Colt SAA to the U.S. Navy since its adoption in 1873, and this was his chance.

Since Colt SAA #16737 was like the Army's 7 ½" version, and intended to be a martial Colt, it was finished in blue with a color case-hardened frame, loading gate and hammer, and had a one-piece walnut stock. However, since it was only a sample, it did not have the normal "US" stamp or inspector's acceptance marks on the stock or the frame.

Modern Features

Also interesting for such an early 1st Generation Colt SAA is #16737 contains features not put into production, some until sometime later. The barrel uses a threaded stud into which the ejector housing screw secures it instead of the screw entering the barrel itself. The face of the cylinder is not radiused around the front of the chambers but

56　　　　　　　　　　　　　　　　　　　　　　　　　　　　　　　　GUNS MAGAZINE OLD WEST • SPECIAL EDITION

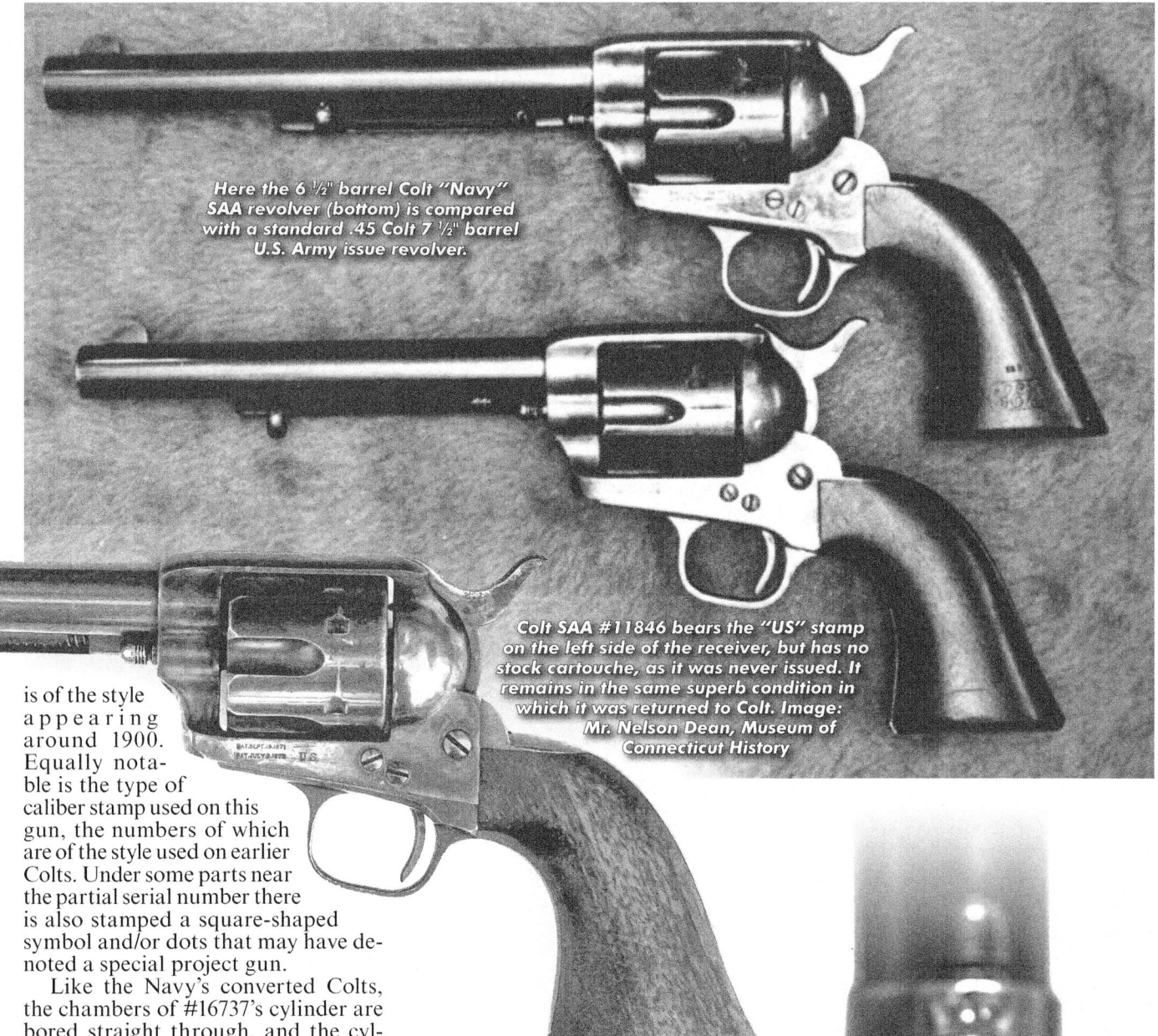

Here the 6 ½" barrel Colt "Navy" SAA revolver (bottom) is compared with a standard .45 Colt 7 ½" barrel U.S. Army issue revolver.

Colt SAA #11846 bears the "US" stamp on the left side of the receiver, but has no stock cartouche, as it was never issued. It remains in the same superb condition in which it was returned to Colt. Image: Mr. Nelson Dean, Museum of Connecticut History

is of the style appearing around 1900. Equally notable is the type of caliber stamp used on this gun, the numbers of which are of the style used on earlier Colts. Under some parts near the partial serial number there is also stamped a square-shaped symbol and/or dots that may have denoted a special project gun.

Like the Navy's converted Colts, the chambers of #16737's cylinder are bored straight through, and the cylinder has no serial number. This may have been because the accuracy of the original cylinder was insufficient, and so another was chosen in a similar manner as with unnumbered replacement cylinders used on .45 Colt SAAs shipped to the U.S. Army. Moore writes Colt may have kept a second identical gun for its own testing, but none has come to light.

General Franklin requested #16737 be tested at 25 yards and Capt. Jeffers acknowledged receipt of the gun July 9, 1875, and on the same day, Capt. Jeffers sent the pistol along with a letter to Commander J.D. Marvin of the Naval Experimental Battery, Annapolis, Md., asking him to test the gun and report the results to the Bureau of Ordnance. A 25-page report outlines extensive comparative testing of the new Colt against the Navy-converted guns. Although #16737 proved superior, the Navy had no funds for new pistols, and it was returned to Colt in August 1875. Now this Colt was at last in the private collection of Mr. Raymond B. Bentley of California, but with no information as to how he obtained it.

The First 6 ½" Colt SAA

Equally fascinating in Moore's book, however, was this Colt Single Action "Navy" was not the first 6 ½" SAA Colt made! All but hidden in the record surrounding the U.S. Navy test Colt, #16737 was mention of an earlier 6 ½" barrel Colt SAA tested by the U.S. Army, and the serial number of yet another mysterious U.S. Army test Colt, which will be also be covered here, both in .45 Colt caliber.

The first 6 ½" barrel Colt SAA was serial number 11846, and although Colt Archives LLC has no record of

The U.S. Army test 6 ½" barrel SAA serial #11846 is matching on all major parts.

Special ordered from Colt in 1893, Arthur C. Gould's 6 ½" barrel Colt SAA revolver bears serial #151992 and was in .44 Russian caliber and shipped with a second cylinder in .44-40 caliber. Image: Courtesy of David M. Brown's book, The 36 Calibers of the Colt Single Action Army

THE .44 RUSSIAN

Colt .44 Russian, Serial Number 151922, made in 1893 and shipped, with two cylinders, to A. C. Gould. Only 154 guns were made in this caliber, and this is one of only 2 known that were made with 6 1/2 inch barrels.

this gun, it and the other "mysterious" Colt SAA was shipped to Springfield Armory for testing August 14, 1874. In his book, Moore only reports "Documentation, illustration and details are contained in 'the Study." However, through no small amount of networking, I was able to not only learn "the Study" was pendulum testing but also the other "mysterious" U.S. Army test Colt, serial number 11916, was a 5 ½" barrel SAA shipped to Springfield with the 6 ½" Colt for the pendulum test!

Before gelatin and electronic ballistic testing equipment, a pendulum test was used to compare the energy of different firearms. In the case in point, the Army wanted to learn the differences in power factor and potential penetration of the issue 7 ½" barrel Colt .45 compared with an SAA with a 6 ½" and a 5 ½" barrel. The 6 ½" barrel Colt, #11846 and the 5 ½" Colt, #11916, are the first Colt SAA revolvers known with these barrel lengths with #11916 possibly being the prototype for Colt's commercial 5 ½" barrel SAA first offered in 1875, that year beginning with Colt SAA #15001. The Army did not convert the SAA to 5 ½" until 1898 with the "Artillery" model.

Resurrection

After the two revolvers were returned to Colt, they were placed in storage and literally forgotten, at least as far as the details of their history were concerned. Then, in 1957, Colt put together a group of 58 rare firearms as a gift to the Museum of Connecticut History in Hartford. In visiting the museum's website, I brought up the photo of its Colt collection, and even though the image was small, I could see a 6 ½" barrel Colt SAA right in the middle.

In contacting the museum's curator, Mr. Nelson Dean, I learned the only information they had on this Colt was it was received as part of the gift from Colt in 1957. You can imagine Mr. Dean's reaction when I informed him of the priceless gun in the museum. Mr. Dean was kind enough to provide the photographs of this wonderful Colt here.

Remaining in nearly new condition, Colt #11846, except for its barrel length, embodies all the features of the very first Colt Model 1873 revolvers, such as the vertical lower front section of the frame, a feature changed within a few months. Being a military version, this gun has "US" stamped in the left side of the frame, but since it was never issued, it has no inspector's cartouche on the stock.

Once again, Colt has no record of this gun being shipped for testing, but when double-checking these serial numbers along with the (first) 5 ½" Colt, #11916, Ms. Beverly Haynes, of Colt Archives LLC found a letter from former Colt Historian, Marty Huber dated February 2, 1978.

In verifying the description of this 5 ½" Colt SAA, Mr. Huber reported while it was originally part of the group donated to the Museum of Connecticut History in 1957, it was thought to be an overrun from production and was held back until sent to auction in 1978 where it was sold in Las Vegas, Nev. One would hope the current owner now knows what a rare prize he or she acquired! Unfortunately, no photo of this Colt was available to include here, but it is probable it too bears the "US" stamp in the frame.

The Third 6 ½" Colt

Once again, in the book, *Colt Revolvers & The U.S. Navy, 1865–1889,* Mr. C. Kenneth Moore makes a vague reference to another rare 6 ½" barrel Colt SAA: "The last one is serial number 151992 and was manufactured on special order." However, there was no other information about this revolver, but seeing it was made in 1893 left no doubt it was a commercial and not a military contract Colt. Once again I went to Colt Archives LLC to ask Beverly Haynes to check on a serial number. What she reported was an equally great find!

Colt SAA #151992 was a 6 ½" barrel revolver in caliber .44 Russian

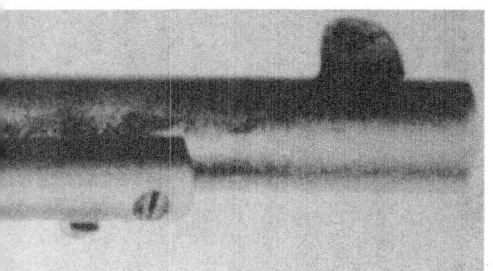

Shipped to the United States Navy for evaluation in 1875, Colt's second 6 ½" barrel SAA revolver, serial #16737, is chambered in .38 Colt, standard Navy issue at the time. It is not stamped "US" and has no stock cartouche. Image: Wayne Eikenberry from the book Colt Revolvers and the U.S. Navy, *collection of Raymond B. Bentley*

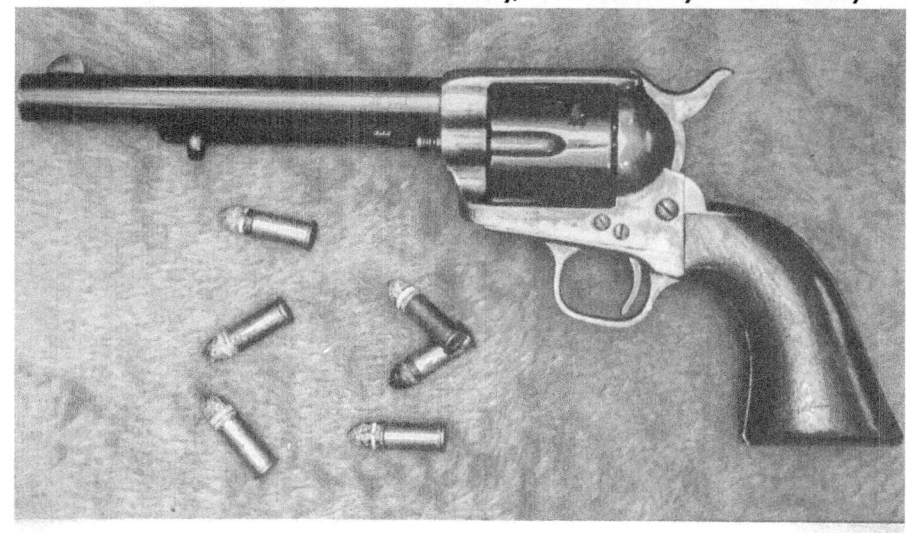

Figure 4–6. Colt Single Action Army revolver serial number 16737. Manufactured and shipped in 1875 especially for testing by the U. S. Navy, it is chambered for the .38 Long Colt cartridge, the Navy standard at that time. Six period cartridges are also shown. (Collection of Raymond B. Bentley) (Photography by Wayne Eikenberry)

and shipped with a spare cylinder in .44-40. It was finished in blue and color/case with type of stock not listed (but they are Colt hard rubber). The gun was a single order shipped May 24, 1893, to A.C. Gould of New York, N.Y. and Boston, Mass. The next question was who was A.C. Gould? The internet provided a great surprise!

Arthur Corbin Gould (1850–1903) was an avid outdoorsman, shooter and a member of the Massachusetts Rifle Association. In 1885, he published *The Rifle*, the forerunner to *The Rifleman*, the official publication of the National Rifle Association, later changing to *The American Rifleman*. Arthur Corbin Gould also published Fishing and Shooting magazine and several other books on guns and shooting.

Historical Colt firearms are virtually everywhere and, while not all may be as interesting or valuable as those featured here, many have a past waiting to be uncovered. One of the best places to start is with a letter of authentication from Colt Archives LLC. I've urged many to "get a letter" on their Colt. Those who did so were always glad.

NORTHERN PRECISION
Custom Swaged Bullets

npcustombullets.com | 315-955-8679

We offer bullets in **.308 to .500** and they are sold worldwide. We are always adding new bullets to our line, and we offer custom weights and styles!

COMING SOON! 6.5, .348, .412, .228

.308 150-250 GRS. to **.500** 300-600 GRS.

WilliamNoody@yahoo.com   329 South James St. Carthage, NY 13619

RUSTY, PITTED AND PRICELESS

John Taffin

Before: 125 years of wear and abuse on a Colt Single Action Army.

Resurrecting a Relic Colt Single Action Army

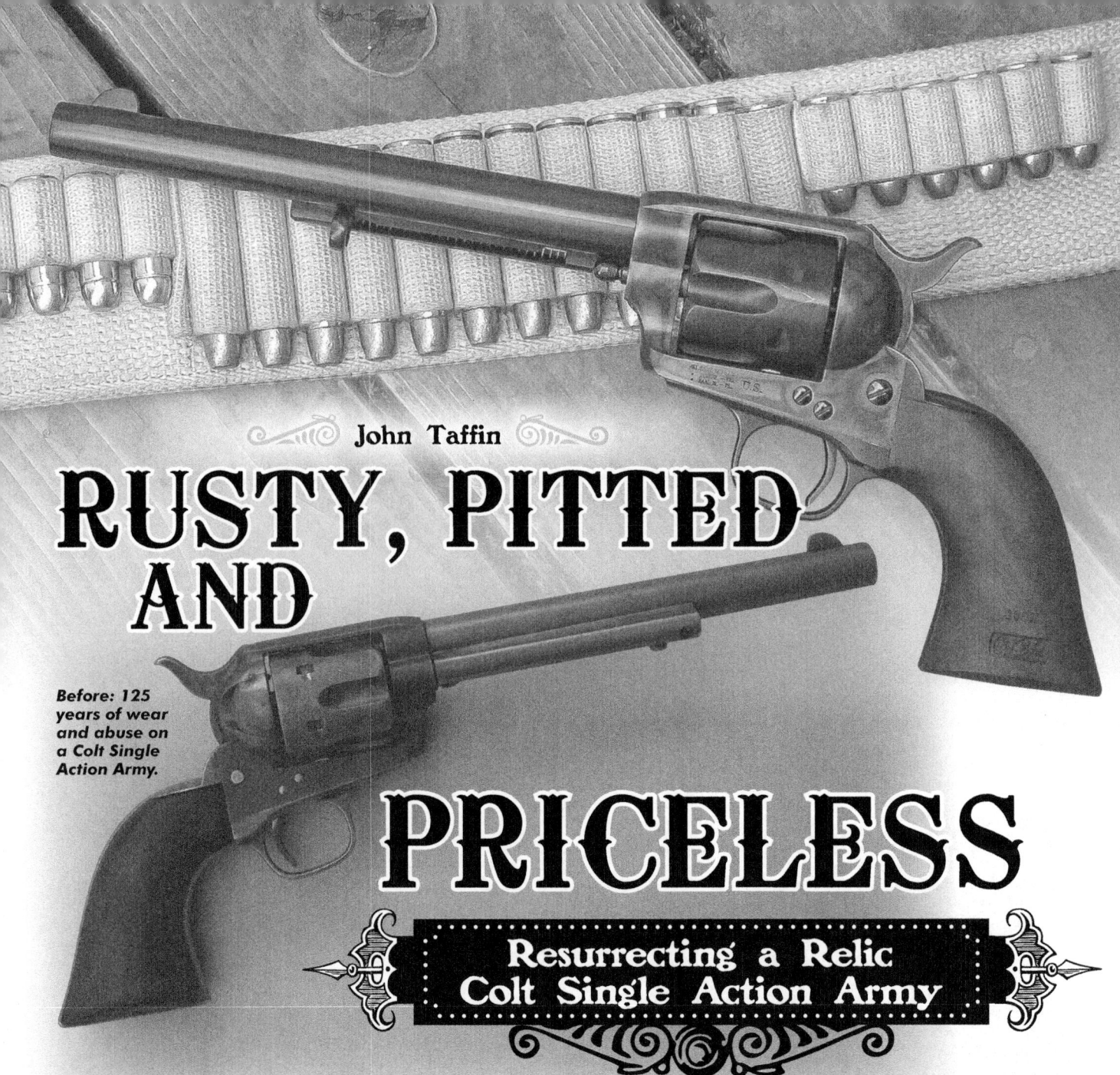

I could say it was just a chance meeting, but I have a hard time believing in chance or coincidence. So, I will just conclude it was meant to be. An estate was being settled with 41 firearms to be sold, however, before I ever heard about it, 40 were already gone and only one remained. It was apparently one no one else wanted. When I heard it was a Colt Single Action my palms started to sweat, my heart beat a little faster and I was prepared to hear about an old sixgun way out of my price range.

"How much will you offer for an old Colt?"

"Depends upon the condition," I responded.

"Well, it's old, it's rusty, pitted just not in very good shape."

"So that's why it remained the last gun to be sold? Well if the frame is okay, I would pay $300 just to get the frame for a rebuild."

"If you will go $300, it's yours and I can call the selling a finished product."

With that I agreed to purchase a Colt sight unseen and we went off to get the one last remaining firearm out of the back of the near-empty safe, a sixgun no one else wanted.

Buyer's Remorse? Or Not ...

Mixed emotions definitely kicked in as I picked up the old Colt. It was a 7 ½" Single Action Army with no caliber marking on the barrel; a very poor and very old appearing re-blue mixed in with patches of rust; one-piece wooden stocks that had shrunk considerably; and the barrel had scratches appearing to be from the teeth of a wrench or jaws of a vise as if someone tried to remove or tighten it.

In addition to the scratches, it appeared someone, who knows when, had filed down the corners of one of the flutes. For the life of me I cannot imagine what in the world this was all about. As I examined the old Colt, my sixgunnin' spirit was on a roller coaster. The old Colt seemed to function okay, certainly much better than it looked. The top of the loading gate where it met the frame shared one-half of a circular dent with the frame and I tried to envision it as a mark made by a 19th-century bullet. Whatever the cause it would require

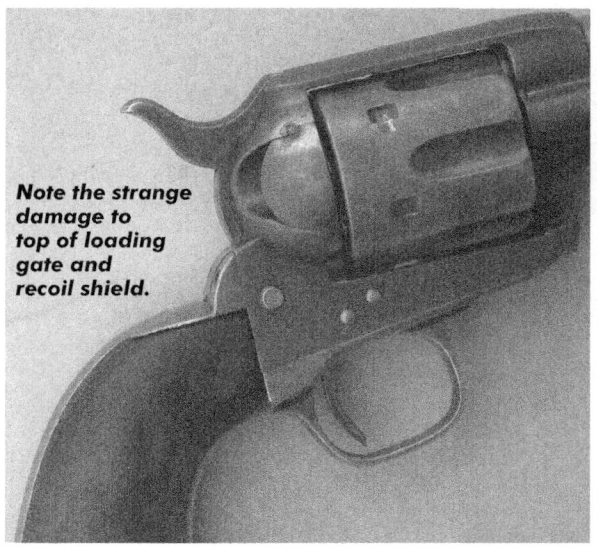

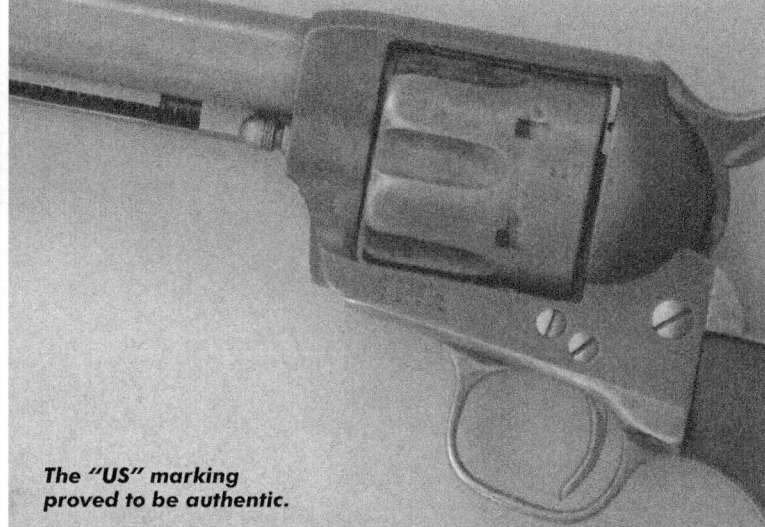

Note the strange damage to top of loading gate and recoil shield.

The "US" marking proved to be authentic.

extensive welding to fix it. So much for a bargain frame!

As I looked further, I discovered mismatched numbers when comparing the serial numbers on the frame, trigger guard and butt. The main serial number really caused my heart to take a leap, as this was a true "One of One Thousand" since the last three digits of the serial number were all zeroes. When one considers the fact less than 358,000 Colt Single Actions were made from 1873 to 1941, at least as to serial numbers, this would be a relatively rare sixgun.

Enter the Cavalry

What I saw next almost stopped my heart! Could it really be? There on the left side of the frame were two small letters. They were not serial numbers, they were not patent dates, they were not caliber markings. They simply said "US." Could it really be? Could this old mistreated relic be an authentic U.S. Cavalry sixgun? Could I be so fortunate as to have found a piece of frontier history for $300? If it really was authentic why didn't someone else buy it much earlier? I decided not to say anything until authenticating or disproving the fact of whether it was a true U.S. Cavalry Single Action Army.

I packed it up and sent it off to John Kopec for inspection and possible authentication. *Kopec lettered it as a true U.S.-marked Colt issued in 1881.* He was even able to tell me where it was originally issued. As with many Single Actions going through the government armory, parts were often separated with different containers for barrels, cylinders, frames and grip frames. *When the sixguns were reassembled no attempt was made to reunite all original parts, hence the mixed serial numbers.* I was offered $1,200 for the parts so I decided to split the difference in the actual pur-

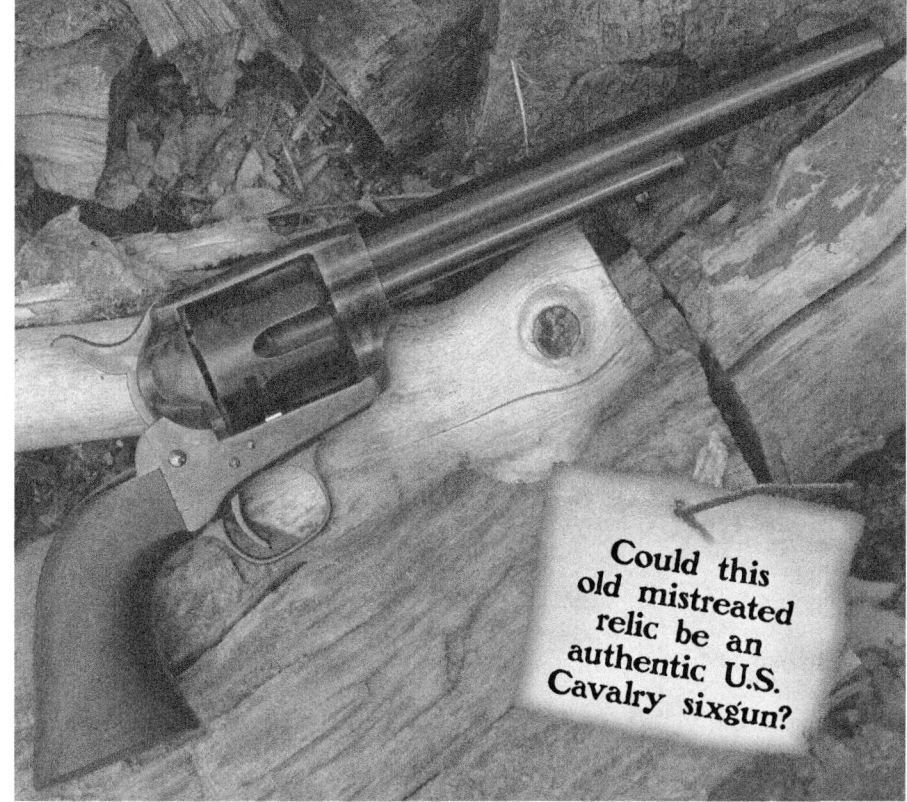

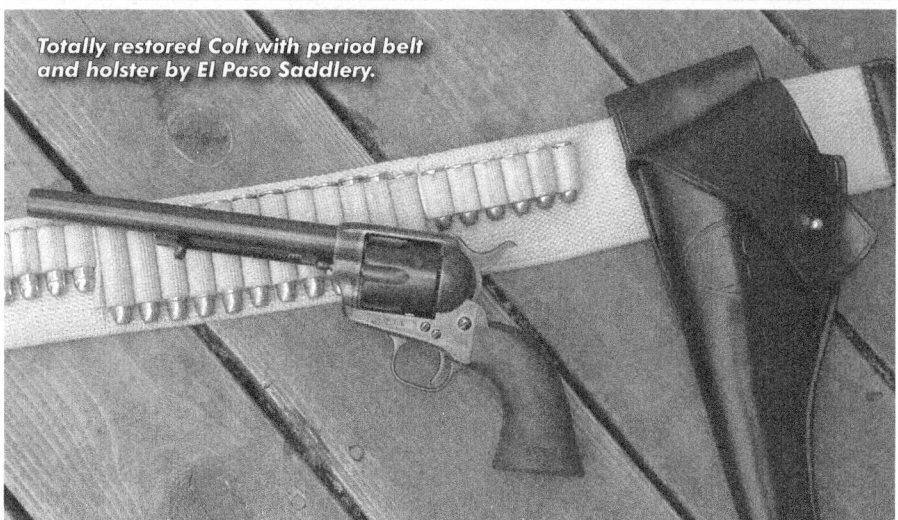

Could this old mistreated relic be an authentic U.S. Cavalry sixgun?

Totally restored Colt with period belt and holster by El Paso Saddlery.

Note the "US" on the left side of the frame.

Fully restored 1881 U.S. Colt with case-hardened hammer and frame.

chase price/authentication expenses, and the true value with the seller. It still gave me a good bargain and I feel better about the whole deal — my conscience remains clear.

Restoration

So now I have an authenticated U.S. Cavalry sixgun in shooting shape, with black powder loads, of course. It proved to be an excellent shooter capable of placing the first five shots in 1" from a rest at 50'. The plan became to shoot it occasionally and have it on hand for photographs. This all changed after talking to Larry Larsen.

Larsen specializes in restoring and custom finishing both old and new Colt Single Actions. The restoration of this Colt Single Action Army would require considerable work to bring it back the way it was in 1881. Neither of us would have considered touching the old sixgun if it had been original. However, the fact the barrel had been considerably marred; cylinder, frame and reloading gate all needed welding and filing; and especially since it had already been refinished poorly, it was an excellent candidate to be totally restored.

The work was considerable. On the frame itself, rust damage was removed, and a small spot weld had to be repaired; the original hammer and trigger were welded and recut to allow perfect timing and lockup; a new black powder-style base pin was installed; and all screws and the base pin were fire blued. Rust was removed from the trigger guard without removing the serial number or inspector's mark and both sides of the trigger guard were properly beveled to meet the frame sharply. The butt had become rounded and worn; this was flat sanded and contoured correctly and a new serial number was cut, one that would assure no intention to faking this as an authentic and all original U.S. Colt. To replace the misshaped original stocks, new one-piece walnut stocks were installed with the correct cartouches and inspector's marks.

All rust was removed from the cylinder, the flutes were polished and beveled, and the damaged flute was repaired all while protecting the original markings. The barrel was polished to remove rust and scratches while still maintaining all original markings, the tip of the ejector housing was beveled, and the correct black powder ejector

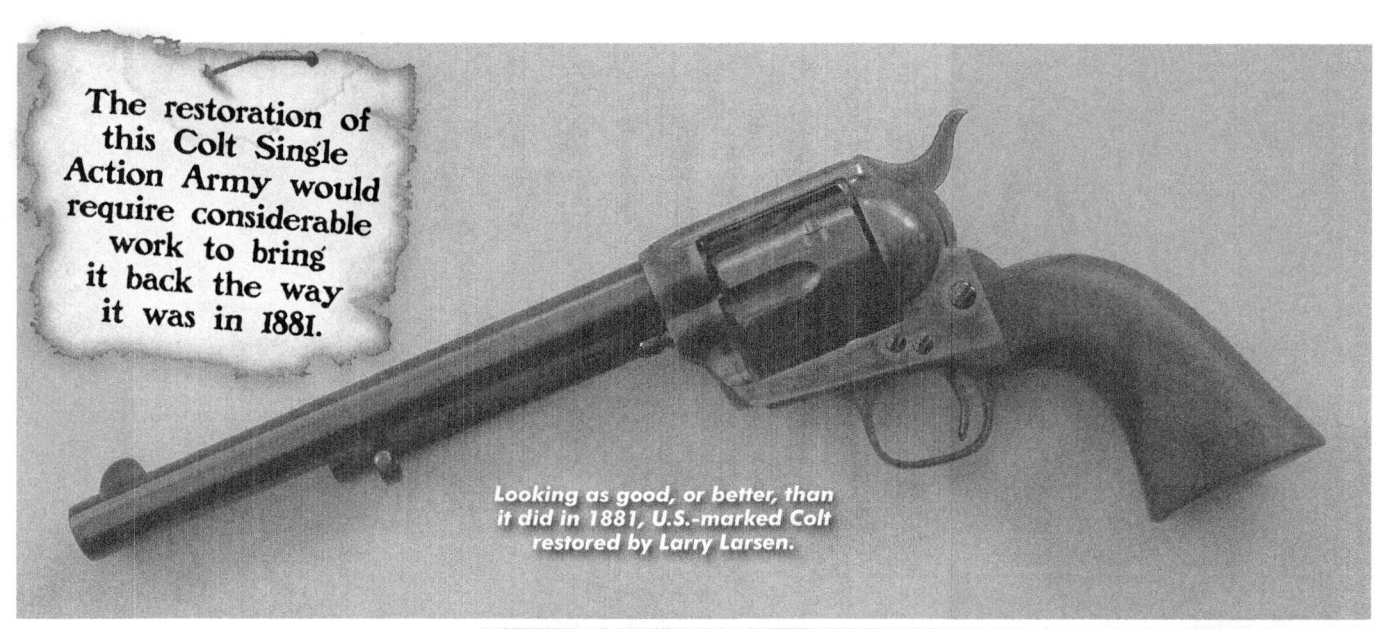

> The restoration of this Colt Single Action Army would require considerable work to bring it back the way it was in 1881.

Looking as good, or better, than it did in 1881, U.S.-marked Colt restored by Larry Larsen.

rod complete with round bull's-eye head was installed.

Except for the case-colored frame and hammer, the entire sixgun was properly and period correctly re-blued; the color case-hardening was performed by Color Case Company and necessary restamping was performed by Dave Lanara.

Original Issue

Larsen also did some research and came up with the following — all of which substantiates the earlier findings. The trigger guard number shows this part to have been on a revolver originally issued to the 8th Cavalry and has the inspection mark of O.W. Ainsworth. The number on the barrel shows it could very well have been issued to the 7th Cavalry in 1875; while the serial number on the cylinder, bearing the "RAC" of Rinaldo A. Carr, shows it originally belonged to the sixgun that went to the New York Militia. The parts of original U.S. Colts really did get around!

Larsen made the one-piece stocks to duplicate the 1900–1903 Factory Refurbishment Regulations and had Dave Lanara cut the 1901 cartouche of Lt. Odus C. Horney on the left-hand stock, and the RAC of Rinaldo A. Carr as it would have originally had in 1881. Put everything together and we have an absolutely stunning resurrection of a U.S. Colt that had suffered outrageous alterations and serious ravages of time.

Such a fine sixgun deserves to be properly carried. For this I turned to El Paso Saddlery for a period-correct U.S.-marked, black butt-to-front flap holster and canvas belt holding both .45 Colt and .45-70 rounds. Now everything is as it should be and as I pick it up and buckle on belt, holster and .45, I think I will be granted understanding if I hear *Bugles in the Afternoon*.

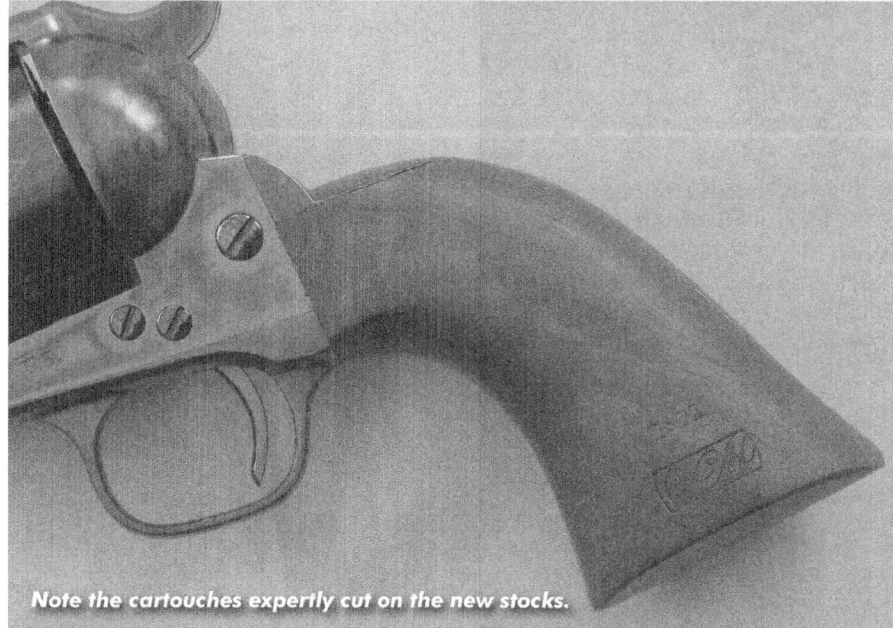

Note the cartouches expertly cut on the new stocks.

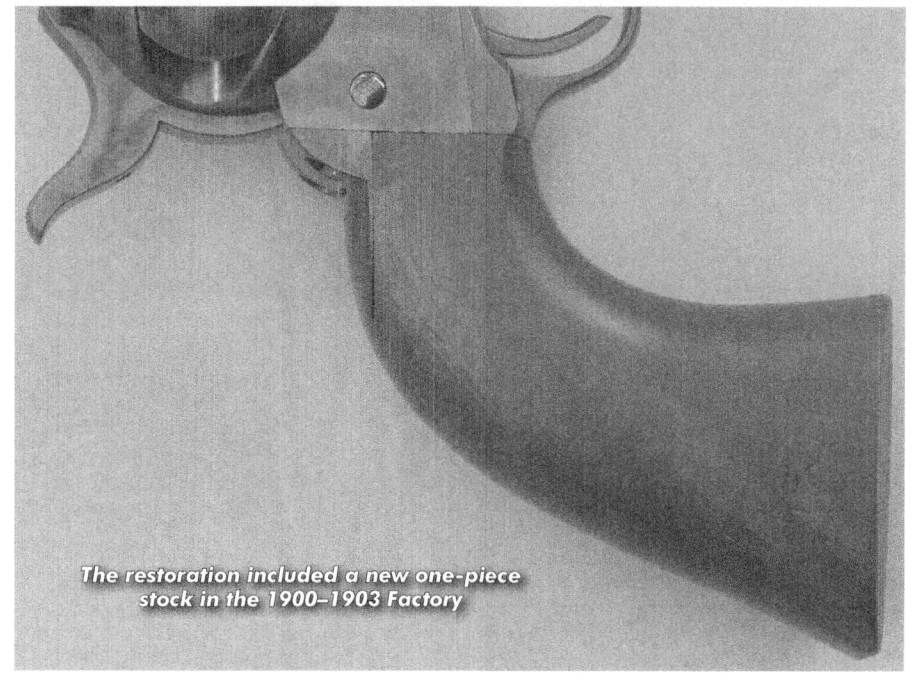

The restoration included a new one-piece stock in the 1900–1903 Factory

Will Dabbs, MD

A COUNTY HANGING

Will Mathis: Crime, Punishment and a Tidy Local Horror

"Familiarity breeds contempt." The first recorded use of this phrase dates back to Chaucer's *Tale of Melibee* in 1386. This means long experience with someone or something can make one so aware of their faults as to become scornful. In a more global sense, we can simply become so familiar with our surroundings they invariably seem mundane.

It is natural to presume nothing interesting ever happened in our own backyard. I rather suspect folks living in places like Jerusalem, Hastings, Normandy and Volgograd feel similarly today. *However, some of the most poignant events took place in some of the most unexpected places.*

I live about a dozen miles outside of Oxford, Miss. My little town is a mere crossroads bisecting a whole swath of nothing deep in rural Mississippi. About a mile as the crow flies

Will Mathis, shown here alongside his wife Cordelia, let alcohol take him down a dark path.

Despite a population of only 800 souls in 1902 when Orlando Lester and Will Mathis were hanged, Oxford, Miss., hosted some 7,000 spectators for the execution.

Whit Owens, Will Mathis' no-good father-in-law, seemed to follow trouble wherever it went.

Apparently the actual murder weapon was a side-by-side shotgun charged with buckshot. Orlando Lester retrieved this weapon from Whit Owens, Will Mathis' father-in-law.

64   GUNS MAGAZINE OLD WEST • SPECIAL EDITION

Thanks to his father's supremely poor life choices, young Clelon Mathis never knew him (left). Will Mathis' widow Cordelia eventually married a man 32 years older than she (below).

After he was hanged September of 1902, Will Mathis was buried in the Kingdom Cemetery just a few miles from where Will (Dabbs) lives today.

Old cemeteries such as these can be a fascinating way to kill a lazy Saturday afternoon.

Whit Owens, Cordelia's dad and Whit Mathis' father-in-law, admitted to the murder of the two federal marshals on his deathbed 26 years later. It seems at least one innocent man went to the gallows for the killings.

Cordelia Mathis, shown here on the right with her young son Clelon around the time her husband Will was executed, avoided jail time herself when Will confessed to two brutal slayings (right).

On Nov. 16, 1901, however, Delay, Miss., was the site of Something Truly Horrible.

from where I sit typing these words rests the tiny community of Delay. Delay likely draws its name from something fairly mundane. On Nov. 16, 1901, however, Delay, Miss., was the site of *Something Truly Horrible*.

The Players

Will Mathis was not necessarily an innately bad man, but like countless others before and since, he had a problem with alcohol. The devil brew robbed the man of his judgment and drove him to do irresponsible things.

In a letter penned to his 3-year-old son Clelon from prison just days before his execution, Mathis wrote, "Intemperance has ruined more men than any other evil in the world. All the demons of hell combined could not contrive or invent anything that would be a worse curse on humanity … as whiskey."

Whit Owens was Will Mathis' ne'er-do-well father-in-law. He did indeed seem an innately bad man. Owens enticed Mathis into brewing moonshine whiskey and was forever in trouble. His daughter Cordelia ("Cordie") was a simple and pious woman. She and Will seemed to love each other genuinely.

Twenty-five-year-old Hugh Montgomery was a field deputy for the U.S. Courts who lived in nearby Pontotoc, Miss. Hugh Montgomery and Will Mathis had a history. Montgomery had arrested Mathis previously for counterfeiting U.S. currency and confiscated his .38-caliber Colt pistol in the process. Mathis had complained bitterly about this to acquaintances. Accompanied by his brother John, Hugh Montgomery struck out from Oxford that Saturday afternoon to arrest Mathis on the charge of illicit distilling of spirits.

John Montgomery, also a special deputy U.S. marshal, was a combat-wounded Confederate Civil War veteran held in high esteem by friends and neighbors. John was married and had a son. Oddly, John Montgomery was actually a friend of Will Mathis and planned to testify on his behalf during his upcoming counterfeiting case.

Orlando Lester was a black man and tenant of Will Mathis. Lester had worked for Mathis' father-in-law Whit Owens for years and was no stranger to trouble himself. He was an experienced distiller of moonshine and had supposedly molested a white girl, an unusually big deal for the time. At the direction of Whit Owens, Lester attempted to shoot a man named Walter Jones to prevent his testifying in an unrelated case. Lester missed Jones and killed Hamp Williams instead. However, that case just seemed to smolder.

The Killings

The two Montgomery brothers got the drop on Mathis fairly late Saturday evening. The dozen miles on horseback from Oxford would have taken awhile, so it was obvious they could not return to town with their fugitive in the daylight remaining. Additionally, Will, Cordie and Orlando had been in the process of slaughtering a pig. Mathis observed that were they to take him into custody, the pig would spoil.

They would all feast on fresh pork, and the marshals could sleep in his spare bedroom. He would go with them peaceably back to Oxford the following Sunday morning.

Federal Marshal Hugh Montgomery confiscated a pistol like this .38-caliber Colt Model 1889 from Will Mathis during a previous arrest for counterfeiting. His refusal to return the gun, despite the ongoing nature of the investigation, precipitated some seriously bad blood between the two men.

Mathis made a counterproposal. He suggested the two lawmen could stay the night. They would all feast on fresh pork, and the marshals could sleep in his spare bedroom. He would go with them peaceably back to Oxford the following Sunday morning. All involved felt it a simply capital idea.

Cordie later testified the two lawmen had consumed a bit more than just fresh pig that evening. Will Mathis was an accomplished moonshiner, and it seems the marshals likely sampled his wares along with dinner. When it was time for them to retire, they were no longer at their best tactically.

Once the two law officers were in bed, Mathis and Lester crept into the room and one of them apparently shot both men. For reasons lost to history they then purportedly dismembered the bodies. Surviving records make mention of a lever-action Winchester rifle and a breechloading shotgun having been ultimately recovered. What came next made it difficult to reliably ascertain the details.

Mathis and Lester took the dead men's possessions and removed a feather mattress along with some baby clothes from the home. Having made a right and proper mess, Mathis then dispatched Cordie to her father's place, sent Lester on his way and put his home to the torch. He then fled on the lawmen's two stolen horses.

The following day neighbors discovered the charred corpses. They first thought them to be those of Mathis and a friend. The Montgomery brothers' family members eventually identified the bodies based upon a gold tooth and a charred pocketknife.

The Guns

It was commonly known Will Mathis owned a Winchester rifle. The lever-action Winchester was one of the most popular utility arms in the world during the latter half of the 19th century. These iconic guns were produced in nine different models from 1866 until the present. Roughly 720,000 copies saw service.

Hugh Montgomery carried a Colt .38 revolver in a shoulder holster. Given the era, this was likely a Model 1889. The Model 1889 was Colt's first double-action revolver with a swing-out cylinder. The Model 1889 differed from previous Colt wheelguns in that the cylinder rotated in a counterclockwise direction. However, the primitive design put undue stress on the cylinder lock and could even allow the cylinder to rotate when holstered.

One of the case's quirkier aspects was apparently this was the revolver Hugh Montgomery had seized from Will Mathis previously. The night of the murder, Montgomery and Mathis had argued vociferously over ownership of the gun. This likely contributed to the evening's bloody outcome.

The murder weapon used to kill the Montgomery brothers was said to be a double-barreled shotgun loaded with buckshot. Hugh was shot in the face, while John was hit in the chest and head. Orlando Lester claimed he had obtained the gun and ammunition from Whit Owens earlier in the evening. The bewildering variety of double-barrel shotguns in service during this period in American history defies ready characterization.

A Different Time

The brutality of these murders both shocked and energized the community. Law enforcement eventually apprehended Mathis, his wife Cordie, Whit Owens, Orlando Lester and an accomplice named Bill Jackson. *Mathis was justifiably terrified a mob would lynch him, his wife and the rest of the conspirators.* The local sheriff said he would speak with the crowd if need be, but refused to intervene physically should they be of a mind to hang him.

Desperate to save his wife, Will Mathis confessed to the murders in exchange for her freedom. The remaining players all related separate versions of the story, each implicating the others while clearing themselves. Mathis' court-appointed defense attorney had never before tried a criminal case. In Mathis' words, "He did the best he knew." The jury deliberated some 40 minutes before returning a verdict of "guilty as charged" and a sentence of death.

Once his wife was free, Mathis rescinded his confession and alleged Lester had been the sole triggerman. Orlando Lester's trial was comparably brief, and the jury returned the same verdict after a mere half hour. He was sentenced to be hanged alongside Mathis.

Whit Owens, Mathis' no-account father-in-law, hired an expensive team of lawyers but was also convicted and sentenced to death. However, his conviction was overturned on appeal. Owens was later convicted of murdering a witness to another crime and spent a decade on the Rankin County Prison farm. He gained early release for "meritorious conduct in preventing the escape of a fellow inmate," whatever that means.

Denouement

Back then a man could be arrested, charged, tried and executed at the county level. At noon on September 24, 1902, a mere 10 months after the crime was committed, Orlando Lester and Will Mathis were hanged in Oxford, Miss. The population of Oxford was only 800 persons at the time. More than 7,000 people showed up to spectate, some having traveled days to gawk.

Tragedy sells, and the garish details of the murders briefly captured the imagination of the country. I even found a San Francisco newspaper clipping describing these sordid events. Will Mathis vehemently asserted his innocence all the way to the gallows. Orlando Lester also denied involvement, but supposedly admitted in prison to having been the one who pulled the trigger.

On his deathbed in 1928, Whit Owens claimed he had actually been the one who did the killing, and that both his son-in-law and his field hand had been executed in innocence. Most of the major players are interred in the Kingdom Cemetery right down the road from where we live. My wife and I enjoy strolling through there on our frequent walks.

I found the graves of Whit Owens, Will and Cordelia Mathis and their son Baxter Clelon. Clelon died at 41, and Cordie subsequently married D.C. Weeks, a man 32 years her senior. Sometimes the most fascinating tales really do arise in your own backyard.

Lever-action Winchester rifles were produced in nine different major variations and saw worldwide distribution. This Model 1873 dates back to the late 19th century.

Frank Jardim

LOW TECH & FEARSOME

Geronimo's Bow: A Formidable Weapon

In 1829, in what is today New Mexico, an Apache man named Goyaałé was born. He would go down in history as Geronimo, and though he was never a chief, he became the most feared Indian warrior of his age. Mexico, and later the United States of America, provided him the opportunity.

Both nations wanted to expand their sovereignty over the land the various Apache tribes occupied to settle for themselves. For their part, the nomadic Apache vigorously opposed these incursions, countering with brutal, and almost continuous, guerilla warfare. Apache raids killed thousands of settlers, men, women and children. What distinguished Geronimo from his brother Apache warriors was his extraordinary excellence as a small unit combat leader and his tenacious resistance into the 1880s, years after other Apache tribes and bands had accepted a negotiated peace.

A Life of Revenge

Though Geronimo and his 16 warriors were not the last Apache to lay down arms when they surrendered September 6, 1886 (small bands were still raiding into the early 20th century), he was the most noteworthy for his ferocity, elusiveness and fearlessness. Ever since his wife, mother and three young children were killed by Mexican soldiers in 1858, he harbored an unwavering, murderous hatred of all Mexicans. In his autobiography he wrote, "I have killed many Mexicans; I do not know how many, for frequently I did not count them. Some of them were not worth counting." In the last five months of his freedom in 1886, the Governor of Sonora, Ariz., credited his little band with the deaths of between 500 and 600 Mexicans.

Geronimo was 57 years old at the end of his last rampage. When he finally surrendered, he was treated as a prisoner-of-war and remained in U.S. Army custody until his death in 1909. Near the end of his life, he asked President Theodore Roosevelt if he could return to his fellow Apache on the reservation in Arizona. Roosevelt would not allow it, telling the old warrior he had "a bad heart" and his crimes against the people of Arizona were not forgotten or forgiven. Perhaps the citizens of Arizona were a greater threat to him than he was to them at that stage, but it is interesting to note on his deathbed, Geronimo regretted his surrender and captivity, wishing instead he had fought until he was the last of his kind.

Like all Apache of his generation, Geronimo was born into the tradition of the bow and spear.

End of the Bow

Like all Apache of his generation, Geronimo was born into the tradition of the bow and spear. When facing an enemy armed with slow-firing muzzleloading guns, the bow still had considerable tactical value; but the advent of metallic cartridge firearms was the bow's death knell as a weapon. When Geronimo and the last of his band were photographed March 26, 1886, all 25 men were carrying rifles (mostly U.S. Army Springfields). The only bow seen was in the hands of a young boy. Geronimo's 1876 Winchester rifle and 1873 Colt pistol turned over at his last surrender are still extant in U.S. Army museums at Fort Sill and West Point.

POW Side Hustle

While a POW, Geronimo realized his infamy was a good source of income. Somewhat ironically, the old warrior returned again to making the bows, arrows and quivers he had long since put aside for war. Geronimo, whose record of torture and murder was widely publicized (and certainly somewhat enhanced in the newspapers of the era) had become a celebrity. He made more money selling his crafts, coat buttons, hats and autographs while in captivity than he had ever had in his life. I had the chance to examine a bow, arrow and quiver set attributed to him held in the collection of the Frazier History Museum in Louisville, Ky.

The Bow in Combat

In our times, sport archery and hunting are such popular hobbies it is easy to forget there was once a time when the bow was a primary weapon of the world's armies. In our American military experience, the Indian Wars are probably the first conflict to jump to mind when one thinks of the bow's use in combat. For a number of reasons, the Plains Indians used bows extensively long after firearms became available to them. The Indians could not make firearms, had difficulty keeping them in repair and most significantly, firearms required ammunition that could only be obtained from the white settlers they were fighting to keep out. Conversely, bows and arrows were made with the materials available in nature. Indians were taught to use bows from childhood and wielded them on foot or horseback with great skill and speed horrifying to their white adversaries.

Close-up of the hand-chipped flint arrowhead. Metal tips, made from salvaged metal, were also used.

Four composite arrows with chipped flint tips and shafts of hardwood and river cane. This style was used by the Apache and seems to fit the bow and Geronimo's area of operations on the U.S./Mexico border.

Close-up of the fletching feathers, attached with sinew.

Geronimo at age 75 at the 1904 World's Fair in St. Louis, Mo., with a self-bow and arrows. He got special permission to attend and participate in the event under military supervision.

A 41" long self-bow purported to be made and owned by Geronimo.

GUNSMAGAZINE.COM 69

Studio portrait of an Apache warrior with self-bow.

In 1860, U.S. Army doctor 1st. Lt. Joseph Howland Bill was stationed in Fort Defiance, N.M. In the year he spent there he treated 80 arrow wounds on 36 men, 22 of whom died.

Studio portrait of Kiowa Chief Satanta with his bow and arrows.

Geronimo at war. Another photograph made by C.S. Fly during the abortive March 1886 surrender agreement. From right to left: Apache leader Geronimo, Yanozha (Geronimo's brother-in-law), Chappo (Geronimo's son by his second wife) and Fun (Yanozha's half-brother).

In 1860, U.S. Army doctor 1st. Lt. Joseph Howland Bill was stationed in Fort Defiance, N.M. In the year he spent there he treated 80 arrow wounds on 36 men, 22 of whom died. Multiple arrow wounds were common. An Apache warrior could fire a lot of arrows in the time a soldier took to reload his muzzleloading rifled musket with powder, Minie ball and cap. Doctor Bill described arrow wounds as having "... a fatality greater than that produced by any other weapon." Bullets frequently passed clear through the body. If they did get stuck, bullets could sometimes be left in — saving the patient from surgery almost as dangerous as the original wound. This was not the case with arrows.

Arrow points often got stuck in the body because blood softened the sinews, fastening them to the arrow shaft causing them to come loose. If left inside, the sharp arrow point would continue to slice its way through tissue as the victim moved. Doctor Bill learned if you didn't get the arrow point out, the victim would die. One of the worst things a soldier could do was try to pull out the arrow in the field. If the arrow point didn't fall off the tip and get stuck in the body, the sharp point would do just as much damage being ripped out as they did going in.

The Geronimo Bow

The Geronimo bow I examined might not look like much of a weapon through 21st century eyes, but to a 19th century soldier, it was a terrifying weapon to face. Carved from a single piece of wood only, this type of bow is called a self-bow. The preferred species of the Southern Plains Indians was Osage Orange, but often ash or juniper were used. Bows could, and were, made from a wide range of natural materials. Nature makes a piece of wood as she sees fit and the Indian craftsman worked from nature's template. The back of a self-bow is shaved along the surface of a single year's growth in the wood so it resists breakage under the stress of the draw. Because of this, it can often look misshapen and have bulges like this one does. The bow can be bent with heat and the draw balanced by shortening one arm or the other. The final result can easily end up looking asymmetrical, though it is completely serviceable.

The Geronimo self-bow is of the type used by the Apache and measures 41" in length. Animal sinew was the most common material for bow strings. Plains Indians preferred the back sinews of buffalo for bow strings because they are the longest. The bow string is actually made up of multiple plies of twisted sinew fibers. This bow had a two-ply string, the most common type, but keep in mind each ply is made from six to 10 individual sinew fibers twisted together. The finished dried string was quite durable, but being a natural fiber, somewhat sensitive to humidity.

The Right Arrow

The Indians knew any bow would shoot an arrow. Success or failure on the hunt or in war depended on straight arrows. They took immense care in making arrows, marked them with both tribal and personal patterns and sought to recover them when possible. The quiver was intended as much to protect their arrows as to carry them. The arrows associated with the Geronimo bow were a composite style the Apache were known to use before they were forced onto the reservations. They have strong but lightweight river cane bodies fitted with hardwood shafts in front and chipped flint points with a very sharp edge. It took a skilled Indian between four and six minutes to make an arrowhead like this. The points are fastened to the shaft with animal sinew that draws tight as it dries.

The feathers attached to the base of the arrow are called fletching. Their purpose is to stabilize the arrow in flight. The feathers are split and cut to length. Some feather is removed from the quill at the front and back leaving a short section of bare quill on each end. The fletching is bound to the arrow shaft at these bare ends with wet sinew. The sinew tightens when dry, securing the fletching tightly to the shaft.

The reader may be wondering if the bow at the museum was actually used by Geronimo before his capture or made during his internment. This is hard to say. The Apache still owned bows long after they were replaced by firearms as weapons. It was remarked at the time of Geronimo's capture that, besides their guns, his warriors had bows as a sort of sidearm. This basic self-bow and arrows made as they were in the same region of his capture might have been taken from him. However, I think it more likely the set was made by him during his captivity. Whites or Mexicans encountering Geronimo outside the reservation or his various post-capture military camps would be lucky to get away with their lives, much less a trophy of this magnitude.

"WHITE BULL" FIRST FRIENDLY INDIAN TO VISIT WHITES IN CUSTER, S.D.

Geronimo's quiver. Quivers both carried and protected arrows (above). The bowstring is made of period correct twisted sinew (below).

The grip is decorated with leather.

A most wanted man — broadside with portrait of Geronimo that is a pretty fair likeness. Seeing Geronimo was one thing. Living to tell the tale was another.

This is what death looks like. Geronimo at 57 years of age and still at war with the United States. This photo was taken in March 1886 (by C.S. Fly) when Geronimo agreed to a surrender to U.S. Army forces, and then reneged and escaped. Note all the men are armed with rifles and most are U.S Trapdoor Springfields. Hmmm ... wonder how they got those?

Lyman and RCBS both offer molds for .44-40 bullets.

John Taffin

POWER THAT SIXGUN

Reloading the .44-40

Loaded .44-40 rounds with Lyman #427666 (200 grain), RCBS #44-200CM (205 grain) and RCBS #44-200FN (213 grain); all cast using wheel weights.

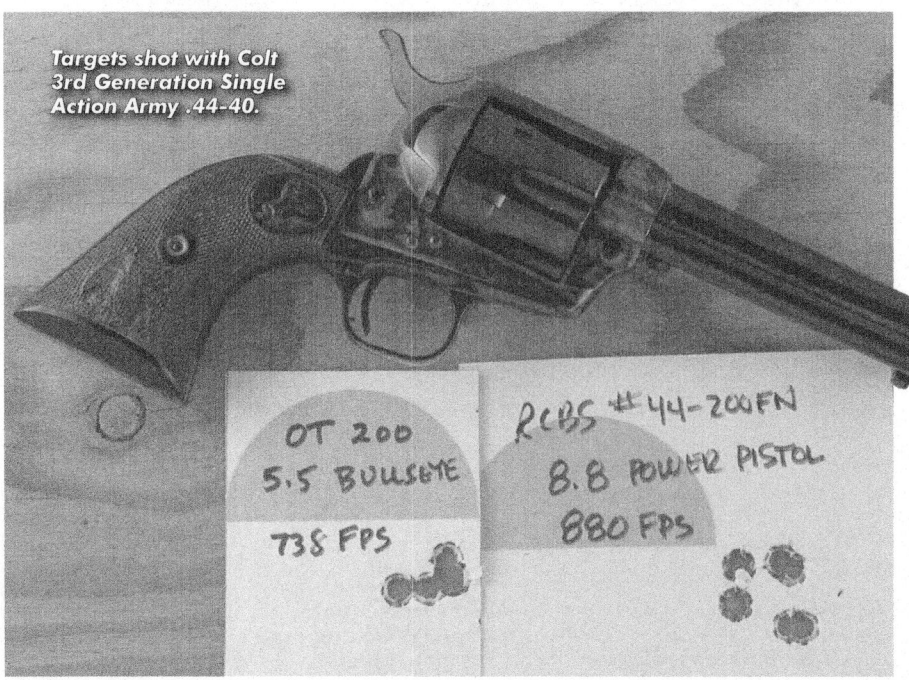

Targets shot with Colt 3rd Generation Single Action Army .44-40.

Everything we could possibly need (not want) arrived in 1873 with the Colt Single Action Army .45 Colt, the Winchester Model 1873 in .44 WCF and the Springfield Armory 1873 Trapdoor chambered in .45-70.

These three firearms gave those on the frontier a powerful sixgun, a very handy short-range lever gun, and a long-range single-shot rifle capable of handling anything with four legs or two. Even with the proliferation of firearms we have today, most of what we need to do could still be done with one of the 1873 originals.

Hand & Lever Standardization

It did not take long for Colt to realize the fact the Winchester cartridge, now mostly known as the .44-40, was about the same length as the .45 Colt and loaded with the same 40 grains of black powder, so by 1878 Colt was chambering their Single Action Army in .44 WCF. There were no caliber markings found on the newly chambered Colt Single Action, rather the barrel was marked "COLT FRONTIER SIXSHOOTER."

The arrival of the .44-40 in the Single Action Army allowed the use of the same ammunition in both rifle and lever gun and many went this direction; however, there were some who simply could not put down the .45 so they continued to carry the 255-grain .45 bulleted load in their sixguns while using the 200-grain .44 bulleted load in their lever guns. In 1892 Winchester introduced their much stronger lever gun in .44 WCF that eventually allowed more powerful loadings of the .44 WCF, which should not be used in revolvers.

Colt chambered the Single Action Army, the Model 1878 Double Action, the Bisley Model and the New Service in .44-40 and then added the New Frontier in the 1980s. S&W offered both single action and double action Top-Break revolvers in .44-40, and both Remington and Merwin-Hulbert chambered their sixguns in the .44 Winchester round. In modern days Ruger has offered a Super Blackhawk Convertible with two cylinders in .44 Magnum and .44-40 as well as their Vaquero chambered in .44-40, and S&W even offered their Model 544 N-Frame in .44-40. Colt Single Action Army replicas are also currently offered in .44-40.

Standardization Troubles

The original loading of the .44 WCF, 40 grains of black powder under a 200-

This custom Ruger Three-Screw by David Clements uses a 4 ¾" Colt New Frontier barrel and has cylinders chambered in both .44-40 and .44 Special.

grain bullet, was a powerful sixgun loading even by today's standards. Modern brass with its solid head will only hold about 35 grains of black powder, however, I have duplicated the old loads using the higher-capacity balloon head brass and 40 grains of black powder, yielding well over 1,000 fps in a 7 ½" Colt SA.

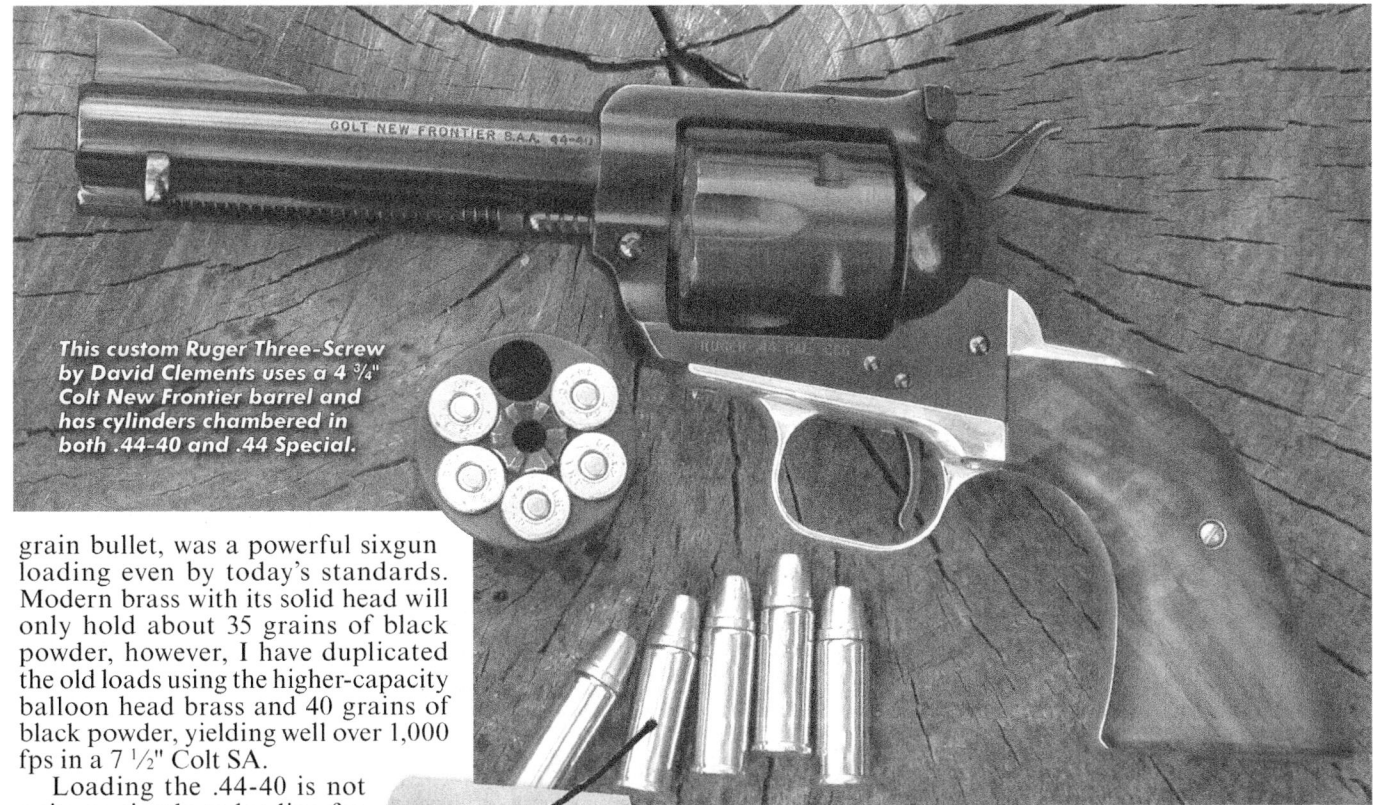

Loading the .44-40 is not quite as simple as loading for more modern cartridges for several reasons. *One is the fact chambering dimensions and barrel dimensions are all over the map.* I have had .44-40 sixguns with chamber throats as tight as 0.424" and as large as 0.432", a few even larger. Barrel-groove diameters can be found from 0.426" to 0.432", so it is necessary to pick the right bullets to match the sixgun. When Ruger brought out the .44-40 Vaquero back in the 1990s, they used tight cylinders and .44 Magnum barrels. Accuracy suffered. Once those cylinders were opened up to allow the use of 0.430–0.431" bullets, groups shrunk considerably.

> The arrival of the .44-40 in the Single Action Army allowed the use of the same ammunition in both rifle and lever gun and many went this direction.

Brass Considerations

Brass for the .44-40 is also thinner at the neck than the .44 Magnum or Special, and if care is not used in lining up the cartridge case with the sizing die the result will be a ruined case. It takes very little effort for the case neck to crumple if it hits the die off center. For many years I used Remington and Winchester .44-40 brass, but Starline brass seems to be a little tougher and heavier and less likely to crumple. However, it is not indestructible and care needs to be taken. Since the .44-40 is a tapered case, basically .45 ahead of the rim and .44 at the mouth, an old-fashioned, non-carbide sizing die is required. This means cases

Taffin loads his .44-40 rounds on the RCBS Model 2000 Progressive Press.

These 3rd Generation Colt Single Actions were engraved by Dale Miller. Top sixgun is .38-40 with ivories while bottom is a .44-40 with ram's horn grips; the custom holster is by Taffin.

Colt offered their excellent heavy-duty New Service in both .44-40 and .38-40.

must be lubed before being re-sized. I normally put about 100 pieces of brass in a shallow cardboard tray and spray them with Hornady wax-based spray-on lubrication. Being wax, it will not compromise primers.

Cast Bullets

When loading cast bullets for use in the .44-40 I normally go with the largest diameter that will fit the cylinder. I have a pair of 7 ½" nickel-plated Colts that appear to be identical. One is a 2nd Generation Peacemaker Centennial Commemorative while the other is a 3rd Generation Single Action. One requires bullets sized to 0.427" while the other will accept those of 0.429–0.430". By tailoring the specific bullet to the specific gun better accuracy results.

My actual loading is done with RCBS .44-40 dies on their Model 2000 Progressive Press. This press allows for the use of four dies, meaning I can use one die for seating and another die for crimping. By separating the steps there is less chance of crumpling a case, which can happen when seating and crimping in one step.

The Right Book

The .44-40 is a perfect example of why we should not use old loading manuals. During the 1950s a standard load for the .44-40 Colt Single Action Army was the Lyman #42798 bullet over 10.7 grains of Unique. It was a very heavy load! I've gotten smarter, or maybe I'm more careful of my guns and my hands now, so I have cut this load back to a new standard of 8.0 grains of Unique or Universal. The latest *Lyman #49 Reloading Manual* lists 7.9 grains of Unique as maximum for this bullet. In a 7 ½" sixgun, this load gives right at 900 fps. If I do want more velocity in a modern large-frame sixgun, I go up to 9.0 grains of Unique which gives me right at 1,000 fps. Both Lyman and RCBS now offer molds for cast bullets that have excellent crimping grooves. These bullets are #427666 and #44-200, respectively.

I recently picked up an old Colt Single Action Army with a heavily pitted barrel and cylinder. However, it also came with a brand-new Christy 7 ½" .44 barrel and .44 Special cylinder. I added a Colt .44-40 cylinder and since both Colt and Christy, which offered Colt parts at mid-century, use the same barrel dimensions for both the .44-40 and .44 Special, this combination works out exceptionally well. In addition to a .44-40 Colt New Frontier 4 ¾" I also have three Colt New Frontier .44 Specials that have been fitted with .44-40 cylinders giving me lots of opportunity for experimenting with loads.

For more info: Colt.com, StarlineBrass.com

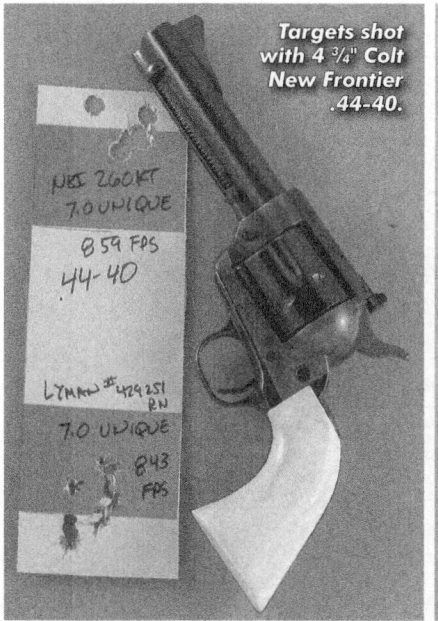

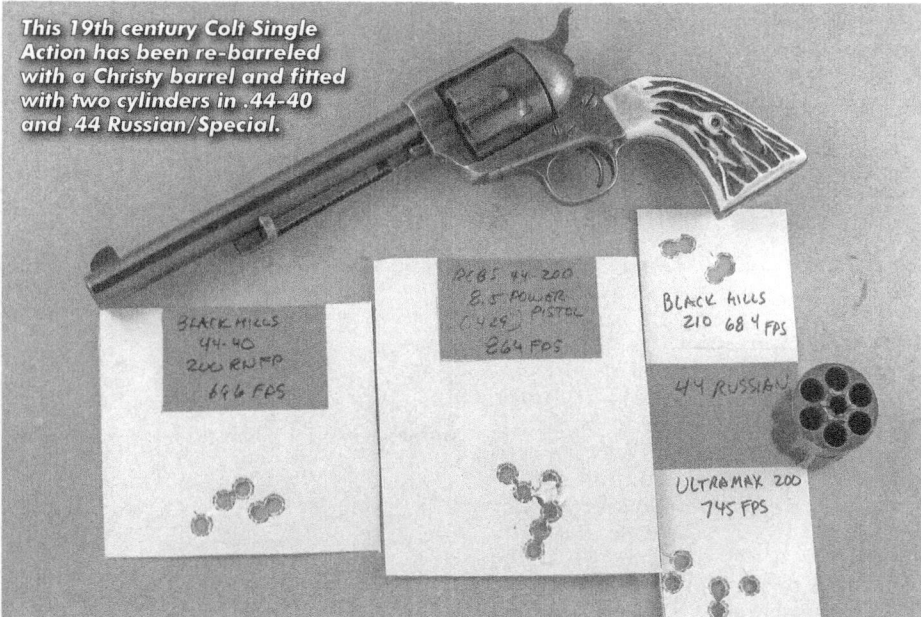

Targets shot with 4 ¾" Colt New Frontier .44-40.

This 19th century Colt Single Action has been re-barreled with a Christy barrel and fitted with two cylinders in .44-40 and .44 Russian/Special.

GUNS MAGAZINE

1-YEAR PRINT SUBSCRIPTION ONLY $24.95!

FREE 2020 Digital Download with your paid order

Call (866) 820-4045
www.fmgpubs.com

M-F 8am-3pm PST ($64.95 outside U.S.)
P.O. Box 509094, San Diego, CA 92150

Mike "Duke" Venturino · Photos: Yvonne Venturino

CARBINES, REPEATERS, MUSKETS & REVOLVERS

Guns of the Indian Wars

Two repeating rifles often mentioned as used on both sides in the Plains Indian Wars were the Henry (top) and Improved Henry (aka Winchester Model 1866) in saddle-ring carbine form. Both chambered the .44 Henry Rimfire cartridge.

These three cartridges were commonly used in various weapons during the years of Plains Indian warfare. From left: .44 Henry Rimfire, .44 Winchester Centerfire (aka .44-40) and .56-50 Spencer Rimfire.

This Indian (tribe unknown) is shown holding a Henry .44 rifle. Chambering would have been .44 Henry Rimfire.

This Piegan (Blackfoot) brave is holding a Winchester Model 1866. Chambering would have been .44 Henry Rimfire.

The Plains Indian Wars began in earnest about 1864 and continued for approximately 15 years. Speaking in general terms, sporadic fighting occurred in the areas between Northern Texas and the Canadian boundary and from western Wyoming to the southern turn of the Missouri River. On the white side, combatants included regular U.S. Army troops, state supplied volunteer units and at times groups composed entirely of civilians. On the Indian side, tribes engaged in fighting included, but were not limited to, Sioux, Cheyenne, Kiowa, Arapaho, Comanche and Plains Apache. It should be noted not all members of those tribes fought in the Plains Wars. Some warriors were belligerent always, some never were and some fought occasionally.

Have Teeth, Will Fight

In the same time frame, American firearms technology changed more than perhaps in any other similar period. In the spring of 1864, when fighting broke out in earnest on the Denver Road in southern Nebraska and eastern Colorado, U.S. infantry troops were still issued .58 muzzleloading muskets.

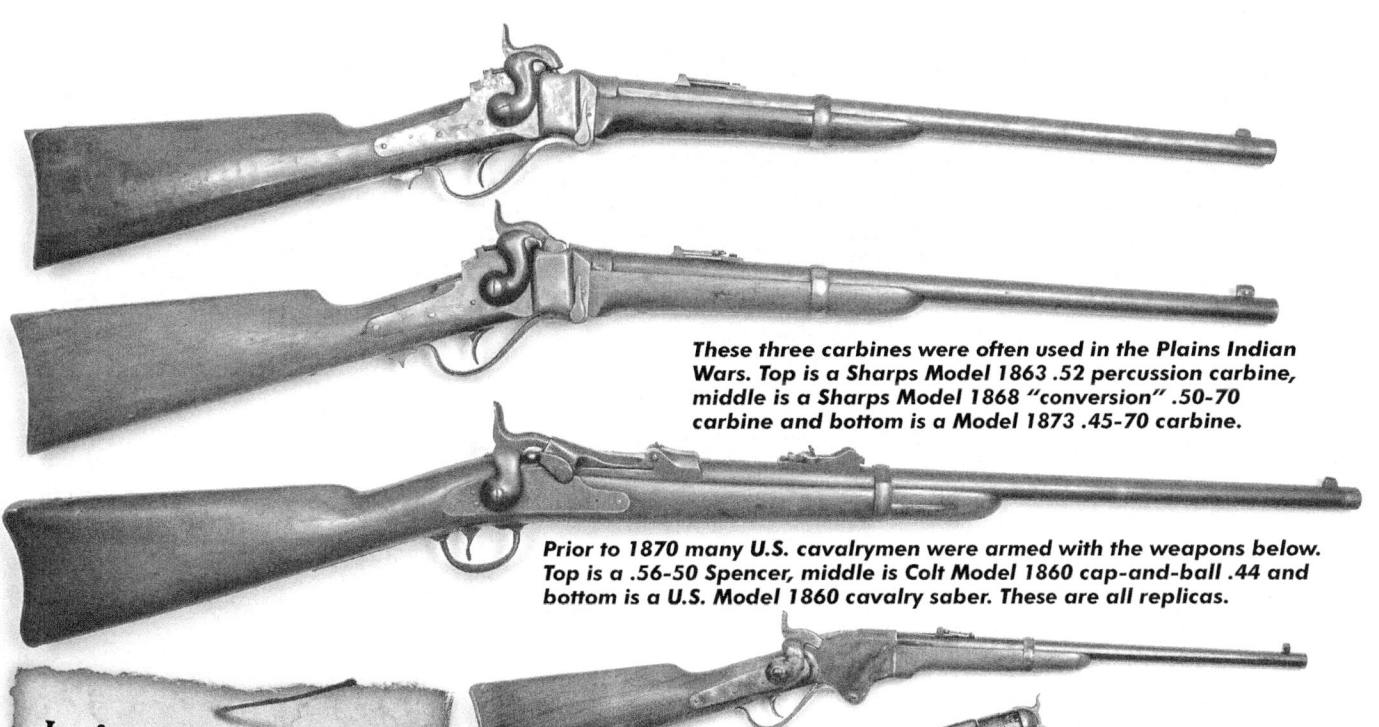

These three carbines were often used in the Plains Indian Wars. Top is a Sharps Model 1863 .52 percussion carbine, middle is a Sharps Model 1868 "conversion" .50-70 carbine and bottom is a Model 1873 .45-70 carbine.

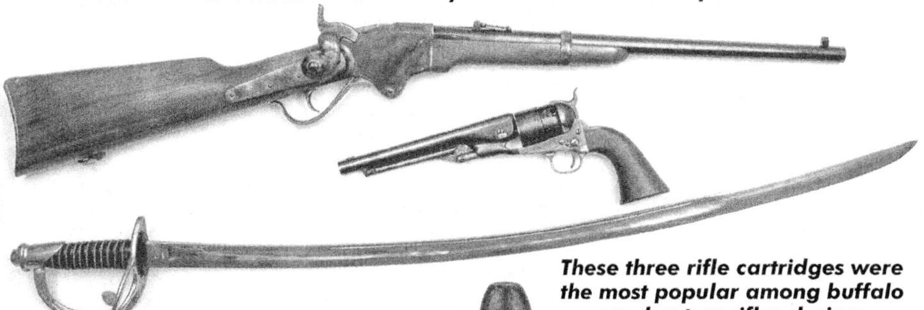

Prior to 1870 many U.S. cavalrymen were armed with the weapons below. Top is a .56-50 Spencer, middle is Colt Model 1860 cap-and-ball .44 and bottom is a U.S. Model 1860 cavalry saber. These are all replicas.

> In fact, during this time U.S. Army regulations stipulated a recruit had to have at least four opposing teeth.

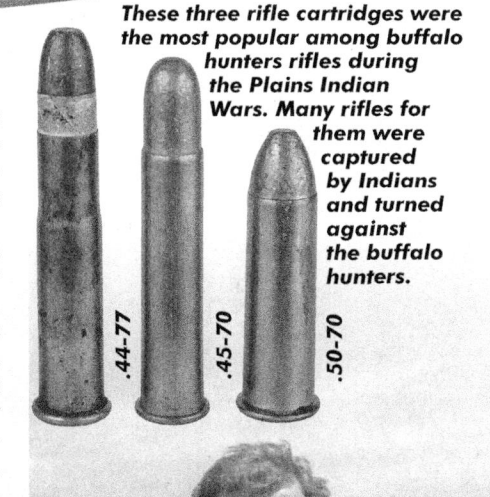

These three rifle cartridges were the most popular among buffalo hunters rifles during the Plains Indian Wars. Many rifles for them were captured by Indians and turned against the buffalo hunters.

.44-77 .45-70 .50-70

Ammunition for them came in the form of nitrated paper cartridges, holding a 60-grain black powder charge and a 450-grain hollowbase Minie "ball" (a conical bullet). In fact, during this time, U.S. Army regulations stipulated a recruit had to have at least four opposing teeth. They were necessary for biting the end of paper cartridges so its powder charge could be dumped down the musket barrel. Then the "ball" was rammed on top with paper still attached. Ignition was supplied by a separate percussion cap.

New Firearms Tech

Some modernization did begin during the Civil War of 1861–1865 when issue began of breech-loading carbines to cavalry troops. The most common were Sharps and Spencers.

Sharps Model 1859 and 1863 carbines in .52 caliber also fired paper cartridges, albeit the cavalryman did not have to bite it. These carbines were breechloaders: Nitrated paper cartridges holding powder and bullet were dropped in chambers. The breechblocks of Sharps were sharp, which had nothing to do with the carbines' name. When raised, breechblocks would shear off the rear of paper cartridges, exposing powder for the ignition flame of a separate cap.

Starting in 1867 the U.S. government began shipping literal boxcar loads of percussion Sharps carbines back to their manufacturer where they were converted to fire the .50 Government metallic cartridges (.50-70).

The other carbine available then was the Spencer, and it is probably correct to say it was ahead of its time. Spencers were repeaters firing metallic cartridges. They loaded through a trapdoor in the buttplate. Magazine capacity was seven rounds. Spencer trigger guards also served as an operating lever. When pulled downward, fired cartridge cases were ejected. When raised, another round was

Duke standing on the site of Adobe Walls.

GUNSMAGAZINE.COM

This buffalo hunter of the 1870s was photographed holding a Sharps Model 1874 rifle.

fed into the chamber. Hammers still needed to be cocked for each shot.

Spencer repeating rifle and carbine cartridges came in a bewildering array. The ones most commonly issued to troops post-Civil War were .56-50. Spencer cartridges were rimfire. Ammunition could be loaded singly into the chamber or inserted through the buttplate into the magazine. Also, a device called the Blakeslee Loader was available consisting of a metal tube holding seven cartridges. They were issued in a round canister holding 10 tubes, although I've never read documentation the Blakeslee boxes and tubes were used in Plains Indian fights.

Bows & Clubs vs. Muskets, Carbines & Repeaters

At Fort Phil Kearny near present day Sheridan, Wyo., in December 1866, a wood cutting detail was attacked by Sioux and Cheyenne warriors. A detachment of combined infantry and cavalry commanded by Captain William Fetterman were sent to their rescue. Two civilian employees at the fort also asked to accompany the troops. Their names were Wheatley and Fisher and both had Henry .44 Rimfire repeating lever-action rifles. Springfield .58 rifle muskets and Spencer .56-50 carbines were carried by infantry and cavalry, respectively. All 81 white fighters were wiped out.

Very few Indians at the Fetterman fight had firearms; most used bows and arrows and war clubs. Other troops sent out later to recover bodies said the two civilians must have sold their lives at great cost judging by the empty .44 Henry Rimfire cartridge cases sur-

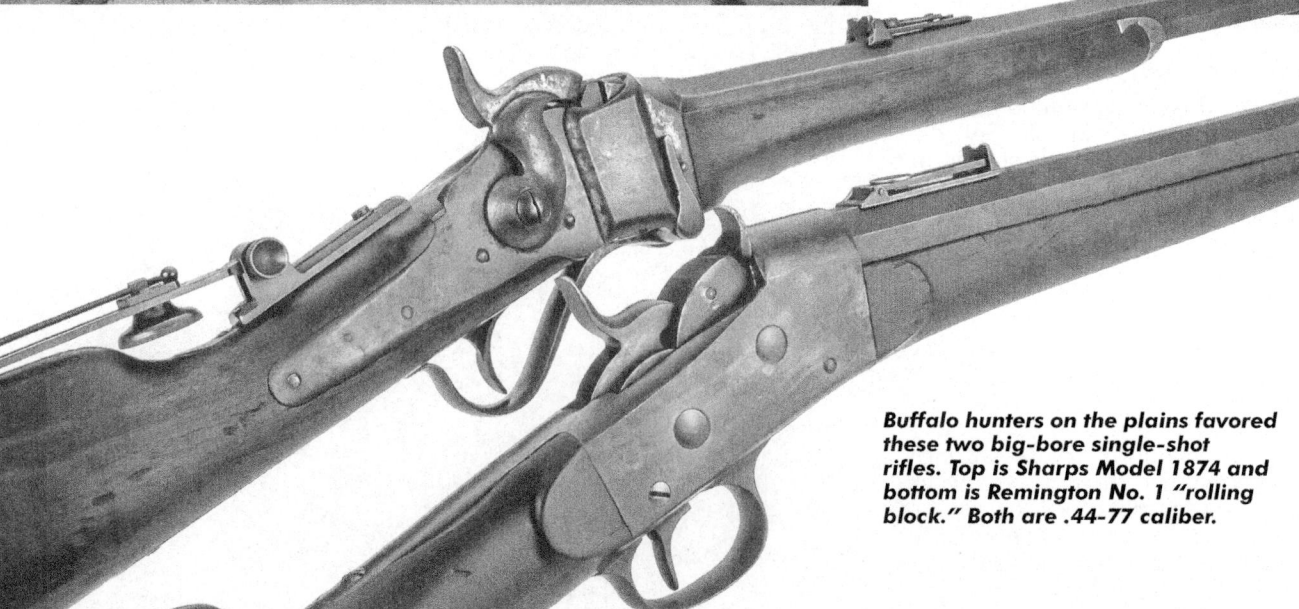

Buffalo hunters on the plains favored these two big-bore single-shot rifles. Top is Sharps Model 1874 and bottom is Remington No. 1 "rolling block." Both are .44-77 caliber.

78   GUNS MAGAZINE OLD WEST • SPECIAL EDITION

rounding their corpses. The Indians captured 29 Spencers in that battle. One young Cheyenne warrior named Two Moons used his captured Spencer until 1877, when he surrendered to troops at Fort Keogh in Montana.

Spencers in Action

An Indian fight where no Spencer carbines were captured was the September 1868 Battle of Beecher's Island near present day Wray, Colo. U.S. Army General Phillip Sheridan got the idea a contingent of "plainsmen" could better catch up to bands of raiding Indians than could ponderous columns of regular army horse soldiers. So, a group of 50 civilians were enlisted as "scouts." They were issued Spencer carbines and Colt Model 1960 .44 revolvers. In command were two regular Army officers: Major George Forsyth and Lt. Frederick Beecher. Instead of chasing down hostiles, at daybreak the morning of the 17th a group of about 500 Cheyenne warriors attacked their campsite. Luckily, the camp was on a branch of the Republican River with an island only a few yards across a small channel. In a hectic mob, all scouts gained the island and immediately began digging rifle pits. With the protection afforded by the pits and with their fast-firing Spencer carbines, the civilians were able to keep the Cheyennes at bay through several fierce charges. Six of the detachment, including Lt. Beecher, were killed and 17 wounded including Major Forsyth. The island was named in honor of Lt. Beecher.

Another very interesting skirmish involving Spencer carbines was with Cheyenne warriors in May 1869. The location was in north-central Kansas. Seven railroad laborers took a handcart from their base several miles to repair tracks. Of the seven, three brought their Spencer carbines, one brought his carbine but forgot his ammunition and the other three went unarmed. During the day Indians charged out of the brush on horseback and all workers ran for their handcart where weapons were stored. The skirmish turned into a running fight, with the Indians charging their horses alongside the cart while two workers pumped furiously toward safety. The three armed men fired their Spencers at the Indians with unknown results. In the chase two workers were shot and killed, falling from the cart. Four others were wounded by arrows and/or bullets. Only one escaped unscathed, but those five did make it to help.

Two items cause wonderment in reading this story. One is why workers left safety in hostile Indian territory without weapons. The other is with a party of Indians charging, one worker was delayed in getting his Spencer into action because in his hurry to load it he inserted a cartridge backward. Naturally in that situation one can be excused for being fumble-fingered, but why would he start this trip with his carbine *unloaded*?

Duke loading a replica Spencer .56-50 through its buttplate.

Prior to the adoption of metallic cartridge firearm rifles, soldiers in the early years of the Plains Indian Wars still used muzzleloading rifle-muskets taking .58-caliber Minie balls.

Henry Repeaters

Among non-military fighters, including frontiersmen and Indians, .44 Henrys were likely preferred at least during the early years of the 15-year period under discussion. Already mentioned were the two civilians with Captain Fetterman. August 1867 near Fort C.F. Smith in southern Montana, a hay-cutting team consisting of 21 soldiers and nine civilians were attacked by an estimated 800 Sioux warriors. In command was Lt. Sigismund Sternberg aided by Sgt. James Norton, both of whom were killed early in the fight. A civilian named Al Colvin took charge. In the hay-cutters' camp, Mr. Colvin had a case of 1,000 rounds for his .44 Henry, of which he fired 300 during that afternoon. However, a great help to Colvin was the brand-new "trapdoor" Model 1866 .50-70 Springfield in the soldiers' hands.

Trapdoor Era

Although during the Indian Wars the U.S. Army didn't adopt a repeating

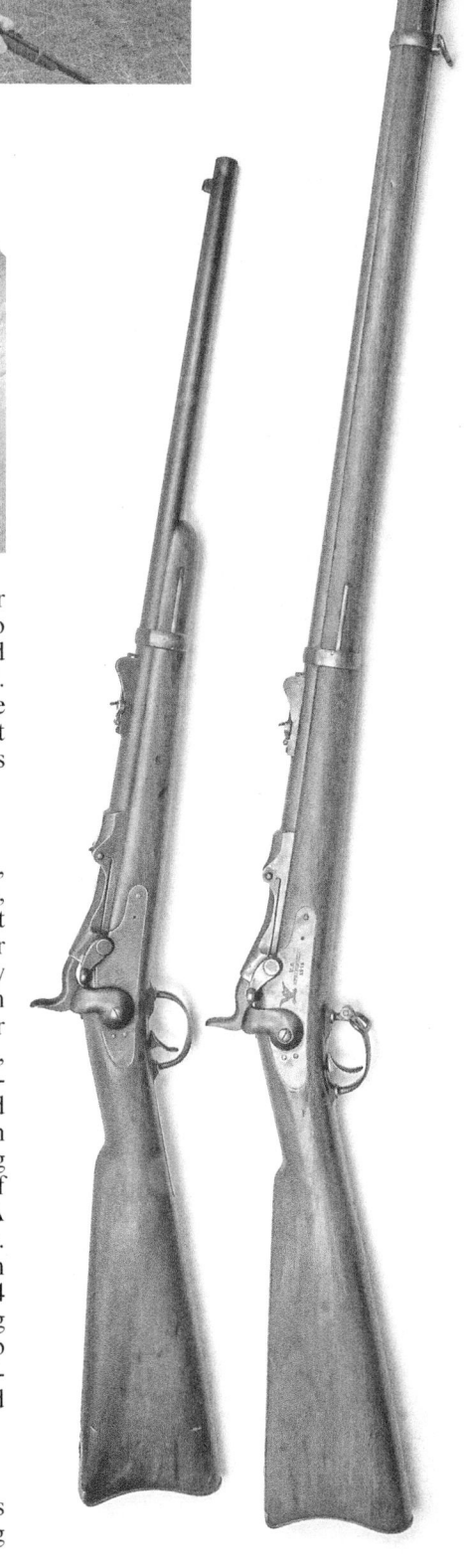

In 1873, the U.S. Army adopted new rifles and carbines chambered for .45 Gov't aka .45-70. These are the U.S. Model 1873 carbine (left) and Model 1873 infantry rifle (right).

In 1871, Colt introduced their Richard's metallic cartridge conversions of Model 1860 cap-and-ball revolvers. Caliber was .44 Colt. At least one of these was fired at the Battle of Adobe Walls. The U.S. Army also purchased 1,200 for issue to cavalry regiments.

> Fast-firing handguns and rifles helped push the attackers away from the buildings far enough that the legendary long-range ability of "buffalo rifles" could take effect.

This is the S&W No. 3 .44 American introduced in 1870. At least one of these revolvers was used at the Battle of Adobe Walls. The U.S. Army purchased 1,000 of these for use by cavalry regiments.

From 1866 to the mid-1890s the U.S. Army used rifles and carbines of the "trapdoor" style. They were .50 Gov't (aka .50-70) from 1866 until 1873 and from then on they were .45 Gov't (aka .45-70.) Shown is a Model 1873 with original .45 Gov't round.

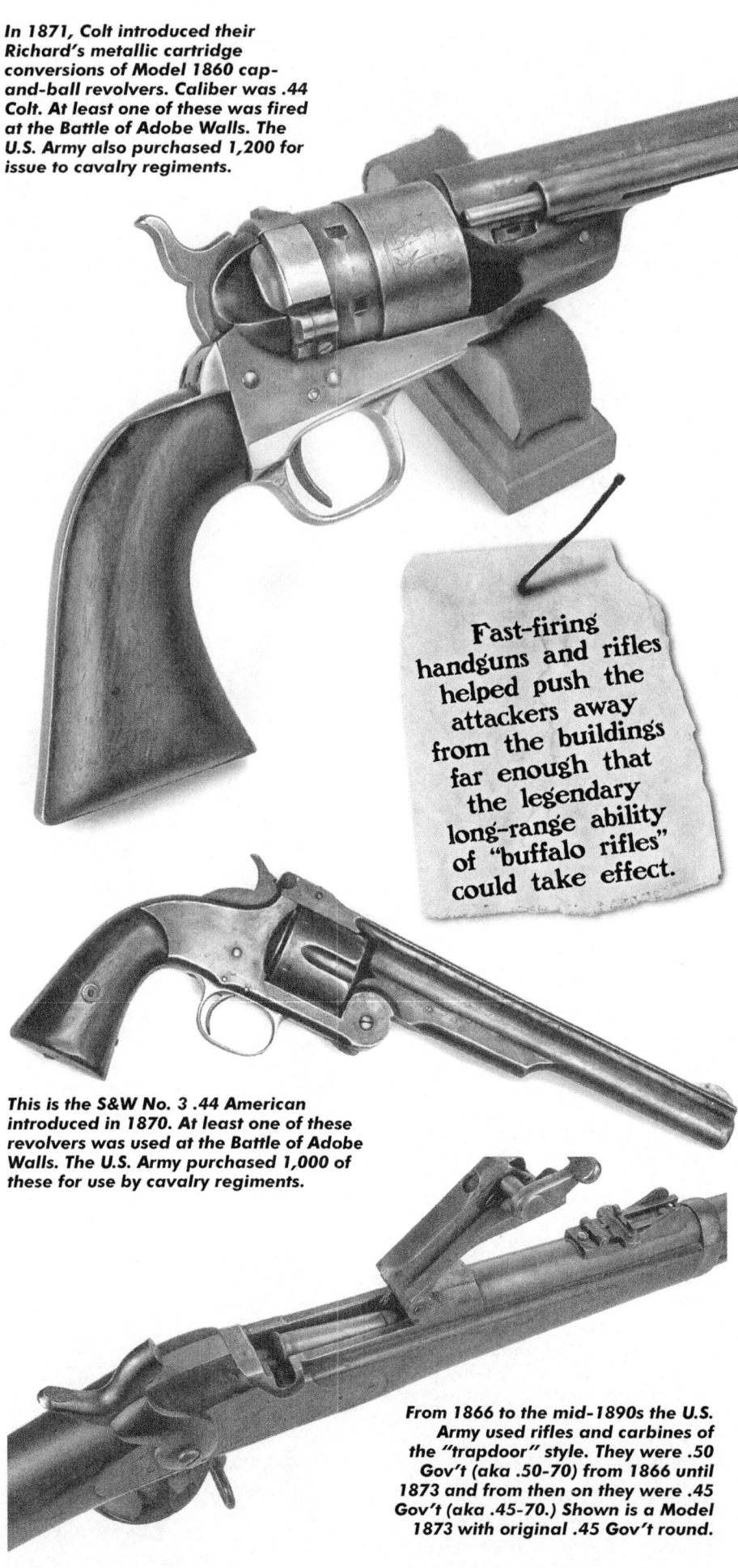

rifle as standard issue except for the cavalry's Spencers, their Ordnance Department did work on replacing muzzleloading rifles-muskets. The government-owned Springfield Armory first began converting .58 caliber Civil War percussion muskets to accept metallic cartridges in 1865. This conversion's system of function was a breechblock that pivoted upward, ejecting a fired cartridge and exposing the chamber for reloading. This became the "trapdoor" action and was used as a basis for American military rifles and carbines until the 1890s. The first trapdoor chambering was a rimfire cartridge of the same, caliber as muskets. By the next year, caliber had been reduced to .50 and priming to centerfire. The cartridge's name was 50 Government but more commonly came to be known as .50-70 because it was the amount of black powder loaded under 450-grain bullets. The government's name for the new conversion was Model 1866 and nominal velocity for .50 Gov't was rated at 1,250 fps.

During this time there were near constant skirmishes between troops and warriors around Fort Phil Kearney about 90 miles south of Fort C.F. Smith. The Sioux and Cheyenne fighters learned if they could induce foot soldiers to fire their muzzleloading rifle-muskets, the delay in reloading offered the warriors time to close in for hand-to-hand fighting.

One day after the Hayfield Fight the new trapdoor .50s got another baptism of fire. With a constant need for wood at Fort Phil Kearney, a crew of civilian wood cutters guarded by 54 soldiers and two officers were camped about five miles northwest of the fort. The heavy hardwood boxes had been removed from 14 wagons so their running gears could haul logs. With foresight those wagon boxes were placed in a circle beside the white men's camp. Early on the morning of August 2, a warning of Indians was sounded, causing wood cutters and their guards to scatter. Twenty-four soldiers, two officers and six civilians made it to the wagon boxes. In command was Capt. James Powell along with Lt. John Jenness.

Between 7:00 a.m. and 1:30 p.m. no fewer than eight charges were made by an estimated 1,000 Sioux warriors. Some individual braves

Besides the Colt Model 1860 cap-and-ball .44 revolver, many cavalry regiments were issued Remington Model 1858 cap-and-ball .44s.

made it to within yards of the wagon boxes before their assaults failed due to the fast-firing trapdoor rifles. Some of the scattered wood cutters and their soldier guards made it to the fort and a relief column with cannon was dispatched to save the wagon-box defenders. Three men were killed inside the wagon-box corral, including Lt. Jenness. Four more died trying to get there. Four soldiers and 14 civilians came out of hiding when the relief column arrived. The soldiers fighting behind wagon boxes credited their new metallic cartridge-firing Springfields with their salvation.

There was an interesting use of the U.S. government's property by civilians in the form of .50-70 trapdoor rifles. That was with the "1874 Yellowstone Wagon Road and Prospecting Expedition" organized in and around Bozeman, Mon. In February 1874, a force of 150 civilians volunteers and with about 22 wagons and 300 head of oxen, mules and horses left their staging area west of what is now Livingston, Mont. They roamed at least 500 miles of southern Montana terrain before returning to Bozeman in May 1874. Besides their own privately owned rifles and handguns, the expedition was "loaned" by Montana Governor Benjamin Potts no less than 150 Model 1870 "trapdoor" Springfield rifles and at least 10,000 rounds of ammunition. Two muzzle-loading cannons also accompanied the expedition. All of these weapons were needed on several occasions. (Note: part of the expedition's staging area was on the acreage I now own.)

One of the most famous but least understood of fights between civilians and Indians happened at a settlement in the Texas Panhandle named Adobe Walls. The first buildings were put up by traders from Dodge City, Kan., about 150 miles to the north. Corrals for stock were built and naturally for the era, so was a saloon. The trader's idea was to make supplies easier to obtain for the many bison-hunting outfits scouring the area. June 25, 1874, there were 28 men and one woman at "The Walls" as it was commonly called. At daybreak several hundred horse-mounted Comanche, Cheyenne and Kiowa warriors charged the settlement. By mid-day three civilians had been killed, but the Indians left 13 warriors' bodies behind and no one knows how many others and wounded they carried away.

The misconception about this fight is the buff-hunters big single-shot Sharps rifles and their owners' expertise in using them saved the day. Only about half the 28 men at Adobe Walls were hunters. The rest were their camp crew — skinners and cooks. Of course, the saloon had a bartender.

What weapons actually saved the day at Adobe Walls were quick-firing repeating rifles and even revolvers. The Indian's charge was so fast and so unexpected they were at the building's walls and doors before being opposed. Reportedly the Indians were beating on doors with rifle butts. At this point the whites began firing their revolvers and .44 Henry and Winchester Model 1866 rifles and carbines through the doors and cracks between the building's log walls. Fast firing handguns and rifles helped push the attackers away from the buildings far enough the legendary long-range ability of "buffalo rifles" could take effect.

Professional archaeology done at "The Walls" in the 1970s recovered both .50-70 and .50-90 cartridge cases and many .44-77s. Also found were many .44 Henry cases and even a few from S&W .44 American and .44 Colt Richards Conversion revolvers. Evidence the buff-hunters were handloaders too were fired primers and bullet-casting sprues found under some of the building sites. Here is a fascinating tidbit: A receipt exists from one of the traders' stores. It shows factory-loaded .50 Sharps rounds priced at 4 ¼ cents each and .44 Sharps rounds for 3 ½ cents.

Handguns on Horseback

Modern Western movies have continually depicted one firearms aspect of the Plains Indian Wars incorrectly. Seldom are warriors shown fighting with handguns. However, they not only used them, but favored them at times for the same reason every cavalryman was issued one by the U.S. Army. They were handy to use on horseback. In the book *The Cheyenne War* by Jeff Broome is an inventory of items captured when a detachment of the 5th Cavalry under Col. Eugene Carr in 1869 took a Cheyenne camp at Summit Springs in northwest Kansas. Among rifles and bow and arrow sets 22 revolvers are listed. Earlier in the same book a civilian participant who survived an Indian attack related they had both "Navy and dragoon" pistols. Those most likely were Colt .36- and .44-caliber revolvers. Until 1873 the U.S. Army armed its cavalry regiments with cap-and-ball Colt and Remington .44s and early Colt and S&W .44s using metallic cartridges.

This article only scratches the surface of firearms used in the Plains Indian Wars and mentions few of the exciting incidents of those historical clashes. For those who might like to delve further into the subject, I've added a listing of the primary books I have studied to obtain these firearms details.

Also conspicuous by its absence is any mention of firearms use at the Battle of The Little Bighorn in June 1876. Not only was this fight the largest of the Plains Indian Wars, but also the most famous. It deserves a work of its own as do some other skirmishes. For those who would like to inform themselves deeper into this subject, I've listed below some of the better books I've studied for details of this work.

Reference:

Fort Phil Kearny: An American Saga by Dee Brown.

Encyclopedia Of Indian Wars: Western Battles and Skirmishes 1850–1890 by Gregory E. Michno.

Cheyenne War: Indian Raids on The Roads to Denver 1864–1869 by Jeff Broome

Adobe Walls, The History & Archaeology of the 1874 Trading Post by T. Lindsay Baker and Billy R. Harrison

Sitting Bull, Crazy Horse, Gold And Guns, The 1874 Yellowstone Wagon Road and Prospecting Expedition by Col. French L. Maclean, U.S. Army (Ret.)

Roger Smith

FRONTIER JUSTICE

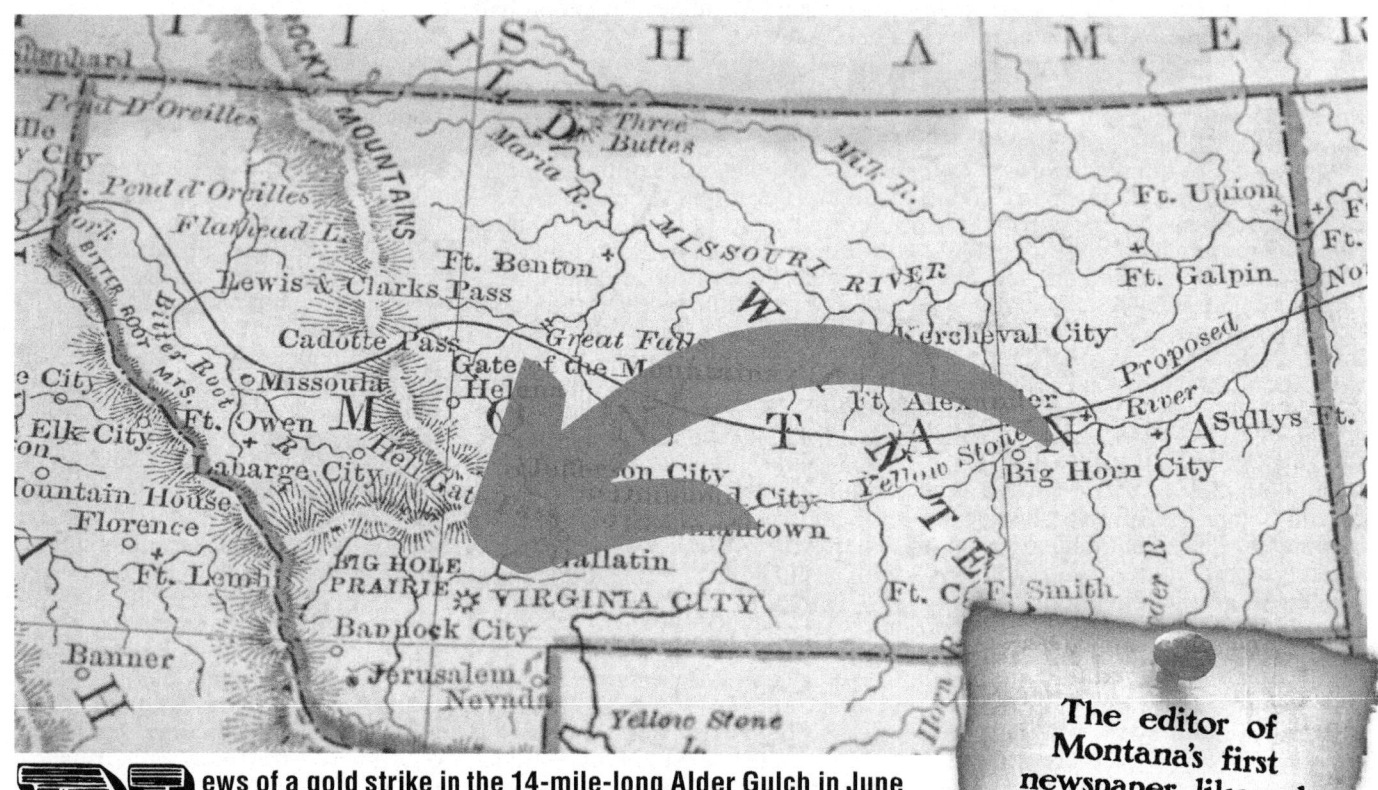

The Secret Vigilantes of Montana

> The editor of Montana's first newspaper likened the situation to what conditions would be like in New York City if all law enforcement were withdrawn for a year.

News of a gold strike in the 14-mile-long Alder Gulch in June 1873 caused a stampede at the miner's camp at Bannack — about 70 miles away from the southwest corner of what is now Montana. Virginia City quickly sprang up on the site of the first strikes to serve the needs of the miners and those who flocked there to serve the miners. By fall 1864 it was a bustling city in the wilderness with bakeries, banks, barbers, boarding houses, brothels, greengrocers, saloons and everything else needed or desired by the local population, including service by two stagecoach lines.

Robberies and fistfights were ordinary everyday occurrences. Shootings and stabbings were the accepted norm for settling differences between men. A killing was considered justifiable if it was the result of settling an argument or an insult. *The editor of Montana's first newspaper likened the situation to what conditions would be like in New York City if all law enforcement were withdrawn for a year.* Except it was worse in Virginia City, because the entire population was composed of easily excited adventure-seeking opportunists. On top of this, an abnormal percentage of the population was the criminal element plaguing every civilized society, hungry for easy spoils and unsuspecting new victims.

Armed Robbery Intelligence Network

The real problem was Virginia City was soon ruled by a good-looking, smooth-talking gambler who got himself elected sheriff. Henry Plummer was secretly the head of a well-organized gang of road agents, run by his newly appointed deputies. His gang robbed and murdered those who left Virginia City with gold dust, money or valuables at will.

Sheriff Plummer and his men had perfected their system at Bannack (where he was also still sheriff) and quickly established a very efficient intelligence network in Virginia City. Bank tellers, store and hotel clerks, waitresses, whores, livery stablemen — everyone who was in a position to converse with those preparing to leave town with their gold seemed to be in on it. Cryptic symbols appeared on certain departing wagons to mark them for the road agents.

Along the primitive routes in and out of Virginia City and Bannack, the robbers built their own buildings out of sight or commandeered ranch buildings and even a stagecoach way station for their use. The owners knew protest would mean death.

Coaches were routinely stopped, and their passengers robbed. While "working," the road agents wore different clothes as disguises and rode different horses to prevent identification. Anyone thought capable of identifying any of the robbers was killed. *More than 100 people were known to have died after leaving Virginia City.* Scores more were believed to have fallen victim to Plummer's gang, never to be heard of again. Some were buried, and the rough country provided countless gorges, gulches, arroyos and canyons within a day's ride to dump more bodies. Wolves and vultures quickly turned corpses into unidentifiable skeletons.

Even the heavily armed messenger services carrying gold dust from Virginia City to Bannack, Salt Lake City and Fort Benton were eventually forced to cease operation.

Anarchy

Law enforcement was a farce. The miners' court was a mockery. The local "judge" was corrupt and Plummer's deputies were the officers of the court. Robbery and murder went unpunished if committed by a member of the road gang. They lied for each other at the mock trials, and fines and legal fees were astronomical for non-members hauled into court for trifling offenses.

Honest citizens gradually realized what was going on and knew they had to somehow band together against the forces of evil ruling them, but most feared to discuss the problem because of the spies everywhere. They had seen firsthand to speak out was fatal. The situation was hopeless. Or so it seemed.

Secret Society

There has been much speculation about how the Vigilantes of Montana came into being, but the most plausible story I have run across was written by John Ellingsen, curator for Bovey Restorations in Virginia City. Ellingsen also happens to be secretary of the Masonic Lodge in Virginia City. He said a man was dying in Bannack in 1863 and requested a Masonic funeral. No

The 3-7-77 above was the warning notice given desperadoes by early day Vigilantes. It meant 3 feet wide, 7 feet long and 77 inches deep, the size of the graves awaiting outlaws if they did not leave the country.

Legends of the meaning of the cryptic 3-7-77 used by the early Vigilantes were enthusiastically adopted into the local lore to titillate the tourists. This postcard is from the 1946–1951 period.

formal lodge existed in the area yet, but word was put out by a few men and to everyone's surprise, 76 Masons showed up for the funeral. Counting the guest of honor, there were 77 Masons there.

There's the old saying the only way two people can keep a secret is if one of them is dead. We should add to it, "unless they're Freemasons." They are known for having their own secret system of signs and gestures to identify themselves with each other — and for their strict adherence to keeping what they know and say among themselves to themselves.

Talk after the funeral soon turned to the problem of the criminal cartel in Virginia City and Bannack. They decided to organize to fight back, with three principal officers and a quorum of seven members necessary to hold a meeting and elect officers. The number of members present that day was the aforementioned 77, who made up the inner circle of what became the Vigilantes. After the first captures and hangings, the great outer body of Vigilantes quickly grew.

Anarchy ... Solved

Despite the miserable winter conditions with often subzero temperatures, between December 21, 1863 and January 11, 1864, *Plummer, his two deputies and nine other members of Plummer's gang were captured and hung.* The Vigilantes then spread out from Virginia City and Bannack and swung nine more of the worst by February 3. The rest of the gang, along with hundreds of other miscreants were able to flee. The so-called judge and the crooked

By 1939, when this photo was taken, the gold miners were long gone and Virginia City was a tourist site. While it was still under construction, the main beam of this building was used to hang five of the road agents terrorizing Virginia City on Jan. 14, 1864. Note the 3-7-77 on the sign for the tourists.

counsel for the road agents were exiled instead of executed because they were not directly involved in the robberies and murders.

Law and Order, Mostly

Montana became its own territory May 26, 1864, and within a year Virginia City's population swelled to 10,000. The Vigilantes found it necessary to hang an additional seven more criminals, the last one on October 31, 1864. The first territorial court, complete with a grand jury, convened in Virginia City on Dec. 5, 1864. As government and honest law and order moved in, most of the original Vigilantes quietly retired from their very distasteful but necessary business. Very few of them ever talked about it except among themselves, but a few of them continued on as needed.

News of even richer gold strikes in Helena, 100 miles to the south, in July 1864 steadily drew most of the miners from Alder Gulch. With civil government and the legal system centered in the new territorial capital in far-away Bannack and a feckless judge appointed to Helena, the rip-roaring ways of Virginia City quickly migrated to Helena in spades.

NEW LOOK AVAILABLE SOON!

The best product for your Old West guns and accessories care *GUARANTEED!*

GUN CARE

Cleans • Lubricates • Protects

- Improves Accuracy
- Prevents Jamming
- Won't Flash Off
- Will Not Freeze
- Non-Hazardous
- Reduces Fouling & Black Powder Issues!
- Won't Harm Wood, Primers, Old Guns, nor stain clothing!
- Bio Preferred by USDA
- Non-Petroleum

ProChemCo LLC
801-569-2763 | 800-248-LUBE (5823)
www.prolixlubricant.com

Although the state's official interpretation of the numbers 3-7-77 has changed, they still appear on the uniform shoulder patch of the Montana Highway Patrol in acknowledgement of the historic importance of the Vigilantes' work to restore law and order to Bannack and Virginia City during the winter of 1863–64.

However, many of the new emigrants were experienced Vigilantes. They boldly adopted the cryptic Masonic number 3-7-77 from the Virginia City founders as their sign or symbol. This number appearing on a man's door, tent flap or any other possession struck terror into the black heart of any criminal. No one outside the inner circle knew what the numbers stood for, but everyone knew what they meant: "Leave or die." *Very soon.* By April 1870, 15 more of the worst dangled in the air, and the Vigilantes at Helena would claim to have retired.

The Grand Lodge of Montana was chartered in Virginia City Jan. 26, 1866, and in 1867 an impressive stone temple was erected on the site of the frame building where the Vigilantes were formally organized in 1863. It cost $30,000, making it the most expensive building in the territory. Its lodge room furniture is said to still be in use today.

Virginia City didn't die when most of the gold miners left in a stampede in late 1864, nor when the territorial capital was moved from Virginia City to Helena in 1875. The population dwindled to 624 in 1880 and 242 by 1930. Its reputation lured curious visitors from the very beginning, however, and its population rose to 380 by 1940 before declining again to only 150 in 2010.

The famed Hangman's Building currently houses a custom hat-making business, and the community struggles on as a tourist destination.

Want More?

Click Here: **gunsmagazine.com**

Frank Jardim

HAVE GUN, WILL TRAVEL

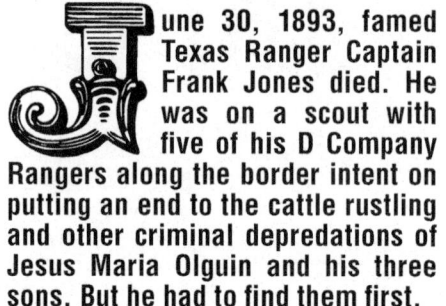

Edward "Jack" Bryant: Lifetime Texas Lawman

June 30, 1893, famed Texas Ranger Captain Frank Jones died. He was on a scout with five of his D Company Rangers along the border intent on putting an end to the cattle rustling and other criminal depredations of Jesus Maria Olguin and his three sons. But he had to find them first.

The Bosque gang, as the outlaws were called, held close to the Rio Grande, allowing them to cross the border into Mexico to evade pursuit. Weeks before, knowing the Bosque gang was large and organized, Jones asked for more Rangers to put them in check. His manpower request was denied, so he went to work with what he had.

Gunfight on the Border

The fatal encounter, often called the Battle of Tres Jacales for the village nearby, was viewed by Jones's second in command Ranger Corporal Bill Kirchner as a carefully laid ambush. His report to headquarters afterward described it as such:

"We had searched several houses and were on our way back [to El Paso] when we saw two men approaching us. When they saw us they began to retreat with all possible haste, of course we followed at once and only ran them out about one half mile when myself and Private Saunders overtook them and demanded a surrender by this time we were not six feet from an adobe [jacal] building along the roadside[.] Two shots were fired at me and about four at the rest of the party[.] One of the shots fired at me struck my Winchester but only ruined the magazine[.] We all at once dismounted and opened fire on them[.] Captain Jones was hit [by] the first volley. His thigh was broken, but he continued to shoot until shot in the breast and killed dead on the

Well dressed and professional looking, Jack Bryant appears to be holding the same make and model Winchester carbine Frank examined in 2013.

Ranger Jack Bryant's 1873 Winchester Saddle Ring Carbine. Its serial number is 236032B, suggesting 1888 manufacture. The "assault rifle" of its day, the 1873 lever action was Winchester's strongest and fastest action to date. Its most popular and powerful chambering was .44-40 WCF. The tapered case of the Winchester Center Fire (WCF) cartridge resisted sticking in the chamber as black powder fouling and heat increased in fast firing. The 200-grain .44 bullet, actually closer to 0.427", was propelled by 40 grains of black powder close to 1,200 fps from the 20" barrel carbine. These handy repeaters held 10 rounds in the magazine, giving the user a tremendous amount of firepower. In his violent line of work in the open frontier, the rifle or carbine, not the pistol, was the primary weapon.

Company D Rangers with their horses in the Leona River Camp preparing for "a scout" as patrols were called. They wore no uniforms and had no badges. Identifiable in this photo are (left to right) Baz Outlaw, Charles Fusselman, Jim Robinson (horseback), Ira Aten (holding handcuffs), Walt Durbin, Calvin Aten, Frank Smith, Capt. John Hughes, Jim King and Ernest Rogers.

Texas Rangers of Company D in camp near Ysleta, Texas, 1894. Jack Bryant is on the far right. On the back of this photo are handwritten notes describing the Rangers pictured as the "Mop Up Crew" and a date between April 30, 1894 and May 24, 1894. After the ambush that killed Capt. Jones, the Rangers of D Company went after the Bosque gang with a vengeance.

spot about 15 ft from the door[.] We continued to fire on them until they retreated and hid in the building[.] Just then a friendly Mexican [Lujan] who was with us in search of stolen horses told me we were in Mexico in the outskirts of Tres Jacales, a small Mexican town and that the people had sent for the Mexican soldiers who would be there in 15 minutes[.] My first decision was to stay with our dead Captain and kill or capture the Mexicans but after waiting about 45 minutes I saw from the appearance of everything we would be overpowered and murdered so we retreated to this side [of the border] ... [sic]."

The firefight lasted less than an hour. Jones was the only Ranger casualty, but two gang members were wounded in the shootout. It's remarkable the Rangers kept up the fight for as long as they did given their weak tactical situation. The Rangers were caught in the open and the gang members, who the Rangers believed were joined by villagers favorably disposed to them, were firing from the cover of adobe buildings, an adobe wall and the surrounding brush.

Bryant's Guns

Among the five lawmen with Jones that bloody day was newly reenlisted Ranger Private Robert Edward Bryant, who was armed with his .44-40 1873 Winchester carbine and Colt six-shooter. A few days earlier, Bryant was an El Paso deputy sheriff. The Olguins were well known to him — Bryant was assaulted by one of the men while attempting to arrest him

> The Rangers were caught in the open and the gang members, who the Rangers believed were joined by villagers favorably disposed to them, were firing from the cover of adobe buildings, an adobe wall and the surrounding brush.

on a cattle-rustling warrant. The man escaped to face Bryant again at the Tres Jacales fight. Though the outlaw escaped again, he withdrew with the bone in his upper arm badly shattered by a Ranger's bullet. Which Ranger shot him is lost to history, but not so the guns of Ranger Bryant, both

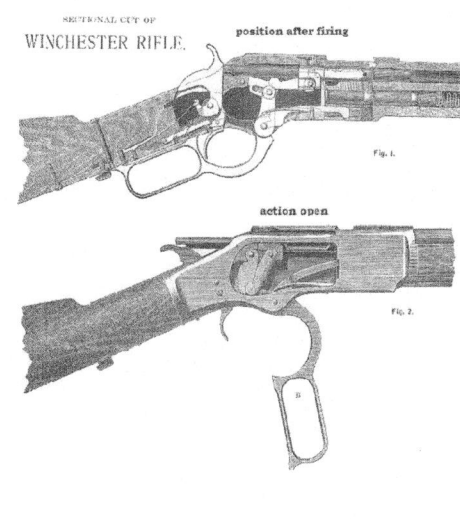

A Mexican prisoner taken by Company D Rangers. In the front row (third and fourth from the left), J.W. "Wood" Saunders and Cpl. Carl Kirchner are seated with Capt. John Hughes to their right. Saunders and Kirchner were with Capt. Jones at the Tres Jacales fight.

SECTIONAL CUT OF WINCHESTER RIFLE.
position after firing
Fig. 1.
action open
Fig. 2.

GUNSMAGAZINE.COM 87

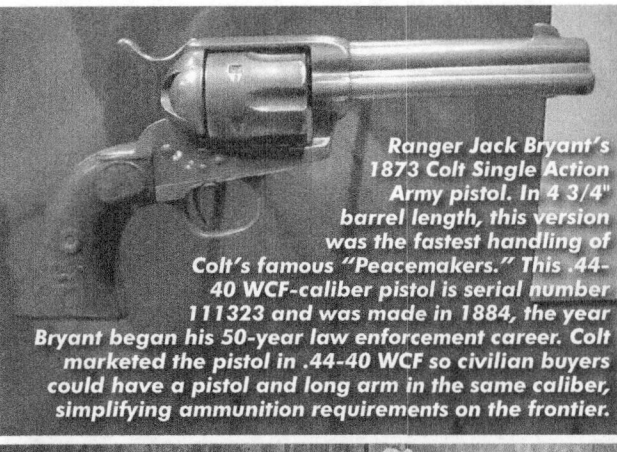

Ranger Jack Bryant's 1873 Colt Single Action Army pistol. In 4 3/4" barrel length, this version was the fastest handling of Colt's famous "Peacemakers." This .44-40 WCF-caliber pistol is serial number 111323 and was made in 1884, the year Bryant began his 50-year law enforcement career. Colt marketed the pistol in .44-40 WCF so civilian buyers could have a pistol and long arm in the same caliber, simplifying ammunition requirements on the frontier.

Rangers lived in the field, not in barracks. Company D is camped under canvas near the Leona River in Uvalde County, probably in 1894. Camps were set up close to the area of operations and Rangers parceled out to meet patrol and law enforcement needs. Rangers brought their own clothes, horse, tack and weapons, and the state provided enough rations, tents, etc., for an austere existence. It was no life for tenderfoots.

Taking advantage of improvements in weaponry, these Company D Rangers upgraded to .30-30 caliber Model 1894 Winchester rifles. Picture shows (standing, left to right) Herff Alexander Carnes, Sam McKenzie, Arthur Beech, (seated left to right) Tom Ross, Albert Mace and Capt. John R. Hughes.

of which I had a chance to examine. Held in his family for years, they were the only guns he ever owned, and their chain of provenance is solid.

The son of a U.S. Army colonel and Mexican mother, Bryant was born in 1866 on the lawless frontier of west Texas near Ysleta. Nicknamed Jack, he became a Texas Ranger in 1883 at the age of 17 and then spent the majority of his adult life, about 50 years, as a lawman working to maintain peace and order in the region of his birth. He moved in and out of Ranger service with the Frontier Battalions until 1898. When he wasn't riding with the Texas Rangers, he was a constable for Precinct 2 in Ysleta, an El Paso County deputy sheriff and a deputy U.S. marshal. He spoke both English and Spanish fluently, which made him a valuable asset to law enforcement.

An 1887 photo of Company D Rangers with Captain Frank Jones (third from left in the front row). Four of these Rangers would die in the line of duty, and a fifth (Baz Oultaw) in a drunken whorehouse shootout.

The highly respected Captain Frank Jones, killed in the Battle of Tres Jacales at age 37.

In 1899, Captain John Hughes (who took command of D Company after Jones was killed) described Bryant as, "… a 1st class detective among Mexicans, but not with Americans." He went on to write, "He is half Mexican and is educated in Spanish and English and is a first-class interpreter. I consider him a first-class Mexican worker, but he is not so good among Americans."

In consideration of the racial biases of the time, it's safe to say while Bryant's mixed ethnicity and intimate understanding of the language and culture of Mexico gained from his mother, and later his wife, equipped him to be especially successful among Texans in the Mexican community, it probably hampered him in his dealings with white Texans. It must have been an especially challenging path for him. Near the end of his career in the 1930s, he acted mostly as an interpreter. He died in 1940 at age 74, 12 days after he retired.

Shots Fired — Frequently

In the 21st century, it's rare for any law enforcement officer to fire their weapon in the line of duty. When they do, it can be the end of their career as they are subjected to investigations and reviews to determine if their actions were justified.

By comparison, on the Texas-Mexico border in late 1800s, there was an expectation from the civil government the lawmen in their employ should readily use deadly force and they were rarely second-guessed after the fact. Gunfights enhanced a lawman's personal reputation, and instilled fear, if not respect, for the law. The dead and shot-up suspects served as a deterrent to crime as good, or better, than the trials and judicial punishment of captured suspects.

The Texas Ranger Frontier Battalions of which Bryant was a part were often the only significant law enforcement entities preventing criminals from acting with impunity outside the few established towns. The criminal element did not fear the courts, or the laws, or attorneys or being sued. They feared being shot and killed by men like Jack Bryant.

To put it in perspective, in El Paso in 1893, a year Jack Bryant happened to be a deputy sheriff there, an arrest was made about every 15 minutes. The historical record reflects El Paso at this time was a den of saloons and vice that attracted an unsavory element as well as outright criminals. A sampling of the arrest warrants executed by Bryant showed many suspects accused of illegally carrying firearms in El Paso. It's dangerous work anytime, but apparently Bryant was the man for the job.

He managed to survive to die of old age, which is pretty remarkable in his line of work.

BATTLE WAVES ON RIO GRANDE EBB AND FLOW

Latest Cotton Field Clash Only One Of Long Series In Area.

By LEO J. TURNER
United Press Staff Correspondent

TRES JACALES, On the Rio Grande, Nov. 19—(UP)—This little island area a few miles east of El Paso, scene of the recent "border war" between Texas farmers and Mexican bandits who raided their cotton fields by night, has a historical background that has contributed much to that general appellation "the bloody Rio border."

In fact, the Tres Jacales area—so named because of three huts which once stood on a spot between the old and new beds of the Rio Grande river—for more than 40 years has gloried in the unofficial title of "Pirate Island."

And there lives in El Paso a man who knows it better than any other, because back in the '90s he fought over it from end to end. He is Capt. John R. Hughes, one of the most famous of the colorful Texas Rangers.

Ranger Captain Killed

The recent "battle of the cotton fields" reminded him of the time when he took his men down to the island to clean out the Olguin bandit gang and avenge the killing of a brother officer, Capt. Frank Jones of the old Frontier Batallion.

The episode minimizes to a mere skirmish the recent rifle-fire exchange between the guards that stood watch over the Texas cotton fields and the Mexican snipers protecting the raiding "cargadores" or cotton pickers.

In the '90s the kings of Pirate Island were the Olguin brothers, Sebastian, Severo and Priscellano. With their father, they were four of the toughest over-the-border raiders who ever robbed a hacienda or lifted a Texas steer.

They chose "Pirate Island" for a base because this plot of ground was at that time enjoying something of a neutral status.

Under terms of a treaty between the United States and Mexico it had been agreed that the Rio Grande should mark the boundary between the nations, but in 1854 the river shifted its channel southward, leaving an island several miles long and several wide between the old and new beds.

Land Status In Doubt

With the ownership of this 3,000 acre island in doubt, law enforcers hesitated to invade it.

Defiantly and arrogantly, the Olguins went about their outlawry. Texas at last decided that it was a job for the Rangers.

The Adjutant General sent Capt. Frank Jones and his border company to Ysleta, Texas, a town filled with Olguin sympathizers who hurled insults from windows and set their dogs on Ranger horses.

Jones nursed his wrath a few days then decided it was time to act. He organized one of the swift night raids which Texas rangers still conduct so successfully.

The few small houses of the place were deserted, but the Rangers found what they had gone for—a fight.

It occurred on the way back, when two Mexican horseman sprang from cover and galloped away, the rangers in pursuit. The riders led the company to the Mexican side of the river—and into a heavily armed ambush.

Leader Shot Down

Too late Jones saw the mistake and ordered a retreat. His men rode back through a crackling hail of lead. The captain did not ride with them. He lay near one of the three small huts of the village of Tres Jacales.

The Olguins challenged the Rangers to cross and get the body, which finally was surrendered after 48 hours of argument. Ranger Bob Ross of El Paso was the man who brought it back.

John R. Hughes, then a Ranger sergeant came down from Alpine to take command. The border seethed with hatred. His rangers descended on the island, kicked down the doors and entered with drawn guns. They took many prisoners, men wanted for murder on the Texas side. They also killed a few, but the Olguins escaped.

In the recent cotton raids, rifle fire again swept across Texas soil from the sand dunes on Tres Jacales, and blood spots on those sand dunes indicate that some of the raiders may have been hit by Texas farmers protecting their crops from raiders who ride in the night.

Bands of butchers often serenaded bridal couples by pounding marrow bones against cleavers in 19th century London. Each cleaver, ground to produce a distinct tone, made the mass effect that of the harmonious chiming of bells.

Even 40 years after the Tres Jacales battle, the area was still a haven for outlaws as this 1937 newspaper article recounts. The border remains a dangerous place to this day.

"We certainly were hard hit in the market slump, else I wouldn't still be using this old 1937 car."

NEW PRODUCTS >>>>>>

SIGNATURE SERIES LONG RANGE MUZZLELOADERS
The Best Of The West

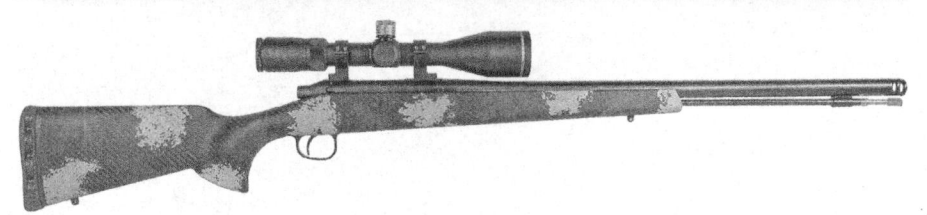

The Best of the West's *Signature Series Long Range Muzzleloaders* are available in .45- and .50-caliber, and shoot between 0.5 and 1 MOA at 550 yards. The shooting system package also includes a Huskemaw Optics long-range riflescope, breech plug tool and breech plug anti-seize, short starter, 12 powder tubes (powder not included), 20 bullets, 100 patches, 10 primer carriers, unloading tool and more. MSRP: $6,099. For more info: (866) 754-7618, TheBestoftheWest.net

SOG-TAC AU
SOG

The *SOG-TAC AU* is one of three knife families introduced by SOG. With a 3.43" blade made of CRYO D2 steel, it is the first automatic with SOG's XR locking mechanism with an opening on both sides of the handle. The SOG-TAC AU comes in three sizes and multiple blades. MSRP: From $138.95 to $166.95. For more info: (425) 771-6230, SOGKnives.com

6.8 WESTERN
Winchester

The *6.8 Western* cartridge was designed by Winchester and Browning to be the all-around long-range hunting and shooting cartridge. The cartridge boasts heavier-weight bullets and more energy than 6.5 Creedmoor or 6.5 PRC cartridges. There is less recoil compared to .300 WSM, .300 Win. Mag. and .300 PRC rounds. The long, heavy bullets are ideal for big-game hunting and long-range precision shooting. MSRP: $39.99 per box of 20 for the 165-grain 6.8 Western. For more info: (618) 258-2000, Winchester.com

14-PIECE 9MM PISTOL FIELD CLEANING KIT
Sport Ridge

Slip the Sport Ridge *14-Piece 9mm Pistol Field Cleaning Kit* into your range bag so you can clean your gun wherever you go. The kit includes a patch slot tip, 9mm brass jag, two brass rods, 9mm bore mop, 9mm bore brush, 25 cleaning patches and more. MSRP: $14.69. For more info: (910) 637-0315, SportRidge.com

SABRE STAR BULLETS
Northern Precision

Sabre Star Bullets from Northern Precision are now made in .452 diameter for the .45 ACP, the 454 Casull and the 450 Bushmaster. They are designed for extreme expansion for both self-defense and varmints. These have cone-shaped hollow points with six sharp expanding points that produce a buzzsaw effect on contact. The Sabre Star is also made in .429 and even .418 caliber for reduced recoil loads. MSRP: $25 for 40 standard bullets; $35 for 25 bonded core bullets. For more info: (315) 955-8679, NPCustomBullets.com

RIMZ MOON CLIPS
EZ Moon Clip

RIMZ Moon Clips are the "world's only hydrocarbon polymer moon clips." Use them to avoid hurting your fingers while loading or unloading. No tools are needed when using these. The RIMZ 625 will fit most 45 ACP revolvers including the S&W Governor. The RIMZ 25 retains rounds more securely and is made of stiffer material. Note RIMZ moon clips only work with rimless ammo. MSRP: $35 for 10 clips. For more info: (937) 919-5910, EZMoonClip.com

HOLSTER CARE KIT
GALCO

Like all products made from natural materials, leather holsters, belts and ammo carriers require periodic care and maintenance. GALCO has assembled the *Holster Care Kit* to make this easy. It includes an application dauber, a synthetic wool buffing pad and a foam scrub pad to make applying GALCO's Leather Lotion and Draw-EZ simple and mess-free. MSRP: $34. For more info: (623) 434-7070, GalcoGunLeather.com

GUNS MAGAZINE OLD WEST • SPECIAL EDITION

MSRP is subject to change without notice. FMG Publications presents the MSRP in good faith and is believed to be correct at the time of printing.
For more information on seeing your product featured in New Products, contact Delano Amaguin at (888) 732-6461

ANACONDA
Colt's Mfg. Inc.

The updated *Anaconda* has been added to Colt's Snake Gun revolver series. With a six-round, large frame, the Anaconda is a U.S. forged stainless steel double-action revolver chambered in 44 Magnum. The 2021 version has been redesigned to use an oversized Python action with a bulked-up frame. Recoil-absorbing Hogue overmolded grips are interchangeable with all Colt Python grips. The sights are elevation- and windage-adjustable, and interchangeable with an Allen key. The full-lug, ventilated rib barrel is offered in 6" (in picture) and 8" lengths. MSRP: $1,499. For more info: (800) 962-2658, *Colt.com*

1873 WESTERN REVOLVER
Davidson's Inc.

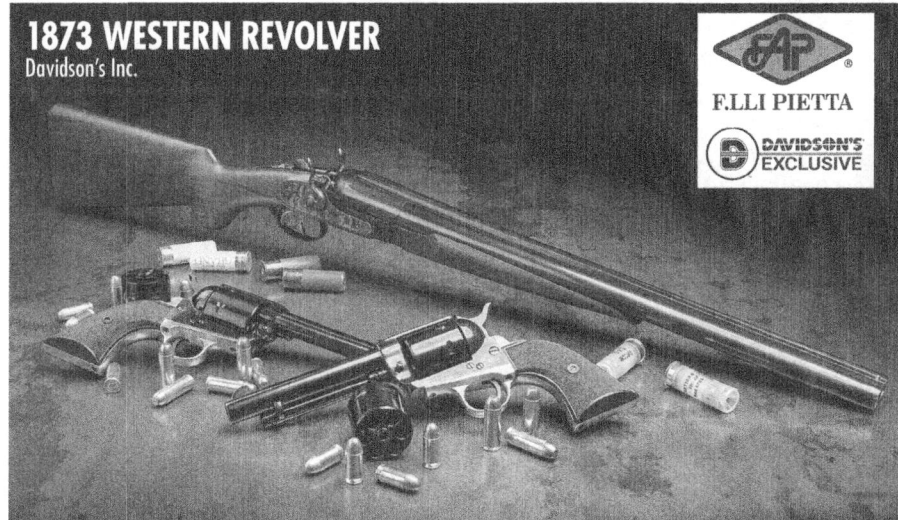

F.LLI PIETTA
DAVIDSON'S EXCLUSIVE

Davidson's now offers two variants of the *1873 Western Revolver*. The new Davidson's Pietta Exclusives are convertible models — each comes with two cylinders. One is chambered in .45 Colt and one in .45 ACP. Offered in a 4.75" and a 5.5" barrel, they both feature a deep blued finish on the frame, cylinder and barrel. The single-action revolvers also come with a companion piece: the 1878 Double Barrel Deluxe Coach side-by-side shotgun. Chambered in 12 gauge, it features a 20" barrel, a walnut stock, a color case-hardened receiver and more. MSRP: Revolvers $559.99 each; Shotgun $989.99. For more info: (928) 776-8055, *DavidsonsInc.com*

200 SERIES AMMO BOXES
MTM Case-Gard

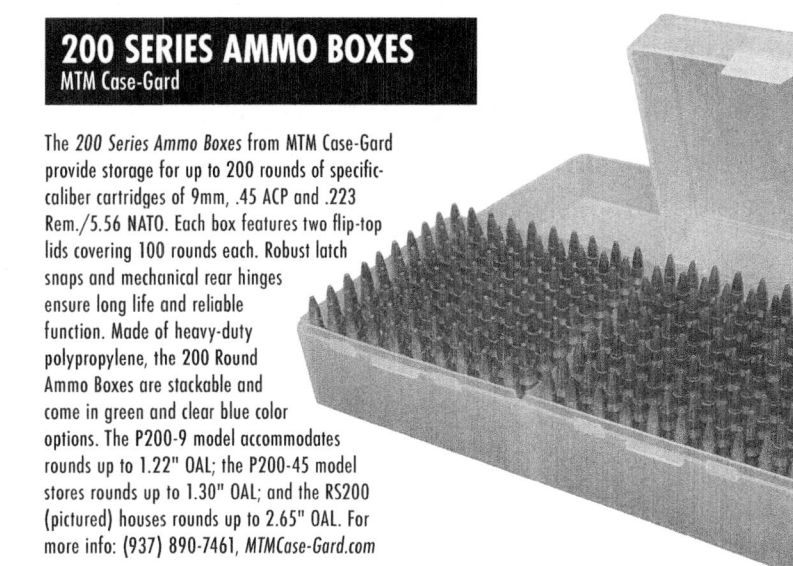

The *200 Series Ammo Boxes* from MTM Case-Gard provide storage for up to 200 rounds of specific-caliber cartridges of 9mm, .45 ACP and .223 Rem./5.56 NATO. Each box features two flip-top lids covering 100 rounds each. Robust latch snaps and mechanical rear hinges ensure long life and reliable function. Made of heavy-duty polypropylene, the 200 Round Ammo Boxes are stackable and come in green and clear blue color options. The P200-9 model accommodates rounds up to 1.22" OAL; the P200-45 model stores rounds up to 1.30" OAL; and the RS200 (pictured) houses rounds up to 2.65" OAL. For more info: (937) 890-7461, *MTMCase-Gard.com*

SAR 9 SPORT
SARSILMAZ ARMS

SAR USA by Sarsilmaz proudly introduces the *SAR 9 Sport Semi-Automatic Pistol*. Built on the same platform as the legendary SAR 9, the SAR 9 Sport is possibly the most rigorously tested pistol and is proudly carried by NATO and elite forces around the world. The striker-fired pistol comes standard with a slightly longer forged steel slide with cooling ports and a lightweight polymer frame. It offers three back straps to customize fit and a safety trigger that's smoother than a double action revolver's. The SAR 9 Sport points naturally and is a pleasure to shoot. MSRP: $799.99. For more info: (833) 727-4867, *SARUSA.com*

NATCHEZ BOWIE IN 3V
Cold Steel

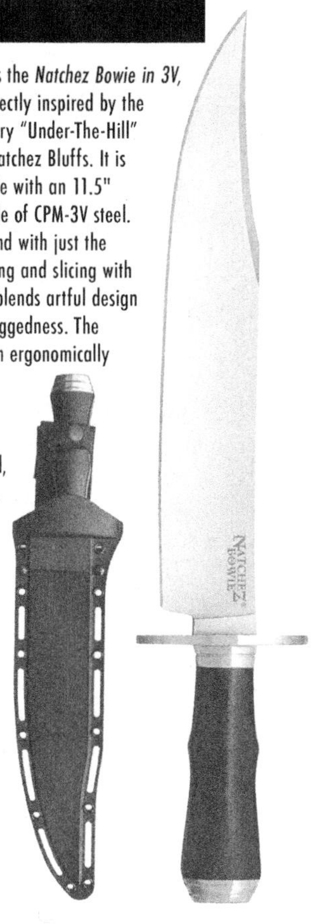

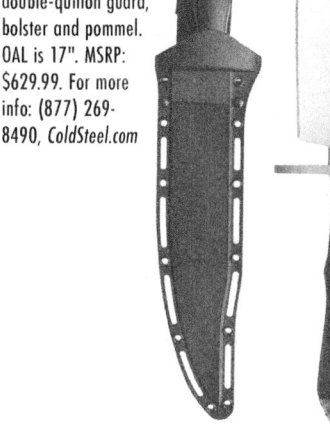

Cold Steel introduces the *Natchez Bowie in 3V*, an elegant blade directly inspired by the infamous 19th century "Under-The-Hill" landing below the Natchez Bluffs. It is a bowie pattern knife with an 11.5" clip-point blade made of CPM-3V steel. Expertly balanced and with just the right heft for chopping and slicing with precision, the knife blends artful design with function and ruggedness. The G10 handle offers an ergonomically contoured grip. Additional features are a polished double-quillon guard, bolster and pommel. OAL is 17". MSRP: $629.99. For more info: (877) 269-8490, *ColdSteel.com*

Mike "Duke" Venturino • Photos: Yvonne Venturino

DEMYSTIFYING COLT SAA GENERATIONS

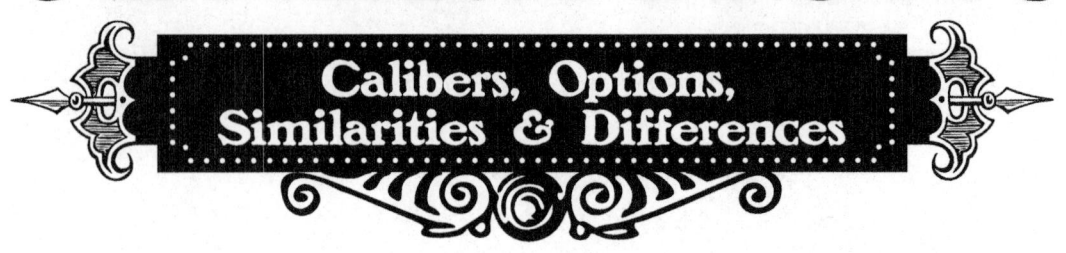

Calibers, Options, Similarities & Differences

Something that seems to baffle newcomers to the Colt Single Action Army (SAA) fraternity is the subject of generations. A corollary to generations is the array of cartridges for which each generation of SAAs were/are chambered. There can be as many as with the 1st Generation or as few as with the 2nd and 3rd Generations.

Please note I am not including the flat top target models in either SAA or Bisley form from the 1st generation or the target-sighted New Frontiers from the 2nd and 3rd Generations. Those deserve an article specific to them. Only fixed-sight SAA and Bisley Colts are covered here.

Chronology

First let's get the SAA's generation chronology stated plainly. The 1st Generation ran from the SAA's 1873 inception until 1941. Starting in 1956 was the 2nd Generation, ceasing production in 1974. Although many small changes were made in the revolver's basic form, most parts were

By my figuring, including Bisleys and the 1,800 or so made as .44 Henry Rimfire, at least 630,000 fixed-sight Colt Single Action Army revolvers have been made to date.

Through its many generations Colt SAAs have been offered with these three finishes. Top is full nickel. Bottom is blue with color case-hardened frame. In between is full blue which has been a special-order option.

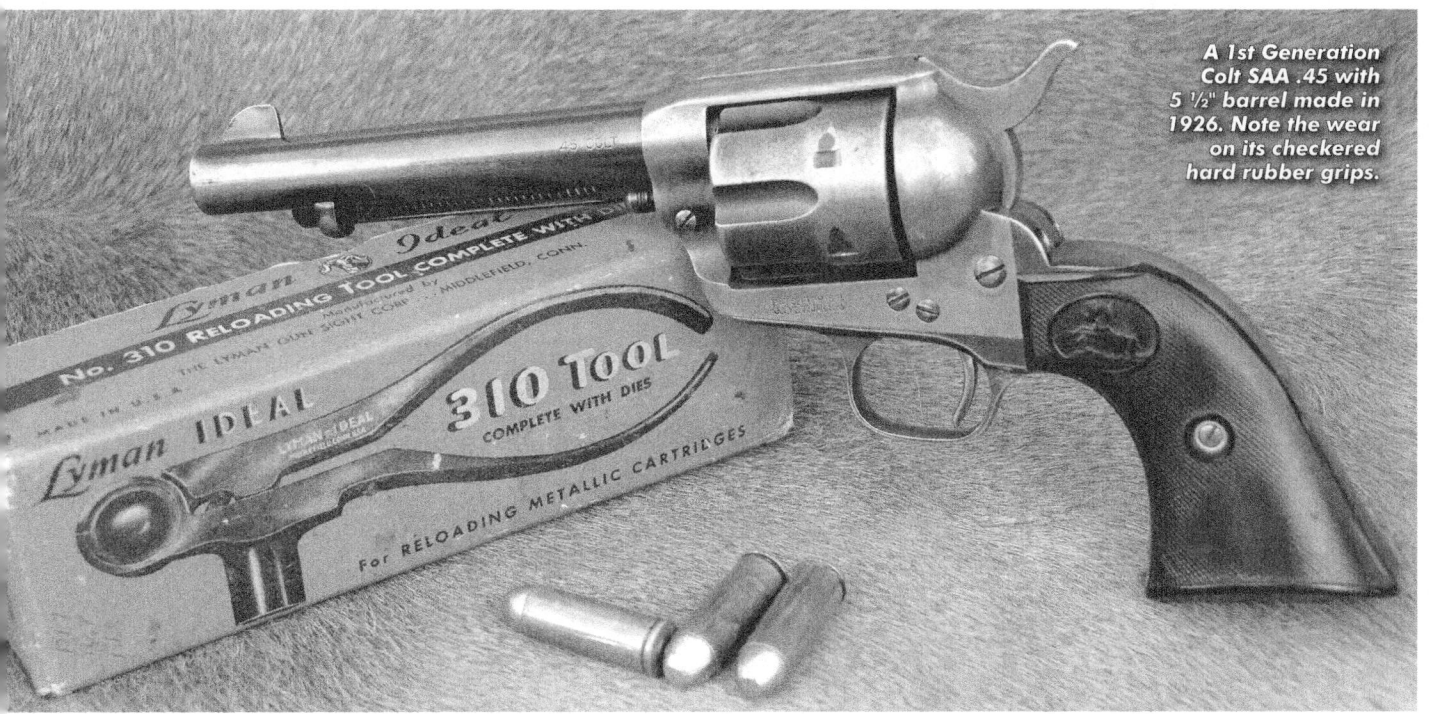

A 1st Generation Colt SAA .45 with 5 1/2" barrel made in 1926. Note the wear on its checkered hard rubber grips.

interchangeable between those two generations. However, serial numbers did not stay the same. In 1873 serial numbers started at 1 and ran to 357859. (Sources vary on the exact number.) This includes the Bisley Model with its unique grip frame. All 1st Generation SAA versions were in the same serial number range except for a special run of about 1,800 made circa 1875 for the .44 Henry Rimfire cartridge.

In 1956 the first serial number was 0001SA and this suffix remained on all 2nd Generation SAAs except for the numerous "commemoratives" offered during those 18 years. According to the book *Colt SAA Post War Models* by George Garton, the last 2nd Generation serial number was 73319SA. (Again, sources vary as to exact numbers.)

In 1976 the 3rd Generation appeared, starting with serial number 80000SA. By 1978, 3rd Generation serial numbers reached 99999SA and started over at SA1001. In 1993, the numbers reached SA99999. This time Colt started over by splitting the SA with S as prefix and A as suffix as in S2001A. Why Colt skipped 1,000 numbers in 1978 and 2,000 in 1993 seems to be a mystery. At this writing 3rd Generation serial numbers have reached S90000A and still counting. By my figuring, including Bisleys and the 1,800 or so

This is the serial number of a 1st Generation SAA.

Duke firing his favorite Colt SAA barrel length — 7 1/2".

GUNSMAGAZINE.COM 93

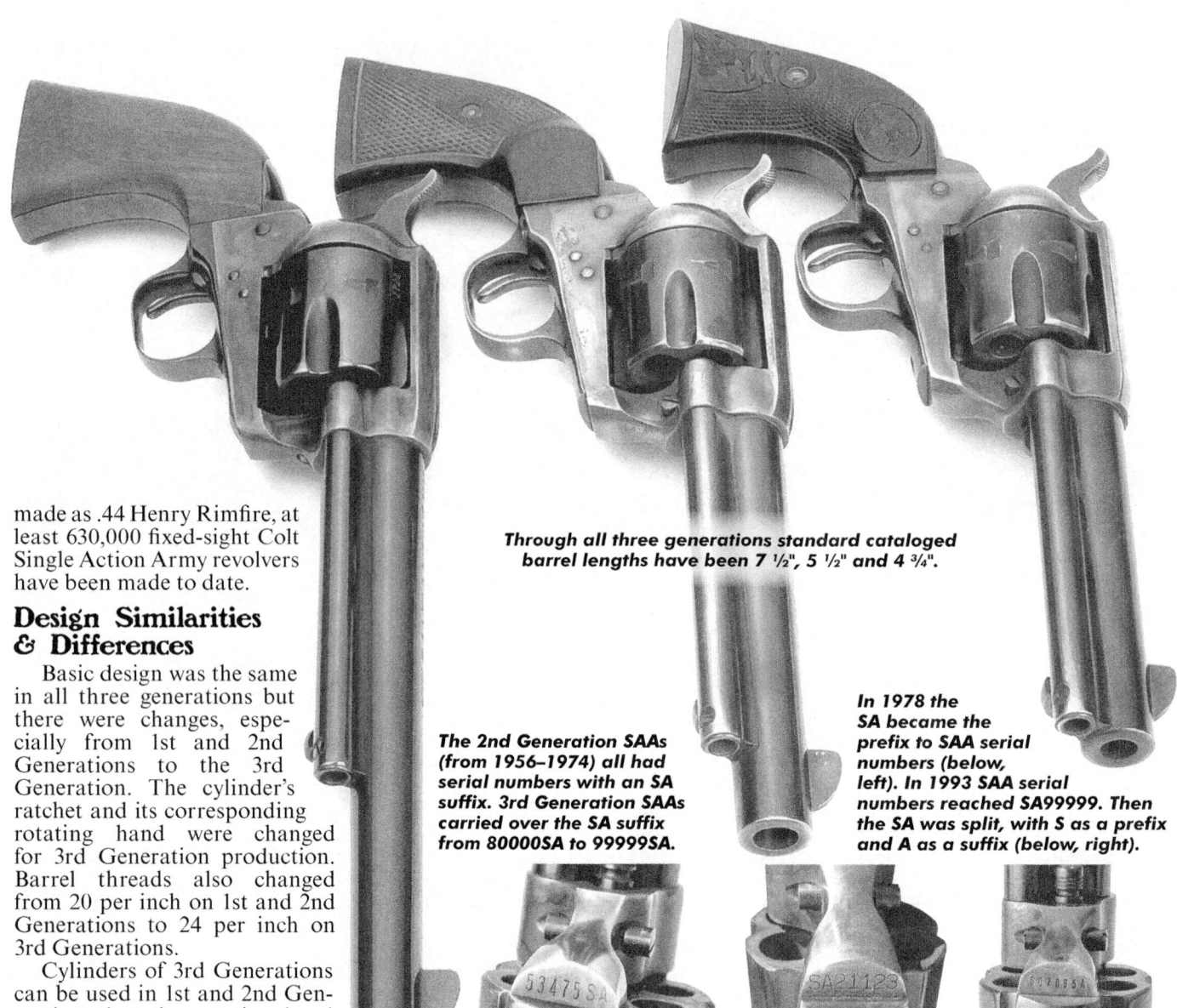

made as .44 Henry Rimfire, at least 630,000 fixed-sight Colt Single Action Army revolvers have been made to date.

Design Similarities & Differences

Basic design was the same in all three generations but there were changes, especially from 1st and 2nd Generations to the 3rd Generation. The cylinder's ratchet and its corresponding rotating hand were changed for 3rd Generation production. Barrel threads also changed from 20 per inch on 1st and 2nd Generations to 24 per inch on 3rd Generations.

Cylinders of 3rd Generations can be used in 1st and 2nd Generations but the rotating hand must be replaced with a proper one. Of course, a competent gunsmith should do the work. The removable cylinder pin bushing, standard with the 1st and 2nd Generations became a fixed type in 1976 only to become the removable type again starting early in the 21st century.

I've read on the internet 3rd Generation barrels can be "crammed" into 1st and 2nd Generation frame threads. I consider that a very poor idea as one set of threads or the other is going to be damaged.

Just the Specs

Let's look at a few details prior to getting into the different cartridges offered per generation. Basic finishes for all generations have been blued with a color case-hardened frame and early on color case-hardened hammers too. Full nickel-plating has been available in all three production runs and full blue finishes have been offered from time to time as special-order options. Grip material from the Colt factory has run the gamut from wood through ivory and a few other natural materials. Starting out, Colt offered one-piece walnut grips as standard and segued to hard rubber in the late 1800s.

Standard barrel lengths began with 7 ½" in 1873 with 5 ½" length as an option in 1875 and 4 ¾" barrels in 1879. (Again, sources vary as to exact years of barrel length introductions.) In the 1st Generation Colt accepted custom orders for barrel lengths and I've read they ranged from 2" to 16".

In the 2nd Generation 4 ¾", 5 ½" and 7 ½" lengths were again standard but a special run of .45 Colt Sheriff's Models were made with 3" lengths and 12"-barreled .45 Colt Buntlines were cataloged from 1957 until the end of 2nd Generation production. Again, this information is according to Garton's book.

Through all three generations standard cataloged barrel lengths have been 7 ½", 5 ½" and 4 ¾".

The 2nd Generation SAAs (from 1956–1974) all had serial numbers with an SA suffix. 3rd Generation SAAs carried over the SA suffix from 80000SA to 99999SA.

In 1978 the SA became the prefix to SAA serial numbers (below, left). In 1993 SAA serial numbers reached SA99999. Then the SA was split, with S as a prefix and A as a suffix (below, right).

For 3rd Generations, Colt offered all mentioned here from 3" to 12" and threw in some special-order 3 ½" and 4" ones to boot.

Cartridge Confusion

Now it's time to discuss SAA cartridges, so prepare for some confusion. There is an out-of-print book titled *The 36 Calibers of the Colt Single Action Army* by David M. Brown. This book only relates to 1st Generation production. Therein Mr. Brown gives a chart of those 36 calibers in terms of rarity. Naturally .45 Colt is least rare with 158,688 made in SAA and Bisley fixed-sight sixguns. *The rarest is the .32 Rimfire with only two made.* Four other cartridges were made in enough numbers to be considered significant. Those were .44-40 (71,292), .38-40 (50,402), .32-20

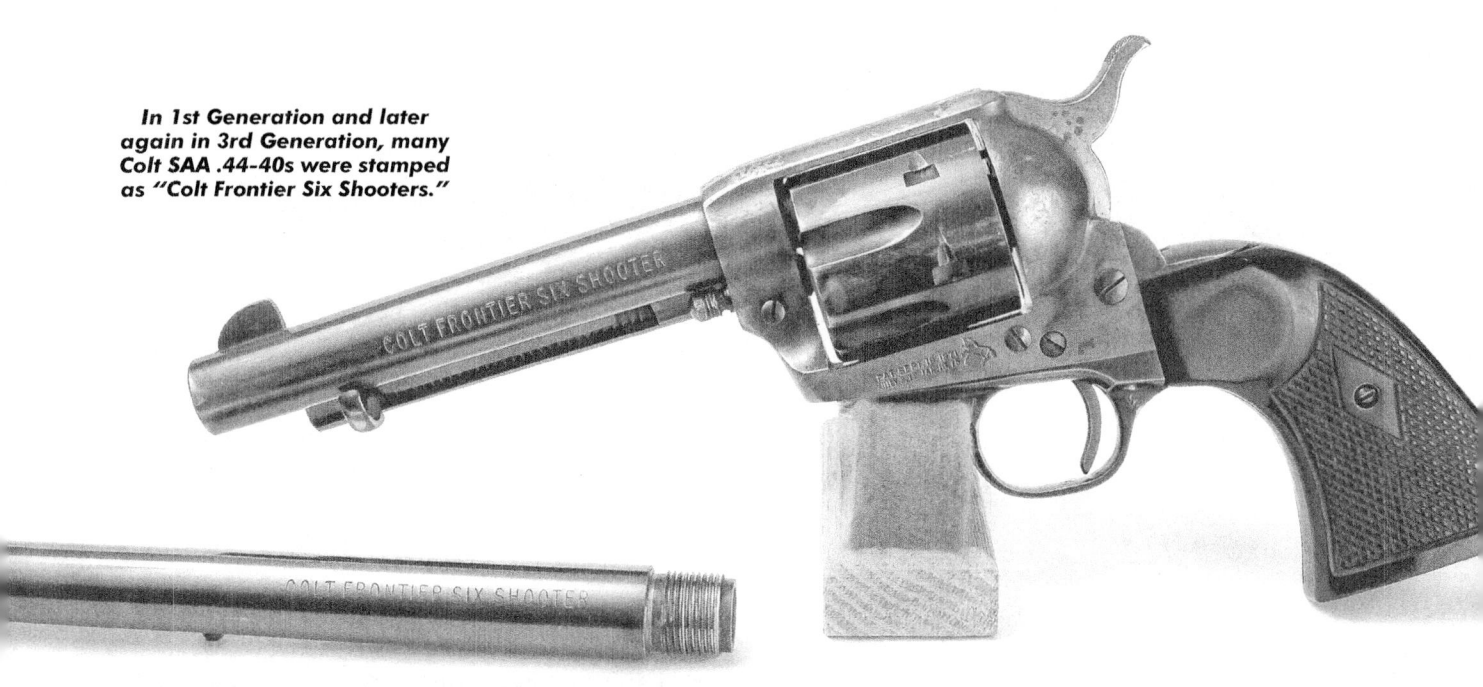

In 1st Generation and later again in 3rd Generation, many Colt SAA .44-40s were stamped as "Colt Frontier Six Shooters."

This is a 3rd Generation SAA .38-40 that was special ordered with a 4" barrel.

3rd Generation Colt SAA .45 with 7½" barrel and custom one-piece grips.

(43,102) and .41 Colt (19,561). Another source gives the same figures except for .38-40 where the figure is 50,853. Like I said, figures vary by sources when studying the Colt SAA/Bisley.

Confusing also at this point are the terms .44-40, .38-40 and .32-20. The .44-40 offering was introduced in 1877 while the .38-40 and .32-20 launched in 1885. However, until very late in 1st Generation production the last two were caliber-stamped .38 WCF and .32 WCF (Winchester Centerfire). However, .44-40 is the only SAA caliber to have had its own name. It was marked at different times and in different ways "COLT FRONTIER SIX SHOOTER" or "COLT FRONTIER SIX SHOOTER .44-40." Early ones even had a tiny ".44 CF" on the trigger guard's rear left side. Later on, its caliber stamp simply became .44-40.

GUNSMAGAZINE.COM

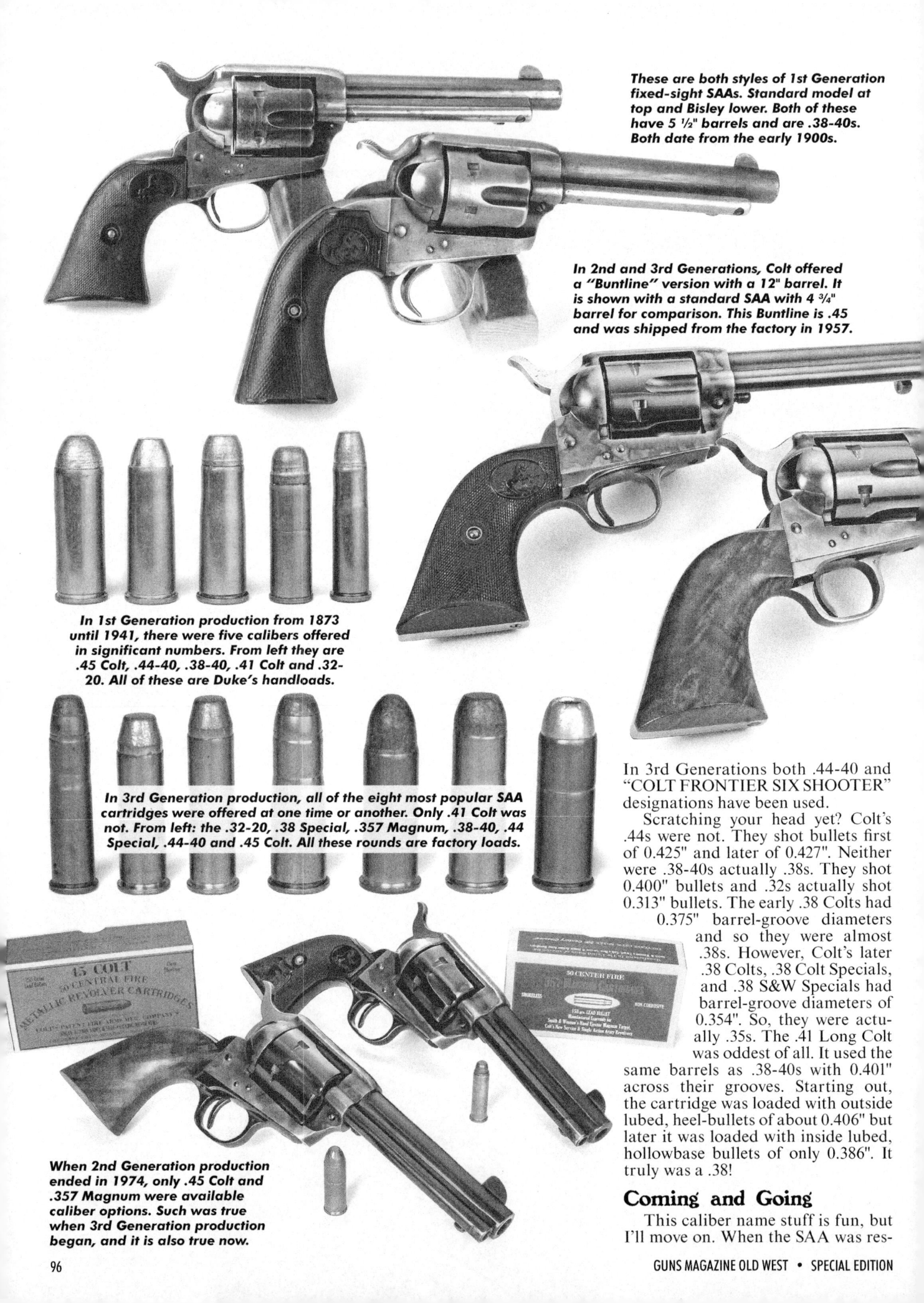

These are both styles of 1st Generation fixed-sight SAAs. Standard model at top and Bisley lower. Both of these have 5 ½" barrels and are .38-40s. Both date from the early 1900s.

In 2nd and 3rd Generations, Colt offered a "Buntline" version with a 12" barrel. It is shown with a standard SAA with 4 ¾" barrel for comparison. This Buntline is .45 and was shipped from the factory in 1957.

In 1st Generation production from 1873 until 1941, there were five calibers offered in significant numbers. From left they are .45 Colt, .44-40, .38-40, .41 Colt and .32-20. All of these are Duke's handloads.

In 3rd Generation production, all of the eight most popular SAA cartridges were offered at one time or another. Only .41 Colt was not. From left: the .32-20, .38 Special, .357 Magnum, .38-40, .44 Special, .44-40 and .45 Colt. All these rounds are factory loads.

In 3rd Generations both .44-40 and "COLT FRONTIER SIX SHOOTER" designations have been used.

Scratching your head yet? Colt's .44s were not. They shot bullets first of 0.425" and later of 0.427". Neither were .38-40s actually .38s. They shot 0.400" bullets and .32s actually shot 0.313" bullets. The early .38 Colts had 0.375" barrel-groove diameters and so they were almost .38s. However, Colt's later .38 Colts, .38 Colt Specials, and .38 S&W Specials had barrel-groove diameters of 0.354". So, they were actually .35s. The .41 Long Colt was oddest of all. It used the same barrels as .38-40s with 0.401" across their grooves. Starting out, the cartridge was loaded with outside lubed, heel-bullets of about 0.406" but later it was loaded with inside lubed, hollowbase bullets of only 0.386". It truly was a .38!

Coming and Going

This caliber name stuff is fun, but I'll move on. When the SAA was res-

When 2nd Generation production ended in 1974, only .45 Colt and .357 Magnum were available caliber options. Such was true when 3rd Generation production began, and it is also true now.

In 2nd Generation production, only four cartridges were cataloged for Colt's SAA. From left they are the .45 Colt, .44 Special, .357 Magnum and .38 Special. All these rounds are factory loads.

urrected in 1956, the first cartridges offered were .45 Colt and .38 Special. The latter one was dropped in 1964. In 1958 the .44 Special was added and dropped in 1967. The .357 Magnum, added in 1960, and the .45 Colt made it all the way to 1974. In his book, Garton stresses his figures for totals are not the same as totals for all production. They're about 7,000 less than the serial numbers. Still, I'll quote what he does present. Top place of course is the .45 Colt (38,291), .357 Magnum (15,821), .38 Special (10,591) and .44 Special (2073).

When the 3rd Generation SAA made its comeback in 1976, the initial calibers were .357 Magnum and .45 Colt. In 1978 the .44 Special appeared and in 1982 so did the .44-40. To the surprise of many, including me, the .38-40 was resurrected in 1993. In the early 21st century the Cowboy Action sport caused the return of the .38 Special and .32-20. As things stand at this writing, only the .45 Colt and .357 Magnum are options. Of course, totals are not possible because production continues.

My SAA study — call it fascination — started upon buying my first at age 19. It was a 2nd Generation (1964) .45, blue/case colored with a 5 ½" barrel. Barely used, I paid $100 for it. That was a lot of money for a college student hustling freight on a truck loading dock for $1.60 an hour. Fifty-three years later, I paid over 30 times more for a 1st Generation (1913) blue/case colored Colt Frontier Six Shooter with 7 ½" barrel and consider it a bargain. In between have been about 100 others. I've never gotten tired of them: any caliber, any finish or any barrel length.

For more info: Colt.com

Will Dabbs, MD

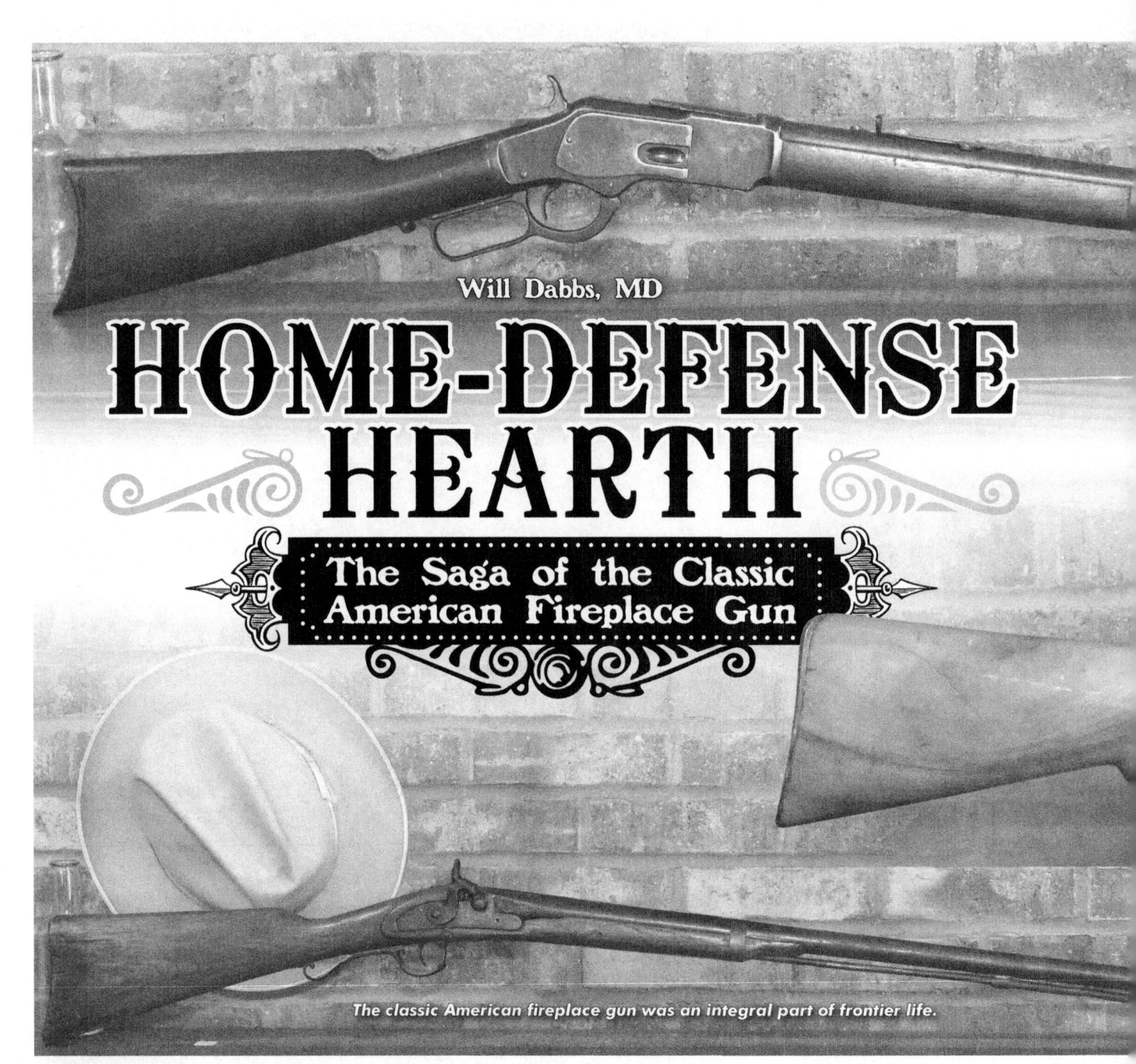

HOME-DEFENSE HEARTH

The Saga of the Classic American Fireplace Gun

The classic American fireplace gun was an integral part of frontier life.

The first Cracker Barrel restaurant opened in 1969 in Lebanon, Tenn. Today they operate 663 stores in 45 states. Cracker Barrels are typically located at prominent crossroads or along high traffic areas on interstate highways. The gimmick that makes Cracker Barrel so successful, in addition to serving supremely unhealthy but undeniably delicious food in simply obscene quantities, is the way each restaurant approximates a stylized rendition of classic Americana.

Each store features exactly the same layout. You walk through an ample gift shop to access the restrooms or restaurant. The walls are adorned with antique trinkets designed to evoke a sense of nostalgia and home. If you look closely, each of these decorative items also includes a numbered identification tag.

I always imagine a warehouse someplace filled with old discarded antique garbage. Some executive might place an order for half a tractor trailer's load of random nostalgic flare. Ten days later a Conex filled with an assortment of framed vintage sepia photos, pressed steel filling station signs, vintage wooden snow skis and dry-rotted horse tack shows up in the parking lot ready for display.

Each restaurant also features an expansive fireplace replete with a generous mantle. The roaring fire greeting patrons during the winter months sets an inimitably inviting tone. Hanging above the mantle in every single Cracker Barrel is a vintage antique shotgun.

Scoping out the shotgun is always my first stop whenever we patronize a new Cracker Barrel while out on the road. Some are single barrels and others doubles, but these nicely aged thundersticks seem to be integral components of the overall ambience. They are typically wired in place to help guard against sticky fingers, but their mere presence says something deep and profound about American culture.

A Gun Culture Like No Other

The United States of America is unique in human history. Carved out of untamed wilderness by sweat,

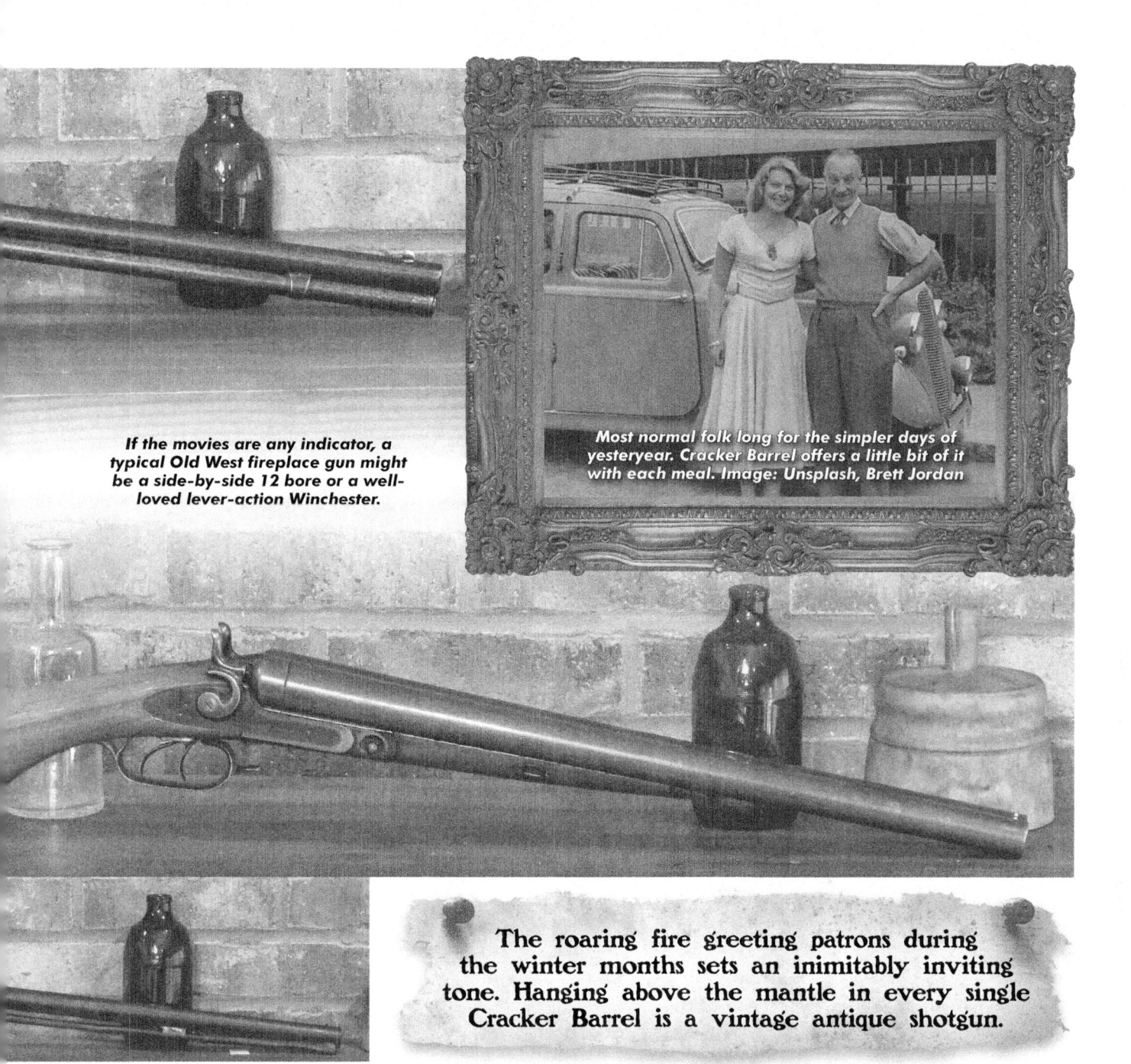

If the movies are any indicator, a typical Old West fireplace gun might be a side-by-side 12 bore or a well-loved lever-action Winchester.

Most normal folk long for the simpler days of yesteryear. Cracker Barrel offers a little bit of it with each meal. Image: Unsplash, Brett Jordan

The roaring fire greeting patrons during the winter months sets an inimitably inviting tone. Hanging above the mantle in every single Cracker Barrel is a vintage antique shotgun.

blood, toil and pure unfiltered will, this great experiment in democracy has for some 245 years done more to promote liberty around the globe than any other human contrivance. Reality is the two massive oceans guarding our borders have likely done more to ensure our security than any mystical sense of exceptional national fortitude. However, we have been, up until recently at least, a nation comprised predominantly of rugged individualists. Biased historical revisionists notwithstanding, firearms are an integral and ongoing component of that frontier ethos.

The image of the hard-bitten family eking a living out of some unforgiving wilderness is classic Americana. An organic component of this stylized tale is the family gun. Usually a shop- worn lever-action rifle or side-by-side shotgun, the family gun was typically maintained above the mantle for both easy access and safety from little fingers. Thusly configured should the family cabin be paid a visit by hostile Native Americans or the errant grizzly all the patriarch need do is reach above the mantle. Thanks to countless Western movies and places like Cracker Barrel, this imagery is still woven into the national consciousness even this deep into the Information Age.

My Personal Fireplace Gun

I began collecting guns at age 13. Suffice it to say my right to keep and bear arms is adequately exercised. *However, amidst myriad firearms of varying values and rarity, one raggedy old beater shotgun occupies a particularly dear place in my heart. This is my personal fireplace gun.*

This vintage scattergun indeed held the place of honor above my own fireplace for years. Before that time, it stood duty over the fireplace in my childhood home. The gun has little intrinsic worth, but its curious origins make it literally priceless to me.

A great uncle purchased a house in the residential area of Hattiesburg, Miss., many decades ago. Little was known concerning the previous owners, and they had moved to a different state by the time my uncle took possession. As my grandfather helped his brother-in-law tidy the place in anticipation of move-in, he took a spin around the attic.

> The ample charge of rocks and metallic detritus ripped down the top of the fence, raking through the assembled fowl.

The old gun has so much mileage the original markings are illegible.

This old shotgun has been repaired many times over the years.

The steel ramrod has long since been lost. Somebody a century or more ago replaced it with this kind-of-straight piece of hickory.

Most of the detritus of human habitation had indeed been removed and discarded prior to their taking possession. However, my grandfather noticed something curious sticking out from under the insulation in the corner of the attic. Further investigation uncovered the shattered remains of a high mileage single-barrel percussion-fired 12-bore shotgun.

The steel was rusted and ugly from neglect, while the furniture showed every minute of its more than a century's worth of hard service. Not a scrap of the original finish remained, and the gun's metallic surfaces were pitted and rough. Despite an obviously hard life the lockwork remained intact and functional.

The steel ramrod was long lost, replaced by a gnarled piece of what appears to me to be hickory. The sort of straight stick just barely fits in the ramrod pipes underneath the long heavy barrel and lends the old gun just scads of character. Worst of all, however, the buttstock was shattered through at the wrist, and the gun rent into two pieces.

Fortunately, my grandfather was both the product of the Great Depression and a woodworking savant. This guy could fix quite literally anything. From holey socks to worn-out power tools, he would just fetch the proper instruments, sit down someplace with decent illumination and fiddle until things were whole. In the case of this old shotgun he shimmed, glued and pegged until the aged smoke pole resembled a proper firearm yet again.

The markings have long since been rendered unintelligible by the toxic combination of age and corrosion.

Will's personal fireplace gun was serendipitously discovered and subsequently resurrected by his grandfather.

When first discovered, the old gun was broken in two. A little attention from Will's grandfather rectified the problem.

Back in 1848 firearms were typically built by hand. Can you tell?

However, I carefully took a rubbing of the lockplate by laying a piece of paper on top and scrubbing it with a pencil. The end result revealed the remains of some kind of seal and the date 1848. At some point the old gun had sported some fairly rarefied engraving. *Guns were handmade instruments back then, and it shows.*

Practical Tactical

My other grandfather had 11 siblings and grew up stone broke on a rural Mississippi farm in the early 1900s. It took the entire brood to ward off rank starvation in the years immediately following the First World War. Their family fireplace gun was a single-barrel muzzleloading 12-gauge much like the one featured in the photos.

Nobody had any money back then, so they couldn't afford store-bought lead shot. Percussion caps and gunpowder strained the budget as it was. When my grandfather was in his early teens part of his household responsibilities involved stalking about the farm in search of game to supplement the family's meager rations. This particular day he had charged the family shotgun in a fairly unconventional fashion.

Loading such a beast involved measuring out a powder charge and then packing it down securely underneath wadding improvised from a scrap of cloth. He would then gather up old screws, nuts, nails and gravel from the barn and load it all on top. Another scrap of cloth tamped down tightly held everything in place. *It's a wonder he never blew himself up.*

There is no buttplate. The stock is just shaped to fit.

This fateful day the blackbirds were in mid-migration, and the sky was dark with the creatures. They had landed everywhere and on everything. Sensing an opportunity, my grandfather stealthily crept along a remote fence line. Judging his angles just so, he lined the heavy scattergun up along the fence, cocked the hammer manually and squeezed.

The ample charge of rocks and metallic detritus ripped down the top of the fence, raking through the assembled fowl. *He dropped 21 birds with that single charge of scrap.* Gathering up the demised blackbirds he scampered home anxious to show off the day's haul. Nearly two dozen birds with a single shot seemed a proper day's work.

His mom accepted the warm carcasses gratefully and retired to the kitchen. Later in the evening, after his dad and older brothers returned from the fields, they all washed for dinner. Once ensconced around the expansive family table, grace was rendered and his mom emerged from the kitchen. The entire family gorged themselves on those 21 blackbirds. All involved retired to bed that evening fully satiated for a pleasant change.

Ruminations

Nowadays if we Americans feel even the least bit peckish we simply zip into the nearest drive-through so some sullen teenager can toss a disposable sack full of greasy bilge through the left window of our car. *America is one of the few countries in the world wherein our poor people struggle with obesity.* However, there was a time when both frontier danger and legitimate hunger were regular companions for the rugged men and women who eked out an existence from the hinterlands.

Today's crop of Americans is not quite so durable as was once the case. I have wondered how Cracker Barrel gets away with such a public display of firearms given our newfound cultural sensitivities. Somewhere, sometime I guarantee some leftist butterfly has felt both triggered and micro-aggressed by the presence of a functional shotgun standing watch over their delicious cornbread and buttermilk biscuits.

I wouldn't attempt to shoot my own fireplace gun for love or money. I suspect the thing would explode like a hand grenade if ever subjected to a proper charge of powder. However, as a trinket to add a little rustic flare to my rural living room, it is simply without peer.

Mike "Duke" Venturino · Photos: Yvonne Venturino

"CONCEALED CARRY?"

Old West Pocket Revolvers

A Colt .31 cap-and-ball Baby Dragoon with a Merwin & Hulbert .38.

By television and cinema portrayals, just about everyone walking the streets of Old West towns were packing big six-shooters on their hips. In some western environs such as Dodge City, this was not only discouraged, but also downright illegal according to city ordinances. Regardless, many men still roamed about towns armed. Their guns just didn't show because they were carrying "pocket revolvers."

Of course almost all of us who avidly watch TV and movie Westerns are aware of derringers. They were tiny weapons of one or two shots, ranging from percussion types such as the one John Wilkes Booth used to assassinate President Lincoln in 1865, to late 1800s metallic-cartridge ones made by Colt and Remington firing tiny .41 Rimfire cartridges. Those were absolutely last-ditch defense weapons and their carriers ought to have also had a Bowie knife after making somebody really mad by shooting them.

Baby Dragoon

One of the first pocket revolvers was Samuel Colt's little .31 five-shooter named by collectors as Baby Dragoon. Obviously, there was a strong market for such a small revolver as evidenced by its year of introduction. Colt's first truly successful revolver was the Goliath-sized .44 Walker/Colt weighing 4.5 lbs. with a 9" barrel. That was in 1847. In 1848, the Colt factory brought out a downsized .44 now called 1st Model Dragoon, but also introduced their first .31 peashooter. It was called the Baby Dragoon.

For a self-defense weapon, Baby Dragoons were odd little guns. Whereas the huge Walker Colt and Dragoon .44s had rammers beneath their barrels to force lead projectiles into their chambers, Baby Dragoons had none. After its five shots were expended, reloading the little gun was an affair requiring it to be disassembled into three parts. The 4" barrel was removed, the cylinder taken off its base pin and then the base pin's cupped end was used to force balls into chambers. Of course, this was *after* a new powder charge had been dispensed from a powder flask meant especially for the .31-size chambers. Only then were percussion caps fitted onto chamber nipples. Luckily men in those days usually wore coats and vests with many pockets because packing a percussion pocket revolver required the accompaniment of powder flask, ball supply and percussion caps.

Despite the hurdles of loading Baby Dragoons, they seem to have sold well enough. About 15,000 were made before it was superseded by the Model 1849 .31s, which had a rammer under the barrel. Colt sold about a quarter-million of that model. Original Baby Dragoons as well as all original Colt cap-and-ball revolvers are rare, expensive and fragile. However, we shooters have been lucky. In the late 1970s and early 1980s Colt brought back most versions of their cap-and-ball revolvers. They used Italian parts

A Pocket Navy (center) and a Pocket Police (right). They are shown for size comparison with a Colt Model 1911A1 .45.

This is how Merwin & Hulbert caliber stamped their Pocket Army when it was chambered for .44-40.

Merwin & Hulbert billed the pointed butt of their Pocket Army .44 as the "skull crusher."

Duke still uses the pocket-revolver concept, often sticking his Colt SAA Sheriff's Model in his hip pocket due to rattlesnakes around his Montana property. It is fitted with a .44 Special cylinder and loaded with shot loads. The hammer is down on the empty sixth chamber so he doesn't shoot himself in the butt!

but were finished here in the states. (For some reason, Colt ignored Model 1849 .31s in its recreation lineup.)

Colt 2nd Generation Baby Dragoons are also rare and expensive but not so fragile. For shooting mine, I cut apart 00 buckshot shotgun shells. Their pellets measured 0.325" and weighed 48 grains. A charge of 13 grains of Goex FFFg black powder propelled them to a whopping 700 fps velocity. *Fired into the baffle box shown in the accompanying photo, those balls penetrated two 1" soft-pine boards and bounced off the third.* Not exactly man-stoppers!

Pocket Updates

Between 1850 — when Colt's first true "belt" .36-caliber pistol arrived on the scene, which collectors have misnamed Model 1851 Navy — until about 1862, the company offered no new "pocket models." Then two versions appeared; both five-shooter .36s on the same frame size, but one with octagon barrel and the other with round barrel, cylinder flutes and edges smoothed. In the same order collectors have named them Model 1862 Pocket Navy and Model 1862 Pocket Police. *Because their barrel lengths were 5 ½" I'd have named them "Deep Pocket Pistols."* They were not likely to fit in many pockets of the era's clothing. However, their weight of 30 oz., compared to the '51 Navy's 44 oz., would have been attractive to many wanting more power than the .31s. (Weights taken from 2nd Generation specimens in my collection.) I bought both of the 2nd Generation Model 1862s. They do offer increased power with 20 grains of Goex FFFg black powder and 80-grain 0.375" round balls: I clocked my Pocket Navy as giving about 850 fps.

Merwin & Hulberts

Two members of my Old West pocket-revolver assortment are Merwin & Hulberts. One is a .38 double-action five-shooter with no particular name I can discover. The second is a .44 single-action six-shooter and was advertised by the company as Pocket Army, although in fact it truly is a

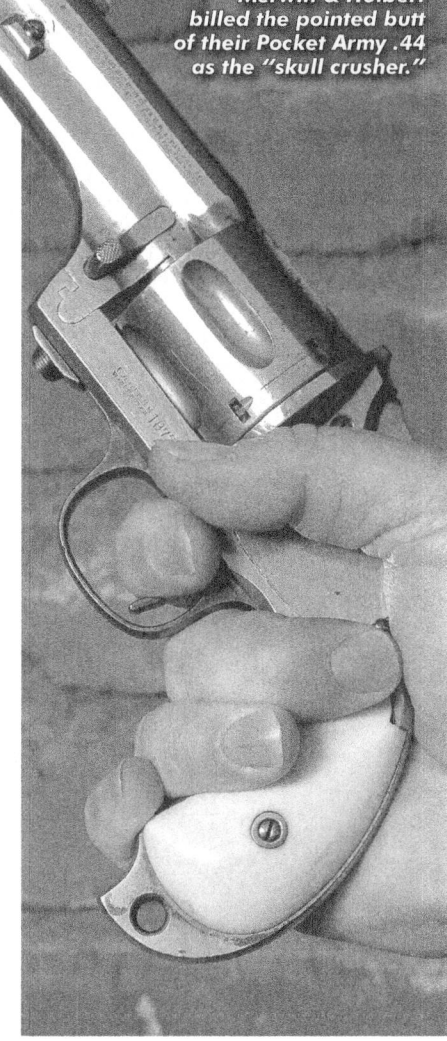

In 1848, Colt brought out two new revolvers. At the top is the huge 1st Model Dragoon .44 and at the bottom is the .31 Baby Dragoon.

> Those were absolutely last-ditch defense weapons and their carriers ought to have also had a Bowie knife after making somebody really mad by shooting them.

These short-barreled full-size revolvers often served as pocket revolvers. From top: Colt Richards Conversion .44 Colt (replica), Colt SAA Sheriff's Model .44-40, Merwin & Hulbert Pocket Army .44-40 and S&W Model 1881DA .44 Russian.

full-size belt pistol. The .38 is a double action and .44 is a single action. Both have 3 ½" barrels, ivory grips and nickel plating. The .38 has the crudest engraving I've ever seen but I'm told it is a factory original.

Regarding function, M&H's are indeed odd ducks as they were probably ahead of their time in design. They load through a port on the frame's left side similar to most revolvers of the day. However, unloading is done by pressing a button just in front of the trigger guard, simultaneously twisting the barrel 90 degrees clockwise. All empty cases fall away and loaded ones remain in their chambers. Their .38 and .44 chamberings are also odd. The .38 M&H is nothing more than the .38 S&W with about a 145-grain bullet. Merwin & Hulbert chambered two .44s. One was the .44 M&H. It was akin to but not exactly a duplicate of the .44 Colt and .44 Remington cartridges. The other .44 used in M&W Pocket Army sixguns was caliber-stamped on the frame's left side "Calibre Winchester 1873." It was the .44 Winchester Centerfire, or .44-40 as we know it today.

Three double-action pocket revolvers. Top: Merwin & Hulbert .38 M&H (actually very similar to .38 S&W). Middle: Colt Model 1877DA .38 Colt. Bottom: Colt Model 1877DA .41 Colt.

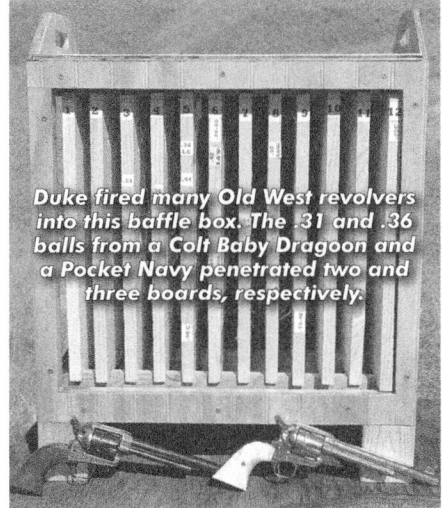

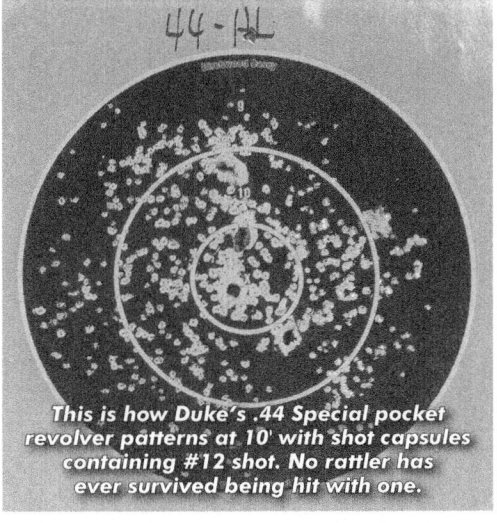

To load a Baby Dragoon it must be dismantled into three parts. After powder is in a chamber, then the cupped end of the base pin is used to force in pure-lead round balls.

Normally Duke carries his Colt Sheriff's Model .44 Special with three shot loads and two normal bullets.

Duke fired many Old West revolvers into this baffle box. The .31 and .36 balls from a Colt Baby Dragoon and a Pocket Navy penetrated two and three boards, respectively.

This is how Duke's .44 Special pocket revolver patterns at 10' with shot capsules containing #12 shot. No rattler has ever survived being hit with one.

The reason Duke feels he needs a modern day pocket revolver.

For comparison: Left is a 230-grain .45 Auto FMJ. At right is an 80-grain .36 round ball.

At this point I must admit a fact that is rare in my more than a half-century as an avid shooter: I have never fired the .38 M&H. Why? Because I did fire the .44-40 Pocket Army and right away it broke. It hasn't been fired again since being repaired. I just don't want to take a chance damaging the .38 also. Remember what I said above about rare, expensive and fragile!

Concealed Carry Expansion

By the mid-to-late 1870s pocket pistols were available in abundance. S&W had a "Baby Russian" .38 and several .32s. Those were the top-end pocket pistols. I've never had the chance to try one of the little late-1800s S&W pocket pistols. And about the lower end, lower quality ones I admit total ignorance.

Colt came out with one more revolver that could be used as a pocket pistol or belt revolver, the Model 1877DAs. These were made as .41 Colt and .38 Colt. A Colt wholesaler gave them nicknames: "Thunderer" for the .41 and "Lightning" for the .38. I've owned several of each and one factor shared by all is this: *It's not a matter if their lockwork will break but when.* Here are the Thunderer and Lightning basics in a nutshell. Those made with barrel lengths shorter than 4 ½" have no ejector rods or housings. They were definitely meant for pocket carry. Those with barrel lengths 4 ½" or 6" do have ejector rods and housings and might be better suited for belt holsters.

Neither .38 or .41 Colt cartridges were powerful, but at least their revolvers were sixguns. I've handloaded for both. In their "short" form both rounds would hit near 750 fps with 130- and 160-grain bullets, respectively. When the "long" variations arrived late in the 1800s, they used 150- and 200-grain bullets again in the same order. Then their bullets' velocities were lucky to break 700 fps. Of course, all this was dependent on barrel lengths.

I'd like to get personal here at the end. I still use a pocket revolver in warm months. It's a Colt SAA .44 Sheriff's Model. It came with .44-40 and .44 Special cylinders. I use the latter loaded with homemade shot loads because our Montana acreage gets rattlers in warm weather. So, the Colt Sheriff's Model goes in my hip pocket. For safety it's only loaded with five rounds and the hammer down on the empty sixth chamber, so I don't shoot myself in the butt. I have dispatched far more rattlesnakes with it than I have wanted to. So, 19th century pocket pistols still have some purpose in the 21st century.

Serena Juchnowski

TWO FOR ONE

Taylor 1858 "The Ace" Black Powder Conversion

A modern twist on an old model ...

The Ace ships with a conversion cylinder allowing use with .45 Long Colt cartridges.

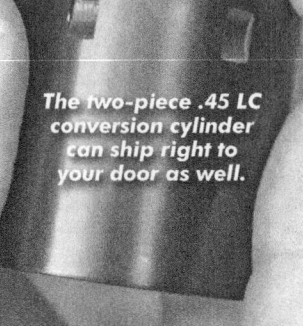

The versatility of Taylor's & Company's Ace first attracted me to it. The .44-caliber black powder revolver also accepts a conversion cylinder to fire smokeless .45 LC/.45 Schofield ammunition. Not only is it two guns in one, but it also ships directly to your house.

Sadly, UPS almost didn't let me have it. The package arrived late in the day. Thinking I'd spare the delivery man a walk across the front yard and a barking dog, I met him halfway across the front lawn. He seemed grateful, then immediately worried. "I'd love to give it to you, but you need to be 21 to sign for it," he said.

"I'm 22," I smiled. He seemed dubious. I offered to grab my license to prove my age, but he declined, still holding my package.

"Your mom's home, right?" he asked, trying to gently find a way to leave it with someone older. By this time, I was grinning, nearly laughing. This isn't the first time my age has been underestimated. I was once asked around age 19 if I could drive. After a few minutes of deliberation, he handed it over, saying "at least it's not alcohol" under his breath.

First Impression

The gun is beautiful at first sight,

The two-piece .45 LC conversion cylinder can ship right to your door as well.

but the case it arrives in is a tad strange. Rather than a zippered triangle, a Velcro fold at one end kept the revolver intact. The Ace comes with three different grip options, smooth walnut checkered walnut or white PVC.

Weighing in at 2 lbs. with an overall length of 8.68", the handgun is smaller than its full-framed sibling. The Ace is built from the design of the 1858 Remington, a model that became popular with military officers after the Civil War. The 1858 Reming-

ton's popularity came from its easy cylinder removal, which unlike the Colt models, did not require taking the firearm completely apart.

The Ace model has a 3" octagonal barrel and includes a lever-latch to retain the cylinder pin in the frame. Due to the small size and snub-nose barrel, this model does not include a loading lever and requires a separate loading stand for black powder revolver cylinders. At least this provides an extra "hand" making the process simpler.

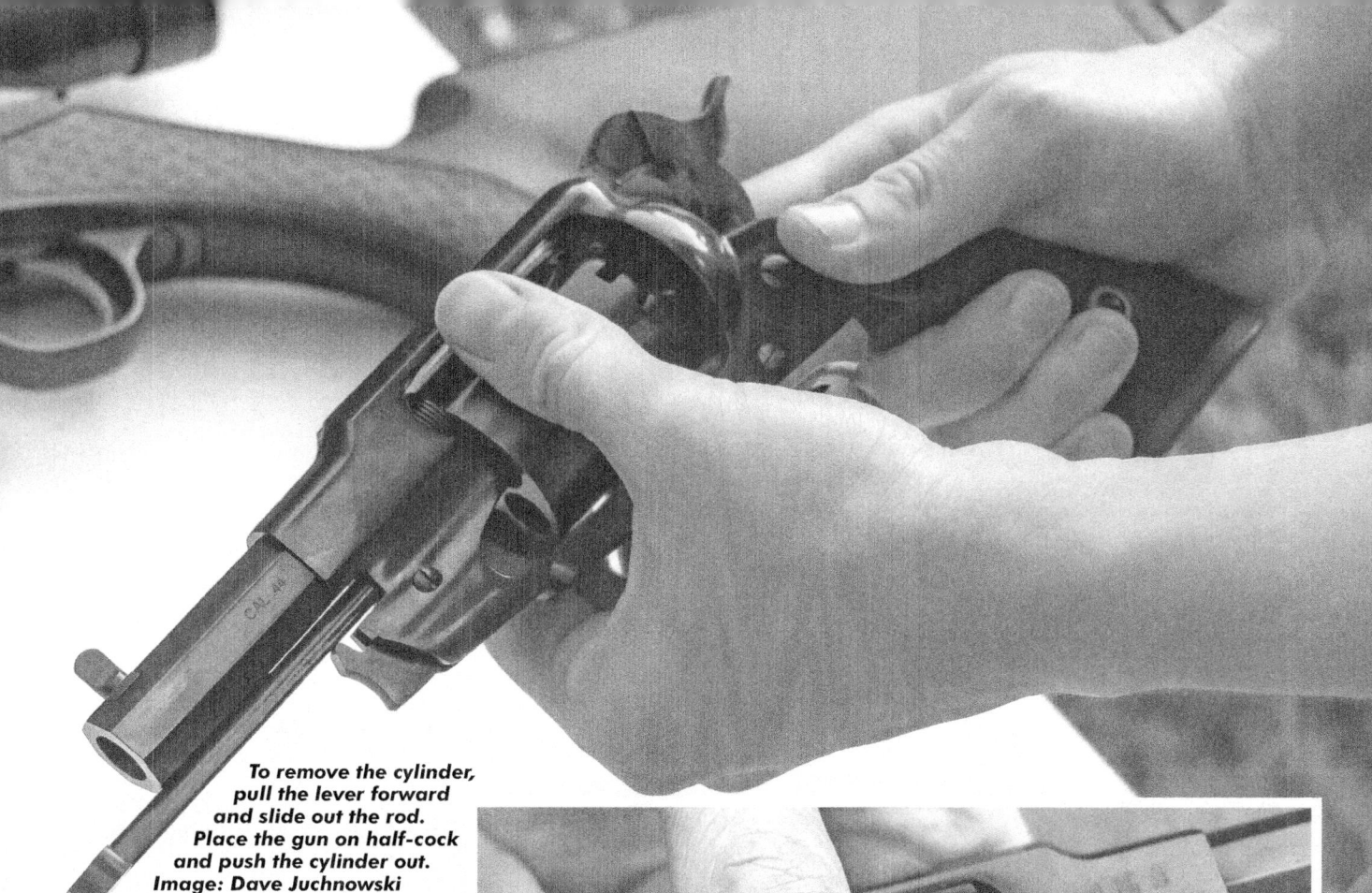

To remove the cylinder, pull the lever forward and slide out the rod. Place the gun on half-cock and push the cylinder out. Image: Dave Juchnowski

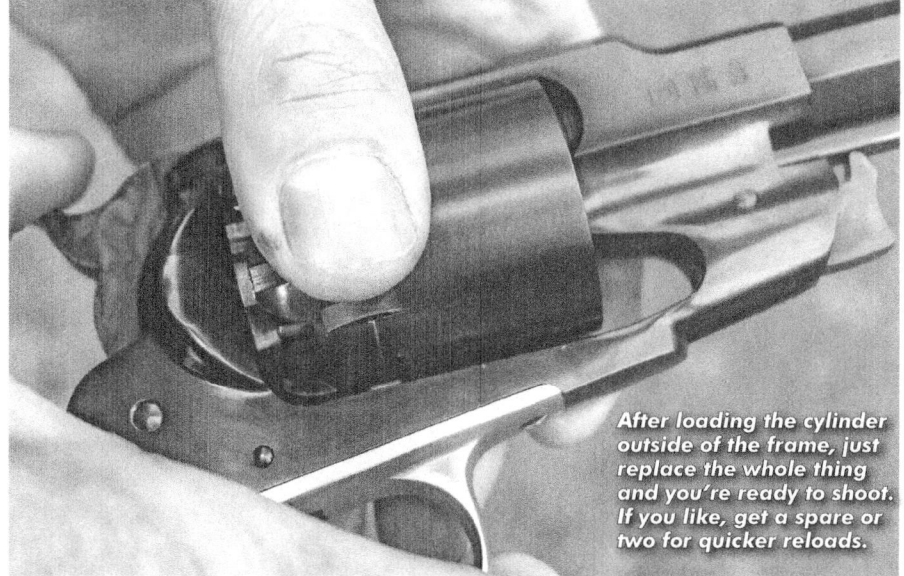

After loading the cylinder outside of the frame, just replace the whole thing and you're ready to shoot. If you like, get a spare or two for quicker reloads.

Note the tight fit as evidenced by the lead shavings.

Changing the Cylinder

Loading was definitely a little different than I'm used to. I first had to remove the cylinder, which was relatively easy. Putting it back in was a slightly different matter. To extract the cylinder, I put the pistol on half-cock and pulled the retention lever forward. A slight push with my thumb sent the cylinder tumbling into my hand. To restore it, I first set the cylinder on the edge of the frame and pushed it in slightly. I pulled the hammer back a little farther while simultaneously pushing the cylinder in farther. I lined the barrel up with one of the cylinders and pushed the retention rod forward until it clicked in. The same process applied to switching to the conversion cylinder, but this cylinder was in two pieces. In both cases, the cylinder needs to be loaded outside of the gun.

Black Powder

Rather than pour powder into the barrel, I had to do so for each chamber. New to black powder revolvers, I mistakenly thought I'd use a ramrod to compress the contents of each chamber. After I had set everything out – powder, wads, balls, cleaning supplies and percussion caps, I realized I was missing something. Most black powder revolvers have a built-in loading lever. The Ace does not. I needed a separate device to load each cylinder.

The 1858 Remington's popularity came from its easy cylinder removal, which unlike the Colt models, did not require taking the firearm completely apart.

The Traditions Loading Tool made refills much easier. Image: Dave Juchnowski

Serena added a ball to the top of each chamber and used the loading stand to compress it.

Percussion cappers are tricky to use, but safer than adding primers by hand. Image: Dave Juchnowski

This revolver is designed to be as compact as possible, so no integral ramrod here!

Shooting black powder guns is ... glorious.

The loading stand was surprisingly fun to use. After removing the cylinder, I secured it on the loading stand by placing the center hole in the cylinder (used for the retention rod on the revolver) on the corresponding rod on the stand. I added one Pyrodex pistol pellet to each chamber and followed with a wonder wad.

Black powder revolvers have the possibility of chainfiring. The spark from the percussion cap and subsequent conflagration can ignite more than one chamber at a time. There are several ways to prevent this. You can place lube or grease on top of each loaded chamber. This method also helps keep the black powder fouling soft and easier to clean. I opted to use wonder wads, a pre-lubed type of patch, which could be placed between the powder and ball or above the ball. Keeping with the traditional powder, patch and ball method, I added a wad to each chamber then a ball. Though the Ace is listed as a .44-caliber black powder revolver, it is really a .45 caliber. I used .451 round balls. As I pressed each ball into the chamber, the loading stand shaved a small ring of lead off each ball, ensuring a tight and complete seal.

After reinstalling the cylinder in the pistol frame, I needed to prime each of the individual nipples with percussion caps. Though number 10s might have fit better, only number 11s were available. The left side of the cylinder was blocked, so I could only add percussion caps to the right side. To reach all chambers, I put the pistol on half-cock and rotated it.

First Shots

I was pleasantly surprised at the near nonexistent recoil of the Ace. I quickly realized when I fired the first shot, all the remaining percussion caps went flying into the surrounding grass. I resolved to priming one chamber at a time by hand. I first attempted to use a percussion capper, but the force used to pull the capper loose from the nipple also upset the cap.

I also had to take extra care to remove each spent percussion cap before firing the next shot as they had

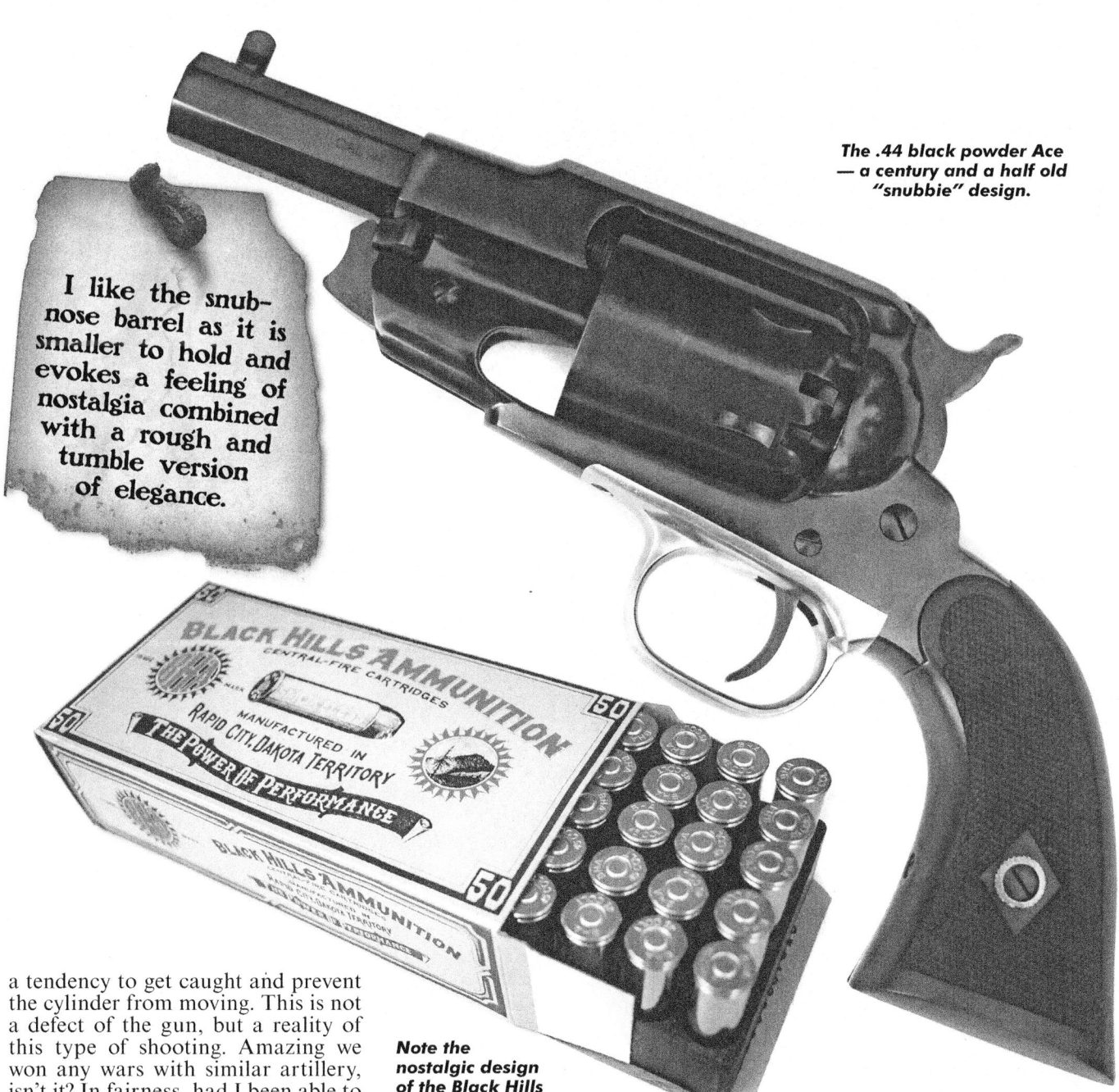

The .44 black powder Ace — a century and a half old "snubbie" design.

I like the snub-nose barrel as it is smaller to hold and evokes a feeling of nostalgia combined with a rough and tumble version of elegance.

Note the nostalgic design of the Black Hills Ammunition .45 LC box.

Be sure to clean out the fouling from the percussion cap nipples for reliable ignition. A small pick does the job nicely.

a tendency to get caught and prevent the cylinder from moving. This is not a defect of the gun, but a reality of this type of shooting. Amazing we won any wars with similar artillery, isn't it? In fairness, had I been able to source the right size caps the process would have been smoother.

I initially loaded all six cylinders. I did have some issues getting the Pyrodex pellets to ignite, sometimes needing to use three or four percussion caps to get the gun to fire. Afterward, I used Goex triple F black powder — zero ignition issues. The black powder also brought along a satisfying puff of smoke. Inlines have much better luck with pellet powder substitutes.

.45 Long Colt Conversion

I had never seen .45 Long Colt before. When I first opened the box of .45 LC from Black Hills Ammunition, I was astounded: a stout and hefty cartridge with a 250-grain bullet and a velocity of 725 fps, and much greater recoil than the black powder load. It nearly jumped out of my hand at first — a problem quickly rectified with a solid grip. Though minute, I cannot go without praising the look of the cartridge box, designed to add to the Old West feeling of firing the cartridge. Old-style lettering, borders and illustrations adorned the sides and top. "Manufactured in Rapid City, Dakota Territory," was also a nice touch.

Overall

This gun was fun to shoot and in today's ammunition and component climate, provides unique ammunition flexibility. I like the snub-nose barrel as it is smaller to hold and evokes a feeling of nostalgia combined with a rough and tumble version of elegance. Cylinder changes were a bit tricky at first, but after doing it once or twice, became second nature. The gun is definitely heavy, but this helps with the recoil.

Sights are nothing fancy, just a fixed blade, but anything more technologically advanced would take away from the experience. Shooting the Ace, or any black powder firearm, isn't about evaluating accuracy and precision as much as it is about the experience and dependability of the arm — two items the Ace checks off.

Frank Jardim

COMPLICATED OR FUTURISTIC?

Starr Model 1858: Double Action from Another Planet?

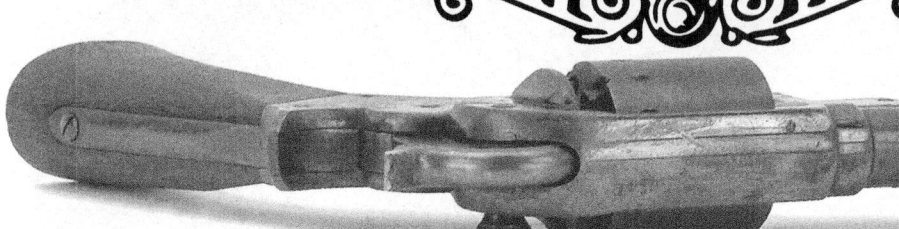

The Model 1858 Starr is most remembered today as the unusual double-action cap-and-ball pistol used by Clint Eastwood's William Mundy character in the 1992 Western film *Unforgiven*. He can't hit a thing with it, and it gets taken from him early in the movie after an epic ass-whooping, never to be seen again. The gun's cameo role was its most notable cinematic appearance. The subsequent films that cast it just weren't nearly as successful at the box office. You might say art mimics life in the case of the Model 1858 Starr. Despite its cutting-edge design, it was destined only for a cameo role as a fighting handgun.

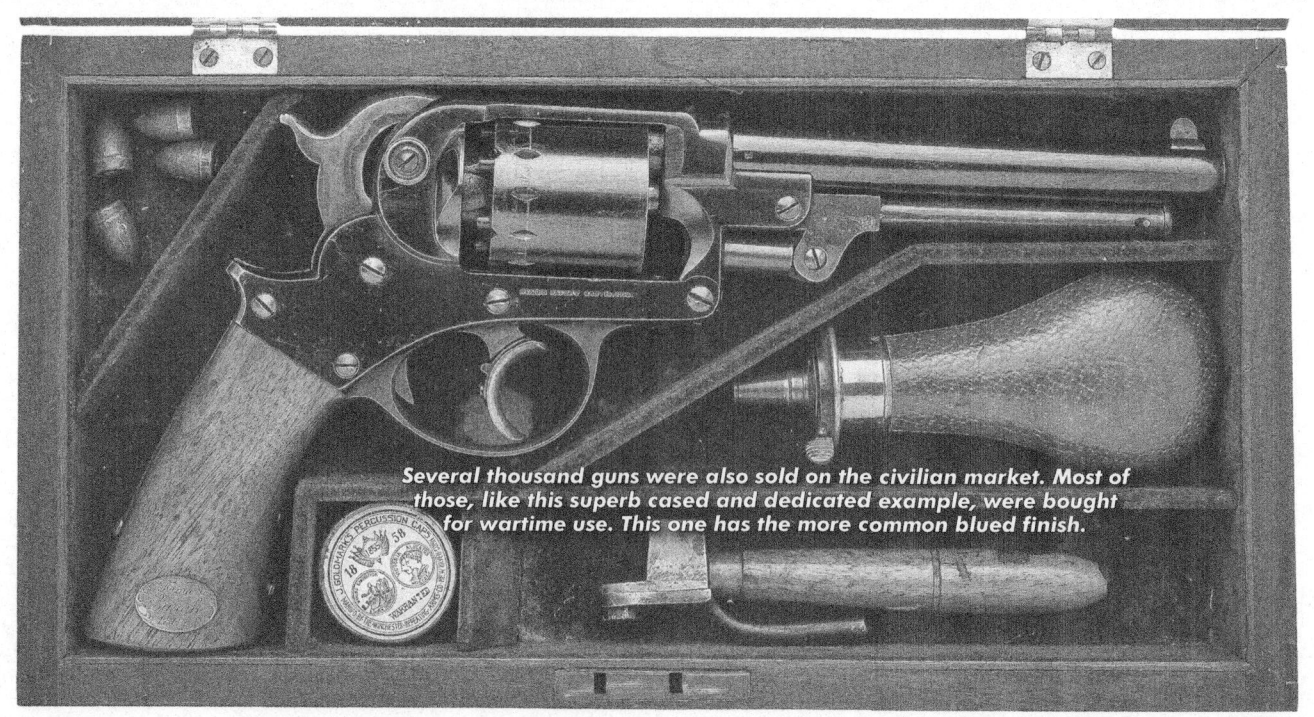

Several thousand guns were also sold on the civilian market. Most of those, like this superb cased and dedicated example, were bought for wartime use. This one has the more common blued finish.

Frank surveyed at least a thousand of those ubiquitous Civil War ambrotype and tintype soldier portraits and came up with a grand total of two 1858 Starr revolvers, and one was blurry!

DA/SA Anomaly

When the Starr Firearms Company of New York introduced their Model 1858 double-action revolver in .36 "Navy" caliber on the eve of the Civil War, it stood in stark contrast with the single actions dominating the market as well as its few double-action peers. Unlike modern double-action revolvers, most pre-Civil War models were actually double-action-only. The Model 1858 Starr could shoot both ways.

This feature was very uncommon and Starr shared it with the Cooper Firearms Company's fine, five-shot, .31-caliber pocket pistols (which strongly resembled the 1849 Colt) and the British made .44 Beaumont–Adams revolver. Both the little Cooper and the beefy Beaumont-Adams were designed for thumb cocking in single-action operation for precise shooting in the familiar way our modern revolvers do. In single action, the 1858 Starr didn't work that way — probably the main source of the tarnish its reputation took during the Civil War.

In double-action mode, the Model 1858 Starr was great and seemed conventional then, and now. You pull the trigger all the way through its arc, the cylinder rotates, the hammer rises and falls and the gun fires. However, then as now, in single action, the Starr proved awkward to operate because of its novel design.

Most Complicated Cocking Ever?

Unlike just about every other single-action revolver with a spurred hammer, you can't simply pull the hammer back to cock it. The Starr was

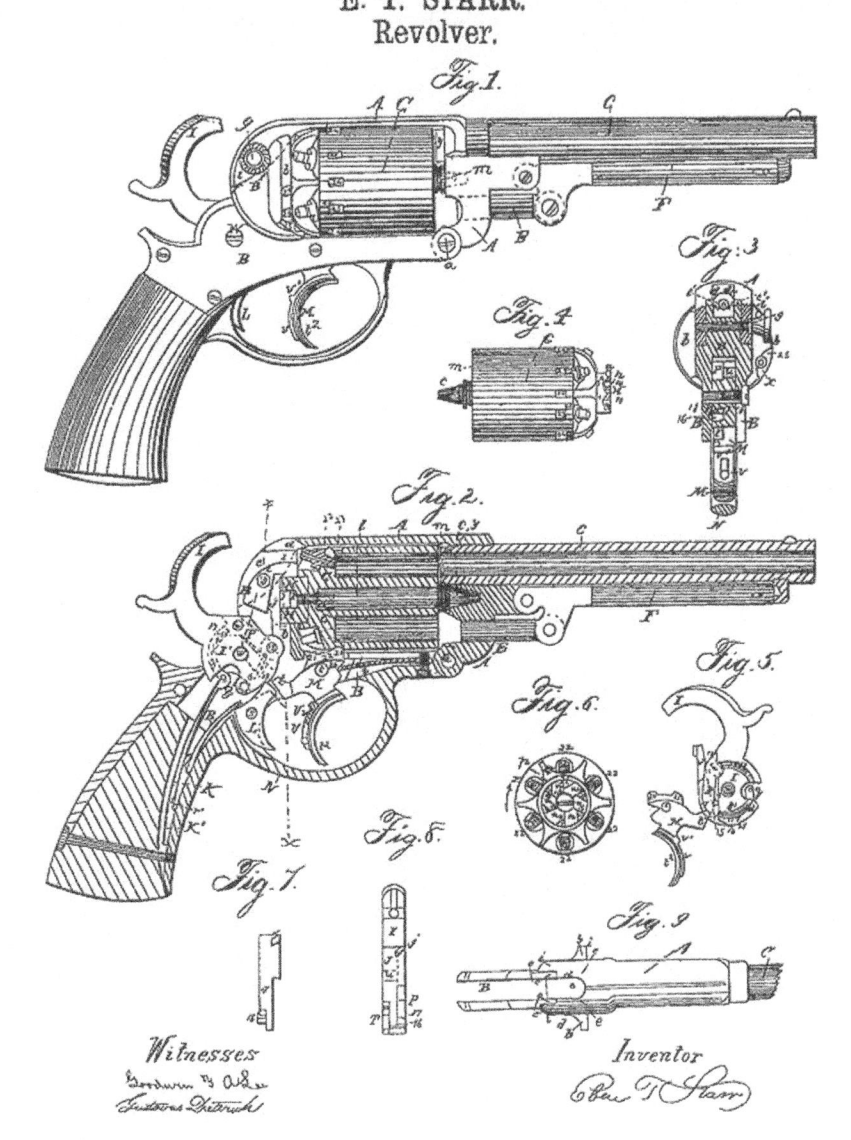

This civilian pistol has a rare non-standard long barrel. Virtually all the Model 1858 Starrs had 6" barrels, regardless of whether they were .36 or .44 caliber.

> It's a fact the U.S. Army didn't want any more of them. They requested the pistol be redesigned as a conventional single action.

Most Model 1858 Starrs will have military inspection cartouches on both sides of the grips.

They point well and the saw-handle is ideal for stabilizing the pistol during double-action shooting.

Note the slots for safety and locking up the cylinder in single action (on the side of the cylinder) and "V" cuts on the rear edge for indexing in double-action firing.

meant to be cocked by pulling what we today, and frankly everyone who has ever seen one in the last 163 years, would consider its trigger. What looks like the Starr's trigger is not actually the trigger. In the gun's instructional literature, the "trigger" is called a firing-lever. The primary purpose of the firing-lever was to cock the hammer. The actual trigger was set in the back of the trigger guard.

The shooter was expected to select between single- or double-action mode by moving a sliding spring switch screwed to the rear of the firing-lever. Slide the switch down for single-action or up for double-action shooting. In the up position, the raised tab clears the back of the trigger guard, allowing the rear face of the firing-lever to depress the trigger at the end of its travel and release the hammer to fire the gun. In the down position, the tab hits the trigger guard and blocks rearward travel of the firing-lever before it touches the trigger. The hammer is cocked, but the sear is not tripped.

To fire a shot in single-action mode, the firing-lever was pulled through its arc to cock the hammer and released. Then the shooter had to shift his trigger finger to the actual trigger in the rear of the trigger guard and squeeze it to fire the shot. The Starr could actually be thumb cocked too, but the shooter had to first depress the trigger slightly to release the hammer. This operation requires some fine motor skills. Exactly the kind of skills people tend to lose in the adrenaline-fueled stress of combat.

Combat Service

The Model 1858 Starr revolver played a notable, if short, role in the Civil War. Around 3,100 in .36 caliber and 23,000 in .44 caliber went to the Union cause, most through government purchases, and the rest by private sales to individuals. In overall production, Starr Firearms Company was actually the third-largest producer of revolvers during the Civil War, though they were a distant third and about 32,000 of the approximately 58,000 pistols produced ended up being plebeian single-action Model 1863s. To put their production numbers in rough perspective, for every three revolvers delivered by Colt or Remington, Starr delivered one.

Though the 1858 Starr was advanced technology, it seems its detractors in the military were more outspoken than its supporters. There is a documentary record showing Model 1858s were gradually withdrawn from the field and most (16,772 of them) were in storage by mid-November 1864.

It's a fact the U.S. Army didn't want any more of them. They requested the pistol be redesigned as a conventional single action. Starr Arms Co. did this, creating the Starr Model 1863 single-action revolver, and the government awarded them a new contract for the simplified pistols that appear to have met military requirements.

Practical Accuracy?

Shooting my own Pietta replica Model 1858 Starr, I had to wonder why this fast-firing sixgun was so unpopular with the troops. Was there really some fatal flaw with the Model 1858? The answer depends on your perspective. My guess is it probably just wasn't as practical for the soldiers of the era as competing, simpler, single-action designs. Reflecting on the unspectacular showing I made when I was first learning to shoot double action, and the time and practice it took to get good, I can imagine why the Union cavalrymen who were issued these pistols might not want them. What good is a fast-shooting gun if you can't hit anything? It's hard enough to shoot accurately from

Most Model 1858 Starr double-action revolvers were made in .44 caliber with 6" barrels to fulfill military contracts for the Union Army. This is an example with a case-hardened frame and loading lever.

The Model 1858 Starr's double-action trigger pull is long by today's standards, but it was head and shoulders a faster shooter than any single action. Frank's Pietta replica is a fun shooter.

The Starr's sights were also better than those on the Colt and Remington. The Starr has the usual "V" notched hammer for a rear sight, but the front sight was dovetailed to the barrel allowing for windage adjustment.

Unlike modern double-action revolvers, most pre-Civil War models were actually double-action-only. The Model 1858 Starr could shoot both ways.

The Starr looks like it has a solid top-strap frame, but it's actually two parts hinged together.

Cocking for SA fire and using the rear trigger.

The Starr's cylinder sprocket is deeply inlet into the frame to protect it from cap debris.

With one takedown bolt, the Starr was easier to break down for cleaning than the Colt, but since the bolt wasn't captive like the Colt's barrel wedge, you can be sure many Starrs were rendered useless in the field when soldiers lost the bolts.

horseback in single-action mode. Had the Model 1858 Starr been capable of easy thumb cocking like the Adams-Beaumont, it might have been a success with the troops.

When the Civil War ended, so did military procurement contracts, and Starr Firearms Company permanently closed in 1867. Most of the pistols in government inventory were sold off and went overseas to European armies (most notably for service in the Franco-Prussian War). As a civilian arm, the 1858 Starr pops up here and there in the Old West, including in the holster of Jesse James who used his to kill at least two lawmen.

Like the Spencer carbine, the '58 Starr briefly held an important niche in the universe of American firearms because there was nothing better to replace it readily available. Though a design dead end, the Spencer was important to people who needed a powerful big-bore repeating rifle. It wore that laurel until the 1876 Winchester came along. The '58 Starr was one of the few serviceable, big-bore, double-action revolvers until the late 1870s when Colt introduced better metallic cartridge designs. From surviving examples, we know some thought enough of their '58 Starrs to have gunsmiths convert them to metallic cartridges. I know from experience with my Pietta replica, once you have some time to practice with it, the '58 Starr can put a lot of lead on a target very, very fast.

GUNSMAGAZINE.COM

Mike "Duke" Venturino

A SUBTLE BUT SIGNIFICANT ROLE

Remington's Old West Sixguns

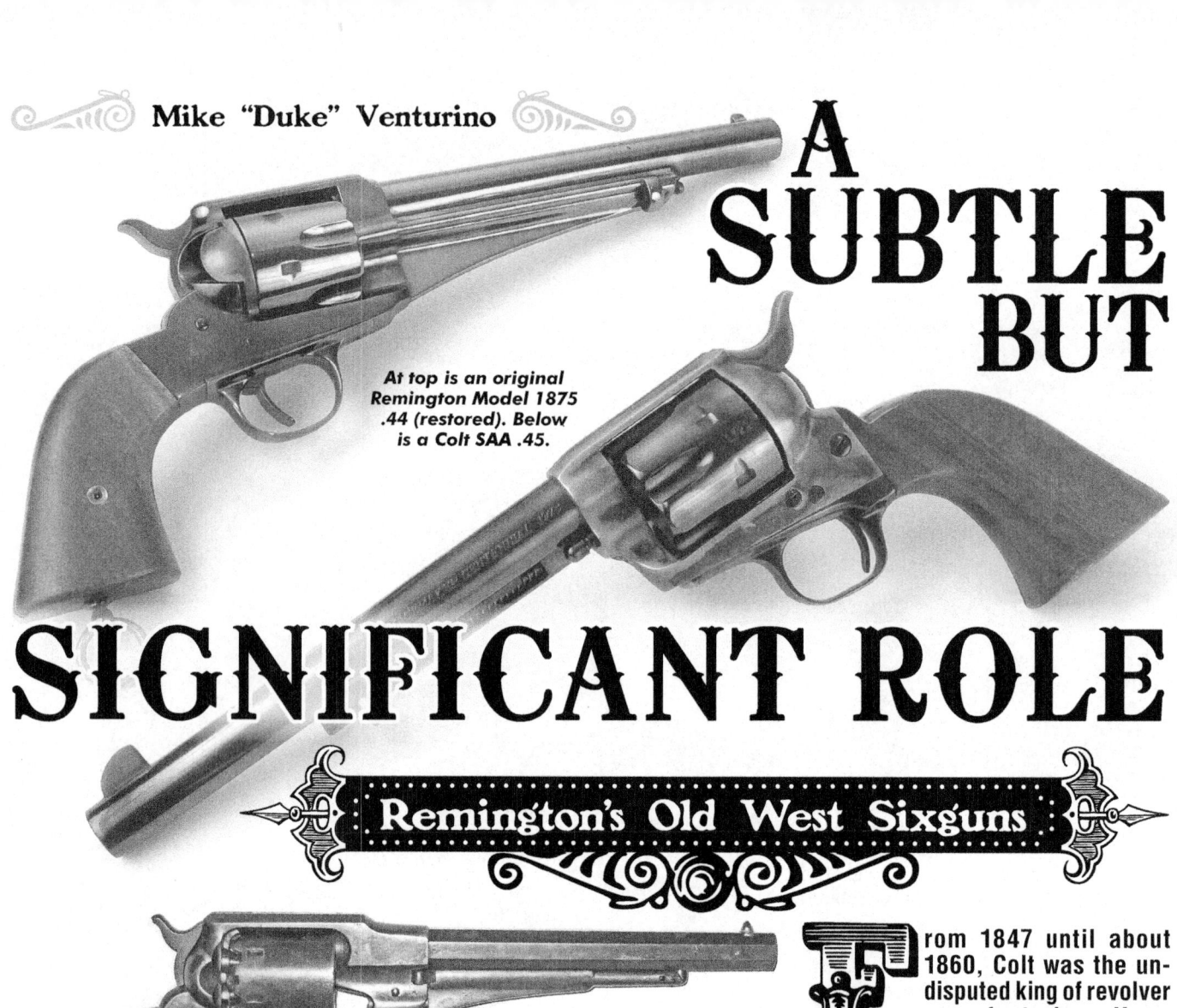

At top is an original Remington Model 1875 .44 (restored). Below is a Colt SAA .45.

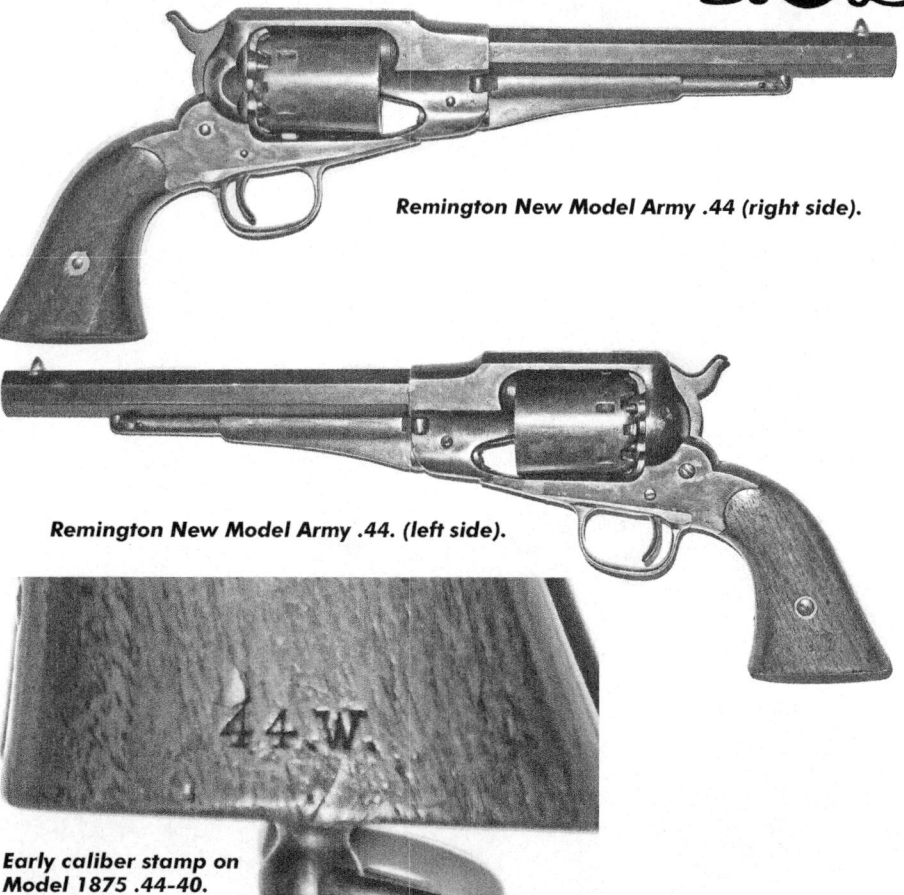

Remington New Model Army .44 (right side).

Remington New Model Army .44 (left side).

Early caliber stamp on Model 1875 .44-40.

From 1847 until about 1860, Colt was the undisputed king of revolver manufacturing. However, there was definitely room for improvement in cap-and-ball revolver design. For instance, their .31-, .36- and .44-caliber revolvers were all open top with a rear sight, a notch in the hammer and a front bead resembling modern shotgun beads. For cleaning, Colt revolvers had to be disassembled into three basic parts: frame, barrel and cylinder.

By about 1860, Remington began making a solid-frame revolver based on patents awarded to Fordyce Beals and William Elliot. Thus was born Remington's New Model Army and New Model Navy revolvers, which were the first significant challenges to Colt's dominance in the revolver world. The "Army" model of .44 caliber was made with a large frame, an 8" barrel and of .44 caliber whereas the "Navy" version was on a slightly smaller frame in .36 caliber with a 7 ½" barrel.

These new solid-frame Remingtons had grooves down their topstraps into which were machined a smaller notch for a rear sight. Front sights were small, German-silver conical beads.

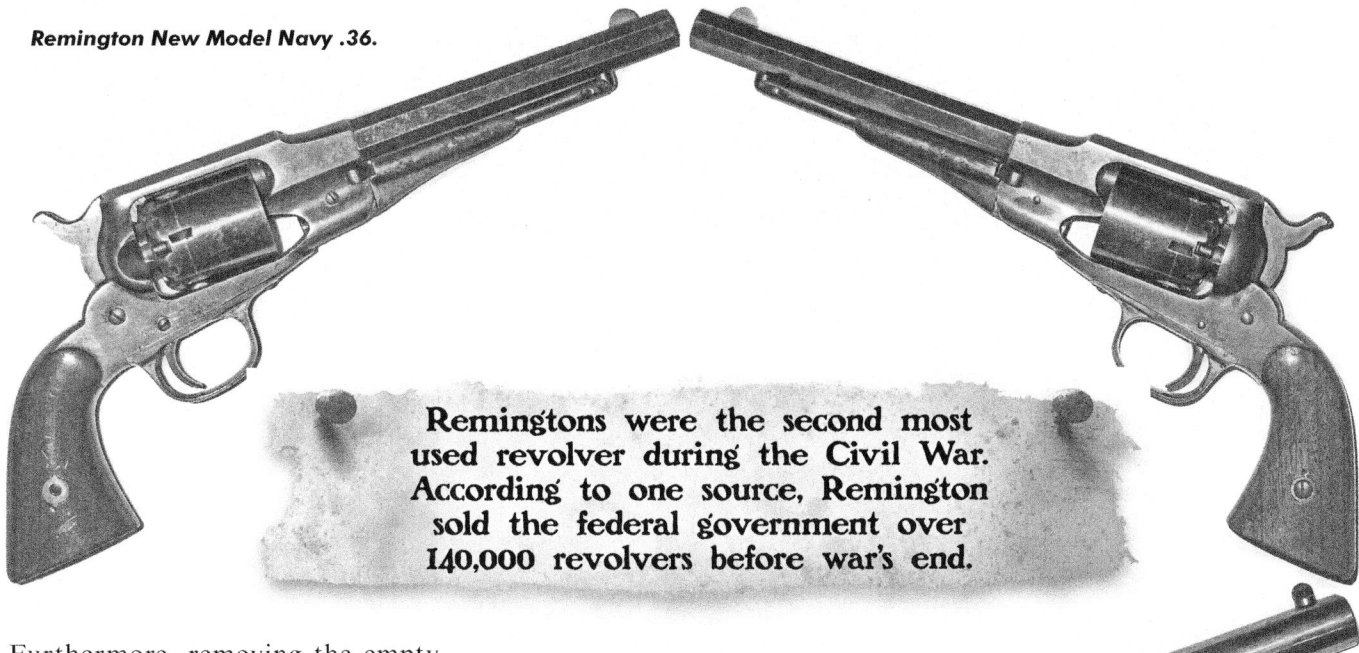

Remington New Model Navy .36.

> Remingtons were the second most used revolver during the Civil War. According to one source, Remington sold the federal government over 140,000 revolvers before war's end.

Remington Model 1875 with 7 ½" barrel.

Later version of Model 1875 caliber stamp on frame's left side.

Furthermore, removing the empty cylinder for cleaning required merely half-cocking the hammer, dropping the loading rammer and pulling forward the base pin. This had to be a benefit in combat, where dropping out an empty cylinder and replacing it with a previously loaded one required only seconds. Another benefit unique to Remington sixguns was a "web" on the loading rammer for strength, and I suspect in combat it also helped turn an empty handgun into a better club. *Remingtons were the second most used revolver during the Civil War.* According to one source, Remington sold the federal government over 140,000 revolvers before war's end.

For decades, Italian replica manufacturers have turned out copies of Remington's cap-and-ball sixguns. The only one I've owned was a New Model Army .44. It was a fine shooter, but I gifted it to a friend to whom I owed a few favors. As I remember it was made by Pietta and of fine quality.

Military Use

Although production of Remington's Army model .44 ended March 1865, military usage of Remington's cap-and-ball .44 revolvers continued. In fact, it didn't end even after metallic cartridge firing revolvers became common. In the book *Bugles, Banners, and War Bonnets* copyrighted 1977 by Ernest L. Reedstrom, there are 7th Cavalry Ordnance Reports listing arms and ammunition in the hands of the regiment's 12 companies. For the second quarter of March through June 1867, 78 Remington .44s are listed. For the same quarter of 1871, the number had increased to 186. However, by the second quarter of 1875 only three of the big Remington .44s remained in 7th Cavalry stores. They had been replaced by the Colt .45 Single Action Army, which stayed in service until the 1890s.

Another fascinating book I've read (and reread) is *Cheyenne War, Indian Raids on the Roads to Denver 1864-1869*, copyright 2013 by Jeff Broome. In it are many firsthand accounts of Indian fights with the U.S. Army, as well as dozens from settlers, teamsters and traders. Spencer carbines and Henry repeating rifles are mentioned prominently. Unfortunately, most accounts concerning handguns only mention "revolvers."

However, in the summer of 1868, Corporal Leander Herron of the U.S. 3rd Infantry, escorted by a 7th Cavalry sergeant, volunteered to carry dispatches from Fort Dodge, Kan. Shortly into their trip they heard firing, rode to it and came to the aid of four soldiers fighting off Indians. In the ensuing melee, all the men excluding Herron were wounded. Herron related: *"I was unwounded. I would load my Remington revolver and pass it to Nolan, who was obliged to fire with his left hand, his right arm having been shattered by a bullet."* When the soldiers were down to only 12 rounds of ammunition for all guns, a troop of cavalry came to the rescue. Herron was later awarded the Medal of Honor.

Cartridge Adoption

One might think with the U.S. Army having purchased so many Remington percussion revolvers the company would be anxious to submit to the government a metallic cartridge firing version. Yet it was not until

Remington Model 1890 with 5 ¾" barrel.

Duke's Hartford Armory Model 1875 .44-40 (top) and Model 1890 .45 Colt (bottom). Both have 7 ½" barrels. Image: Yvonne Venturino

March 1876 that they did so, which was 2 ½ years after the Army had settled on Colt's new .45. Perhaps the reason was Remington's factory was immensely busy at the time producing Number One "rolling block" single-shot, military rifles. They were shipped literally around the world.

When Remington did get around to producing their new cartridge revolver we call the Model 1875, it shared many characteristics with the Colt SAA. Both manufacturers' 7 ½" barreled revolvers now had topstrapped frames with grooves for rear sights. Remington proponents correctly point out this made Colt's first "strap pistol" a copy of Remington's design from 15 years earlier. With both revolvers, half-cocking their hammers freed cylinders for rotation. Cartridges were then loaded into chambers via a loading gate on the frame's right side. Fired cases were ejected by means of a rod located on the barrel's right side.

Remington's new metallic-cartridge revolver did have some advantages. Its grip frame was forged integrally with the frame. A trigger guard was inset and held with a single screw. Conversely, Colt Single Action Army backstraps and trigger guards were two pieces held by six screws. *Perhaps this is why each SAA sold to the Army came with a screwdriver.* Also, Colt base pins were secured by a screw until the inception of the spring-loaded transverse latch in the mid-1890s. Remington '75 base pins could be removed without tools. Remington also retained the distinct web running from frame to barrel.

The first cartridge Remington chambered in their new revolver was .44 Remington, which was similar but not identical to the .44 Colt. This was the caliber of the first '75 sent to the U.S. government. The Army insisted a test model had to be for their .45 Gov't. round. (Also called .45 S&W and .45 Schofield.) Remington did this by making the cylinder 0.010" thicker and 0.015" longer. Since the chamber was not "necked" it would also contain full-length .45 Colt cartridges. The .45 Gov't. used a 1.10" case and the .45 Colt a 1.285" case.

Sales Ups & Downs

In 1877, U.S. Army testing officers gave Remington's .45 excellent reviews,

Duke's Hartford Armory .44-40 Model 1875 replica serial number HA0007P. Image: Yvonne Venturino

Remington Model 1890 with 7 ½" barrel.

Italian replica of Remington New Model Army .44.
Image: Mike Beliveau

but the government declined to purchase any. However, in the late 1870s the Mexican government contracted for 1,000 Remington Model 1875 .45s. Also, the U.S. Department of the Interior purchased a total of 639 Model 1875 .44-40s to arm Native American police on various reservations.

Model 1875s chambering .44 Remington did not sell well on the civilian market and so the .44 WCF (Winchester Center Fire) replaced it in the later 1870s. No .44 Remington chambered Model 1875s were made thereafter. Caliber marking on .44-40s was by a simple .44 or .44W on the left grip. Later, a .44 or .45 was stamped on the left side of frame between cylinder port and barrel and finally on the left rear of the trigger guard.

An 1880 advertisement related the two .44 cartridge options, along with the .45 Government, were offered. (Those as .44 Remington were old stock.) Also in the ad is the price of $12.50 for a '75 with blue finish, $1 for more nickel plating. And instead of the Model 1875 name used now, they billed the big six-shooter as the Remington Improved Army or Frontier Revolver.

Manufacture of Model 1875 Remingtons lasted only 12 years, ceasing when E. Remington & Son declared bankruptcy in 1886. Exact figures as to the total produced are not available. The number 25,000 is usually given, but some knowledgeable collectors think the total was closer to 30,000. Perhaps the most famous user of Model 1875 Remington was Frank James, who surrendered to Missouri authorities after the 1882 assassination of his brother Jesse. He turned in a brace of .44-40s. I've only owned one original Model 1875 chambered for .44 Remington. It was a handful of a sixgun and shot decently if not dramatically with black powder handloads.

Remington Resurrection

Old West Remington sixguns were not quite done. January 1888, a group of investors formed the Remington Arms Company. Among their purchased inventory were leftover Model 1875 parts. A few hundred revolvers were assembled from them. The leftover 7 ½" barrels were shortened to 5 ¾" for the "New Model Pocket Revolvers" which today's collectors call the Model 1888. All were .44-40s with wood grips with the large under-barrel web trimmed down. Most were nickeled, but some wore a blue finish.

Two years later Remington made its last bid for a portion of the big-bore sixgun market. Model 1890s were made with both 5 ¾" and 7 ½" barrels, both nickeled and blued finish and all were .44-40s. Models 1888 and 1890s are virtually identical in profile but are easily discerned by the company markings atop barrels. The '88s were stamped "E. Remington & Sons" and the '90s were marked "Remington Arms Company." Manufacture ceased after only two years with just over 2,000 made.

Italian replica manufacturers have produced copies of both Model 1875s and 1890s, which are less than true clones. However, in the early 21st century a company named Hartford Armory began making very close copies of both Remington models. The gent heading the outfit brought some of his first '75s and '90s to shoot with me and I was impressed with their quality. Then he disappeared, and I never heard from him again. Some of the HA Remington clones did appear on the market with the highest serial numbers I've seen being HA0071 and HA0072.

By happenstance a few years back I was able to buy HA006P, a Model 1875 .44-40 and HA0010P, a Model 1890 .45 Colt. Since the serial numbers listed in the above paragraph do not have a "P" suffix I think perhaps on my pair it stands for prototype. Who knows? Perhaps HA0007P was one I shot nearly 20 years back. Except for the .45 chambering of the Model 1890, both are very close copies of original Remingtons. The Model 1890 appears unfired and will remain so, but I've enjoyed shooting the Model 1875 immensely.

Remington revolvers of the 19th century played important roles in some of the nation's most dramatic times, but they are little known compared to their Colt counterparts. As with Colts, there is also a collector's organization named Remington Society of America.

I owe my thanks and credit to Daniel J. Pozarek, a member of the Remington Society of America. Without his extensive knowledge of Remington revolvers and willingness to share it with me, this article would not have been possible. Also, unless otherwise noted the photos accompanying this article were his work.

Roger Smith

MINI BIG BORE?

The Truly Short .45 Colt

From left: Lee 452-160-RF, 185-grain SWC, 200-grain RFP, Lee TL452-230-2R, Lyman 452423, with a .45 Colt case for comparison.

Lee Liquid Alox in a 4-oz. bottle. A quart of what appears to be similar, Alox 606-55 made by the Lubrizol company and repackaged from a 55-gallon drum. They call it White Label Liquid Xlox.

It's no news the .44 Russian evolved into the longer .44 Special and then into the still longer .44 Magnum. The story of the .38 Short, .38 Long, .38 Special, 357 Magnum and .357 Maximum is similar.

The .45 Colt case first evolved in the opposite direction. Some writers (and even Lyman since the 1992 47th edition of their *Reloading Handbook*) have attempted to contradict or discredit what J.R. Mattern and Elmer Keith wrote in their books *Handloading Ammunition* (1926) and *Sixguns by Keith* (1955) about the existence of Short .45 Colt factory loads. And we're not talking about the .45 S&W/Schofield, either. The accompanying photos prove that Short .45 Colt cartridges really were made during the early 20th century.

The Short version faded away after World War I, and eventually the .45 Colt grew to become the .454 Casull and then the .460 S&W Magnum. Then in 2006 it went back the other way when Cowboy Action Shooter Bruce Young, a.k.a. Adirondack Jack, dreamed up the Cowboy .45 Special. The original purpose was to be able to shoot pipsqueak black powder loads in Cowboy competition games. Black powder burns very poorly unless the case is filled to the base of the bullet, and full-size loads are a real boomer of a handful.

At 0.894" long, the Cowboy Special case has the capacity of the .45 ACP and .45 Auto Rim and was originally available online from Adirondack Jack's Trading Post. By the time he closed the Trading Post in 2012, AJ sold over half a million pieces of brass. Cowboy Action Shooters don't get to have all the fun, though. Loaded with Trail Boss or other fast burning smokeless powders and a lightweight cast bullet, Cowboy brass makes very pleasant plinking loads. It's also a great way to introduce folks to the pleasures of shooting a big-bore revolver. After a too-long spell of intermittent availability, new brass is readily available again, directly from Starline.

DIY Cowboy

The Cowboy .45 Special has usually been considered a do-it-yourself proposition, using normal .45 ACP dies and a .45 Colt shell holder. Full power smokeless .45 ACP loads can be used straight from the book in Rugers, but are too high pressure for original black powder Colt SAAs. I began with published starting loads and, frequently playing "what if" with the computer program QuickLOAD, carefully worked my way down. My "regular" .45 Colt load is the Lee 452-252-SWC grain bullet cast from wheelweights, over 8 grains of Unique powder. The accompanying table shows the results for light plinking loads that shoot very close to the same point of aim at 8 to 15 yards with my favorite 4 ⅝" Ruger Blackhawk.

BULLET	C.O.A.L	USEABLE CC	POWDER	CHARGE	% FILL	VELOCITY (FPS)	EXTREME SPREAD
Lee 452-160-RF Wheelweights	1.109"	1.054	Trail Boss	3.5 gr.	73.8	501	73
			Trail Boss	4.0 gr.	84.3	551	82
			Trail Boss	4.5 gr.	94.9	673	74
			Clays	2.5 gr.	34.9	322	142
			Clays	3.0 gr.	41.8	400	81
			Clays	3.5 gr.	48.9	471	69
			Clays	4.0 gr.	55.8	682	52
			Clays	4.5 gr.	63	788	13
Shooter's Choice 185-grain SWC	1.107"	0.758	Trail Boss	3.5 gr.	103	602	46
			AA No. 2	3.0 gr.	33.2	510	105
			AA No. 2	3.5 gr.	38.9	552	62
			AA No. 2	4.0 gr.	44.4	737	59
Shooter's Choice 200-grain RFP	1.208"	0.954	Trail Boss	3.5 gr.	81.5	535	72
			Trail Boss	4.0 gr.	93.2	593	54
			Red Dot	3.5 gr.	52	550	46
			Red Dot	4.0 gr.	59.3	610	60

Loads with velocities lower than around 550–600 fps leave the cases and chambers sooty and coated with a film of lube. This is because even with the fastest-burning powders, pressures are still not high enough to make an adequate seal between cases and chamber walls to prevent blowback. Even so, the fantasy Cowboy Single Action Shooting Society allows a minimum velocity of 400 fps with 150-grain bullets.

The 160-grain bullets were cast from clip-on wheelweights in a Lee mold. The 185- and 200-grain bullets came from a now-defunct company whose bullets I used to find at gun shows and local gun shops. All bullets were coated with Lee Liquid Alox or White Label Liquid Xlox, including

From left: .460 S&W Magnum, .454 Casull, modern .45 Colt case, Western .45 Colt folded-head case (note lack of extractor groove), modern .45 Schofield case, Cowboy .45 Special and the Cowboy .45 Special head stamp.

Rave reviews? Not exactly. Scan of partial paragraph from Sixguns by Keith by Elmer Keith, 1955, reprinted 1961, p. 285.

> The old .45 Smith & Wesson cartridge with its short case has long been obsolete and also the short Remington cartridge for the .45 Colt. Today we often hear the .45 Colt Peacemaker cartridge referred to as the .45 Long Colt. Some newcomers to the game claim there is no such animal, but if they had shot the short variety that Remington turned out in such profusion before, during, and after World War I, they would see there was some basis in referring to the .45 Colt as the .45 Long. These short .45 Remington cartridges for the .45 Colt were never very accurate due to the long bullet jump and the only thing that was standard about them was a 250 grain bullet. They were soundly cussed out in all the sporting magazines of the time and all old sixgun cranks deplored their use if either accuracy, or power was wanted. They were a disgrace to the .45 Colt gun. I never tried them, but believe

There really, truly were factory loaded Short .45 Colt cartridges.

From left: Current Winchester Cowboy load with 0.4675" case head diameter and 0.509" rim diameter and machined groove above rim. Only since the modern solid head case typified by this Winchester case has the .45 Colt become practical as a rifle load. Next, a 1900–1910 Winchester Long .45 Colt load, 0.479" at the head and with a 0.505" rim. No way could this be used as a rifle round. Next are two Short .45 Colt factory rounds, a 1910–1920 black powder Winchester, the other a 1913–1922 Remington-UMC. Far right is a 1913–1922 REM-UMC .45 S&W with a significantly larger rim diameter than the .45 Colts, Short or Long. The four older cartridges were supplied by early cartridge expert Joe St. Charles, seller, Old West Cartridges on GunBroker.com.

Roger's favorite load in the Cowboy .45 Special is a 200-grain RNFP bullet powered by 4.0 grains of Red Dot and a Winchester Large Pistol primer. Fired standing using a two-hand hold on a Ruger Blackhawk with a 4 5/8" barrel at 8 yards, using a post for support.

(handwritten: Cowboy .45 Special 200 gr. RNFP 8 yds 4.0 gr. Red Dot WLP 610 fps)

Cowboy Action Shooter Bruce Young, a.k.a. Adirondack Jack, dreamed up the Cowboy .45 Special.

Cowboy .45 Special cartridge headstamp.

Closeups of the headstamps on the two Short .45 Colt factory loads, left and center, and the .45 S&W (a.k.a. Schofield) on the right. Again, note the S&W's larger rim diameter.

the ready-mades which came already conventionally lubed. All loads were taper crimped with a .45 ACP die, resulting in exceptional case life. My favorite is the 200-grain RNFP bullet over 4.0 grains of Red Dot. They shoot satisfyingly small groups right to point of aim. My original box was soon empty, so I bought a six-cavity Lee mold to make more.

Performance

Grouping with 230- to 240-grain bullets was generally okay, but they shoot higher enough than the point of aim I fail to see the point in wasting the lead to make and shoot them at these low velocities. Be happy with the lighter recoil from the lighter (and less expensive) bullets that shoot where intended. They're just plain fun for everyone.

An additional benefit of those Short Cowboy cases is easy extraction, especially from gunked up chambers needing cleaning. The .45 Colt brass does not fully eject from either Colt or Ruger cylinders, requiring you to pick them out with your fingers if they don't fall clear from their own weight because of chamber crud. Schofield cases will fully clear both Colt and New Vaquero cylinders, but not from the longer Blackhawk and old Vaquero cylinders. Cowboy cases are short enough that with customary barrel lengths of 4 5/8" and longer, they clear the larger Ruger cylinders with ease. In fact, they even fully extract from my 2 1/8" barreled pocket rocket Taurus.

Another Short Contender

Besides the .45 Cowboy Special, there's another contender to the title of The Truly Short .45 Colt — the .455 Colt, also known as the .455 Eley, which itself was a slightly more powerful version of the .455 Webley.

Colt's fourth shot at the British market, the double-action 1889 New Service with the swing-out cylinder was a real hit with both the British and Canadian military and police

> pared to strength of cases to resist, that the better cases, that is the straight sided ones, seldom or never need full length resizing. I except 45 A. C. P., which, like the bottle-necked, thin cases, must be resized full length every two or three firings.
> The 45 Colts case is furnished in short and long model; 1.1 inches and 1.3 inches respectively. The short one is best for all-round smokeless loading; the long one for black powder. Some of the others also are made both short and long.
> Reduced loads for the better revolver cartridges are given in the tables. They are pleasant to shoot and both cheap and easy to handload, as well as very accurate. Bullseye powder ignites well in light charges, but in my experience fouls the gun too much, a peculiar

An excerpt from Handloading Ammunition by J.R. Mattern, 1926, p. 275.

Dominion .455 COLT headstamp flanked by two different Winchester .455 COLT headstamps.

122   GUNS MAGAZINE OLD WEST • SPECIAL EDITION

The 1924 Dominion ammunition catalog for the Canadian market shows .45 Colt and .455 Colt cartridges, but no .455 Eley or .455 Webley. What does this tell you?

.45 Colt

Smokeless Powder, per 1,000.......... 86.00

Weight of bullet, (lead) 255 grains.

Packed 50 in a box, 2,000 in a case, weight of case, 110 lbs.

Adapted to Colt single and double action, Army and New Service Revolvers.

.455 Colt

Smokeless Powder, Lead Bullet, per 1,000 84.00

Weight of bullet, 272 grains.

Packed 50 in a box, 2,000 in a case, weight of case, 108 lbs.

Adapted to Webley-Fosbury Automatic, English Government Service and Colt New Service Revolvers.

markets. They bought the New Service in both .45 Colt and .45 Eley versions. Barrels of the latter intended for North America were frequently stamped with .455 ELEY on the left side and .455 COLT on the top.

Exactly when and how long Colt and the ammo makers used the .455 COLT barrel and cartridge headstamps makes for interesting debates, but it's not the point here. The point is ".45 Short Colt" and ".45 Long Colt" were mere colloquialisms and never used by Colt or any of the ammo makers, even though "45LC" still persists in gun advertising to this day. The term ".455 Colt" WAS invented by Colt. The Canadian company Dominion loaded properly headstamped .455 Colt cartridges with the Webley's conical hollowbase 265-grain bullet, while Winchester used a slightly blunter version of the same bullet.

So what do you think? Colt officially gave it the family name, and its first name does begin with "45," but its thin rim is even larger in diameter than the .45 S&W/Schofield cartridge. The .455 Colt does chamber and fire in .45 Colt (and S&W) revolvers, but not vice versa. Is the .455 truly a member of the Colt family to be publicly acknowledged, a much older brother than the .45 Cowboy Special, older and shorter than even those commonly called old "short" .45 Colts? Or is it a "woods Colt" family members only privately speak of in hushed tones to one another?

For more info: StarlineBrass.com

Roger Smith
HIT OR MISS
Shotshells for Pistols and Rifles

What inspired the fad of factory-made pistol and rifle metallic cartridges loaded with birdshot? The appearance of Wild West shows feeding the fantasies and fascinations of the Easterners.

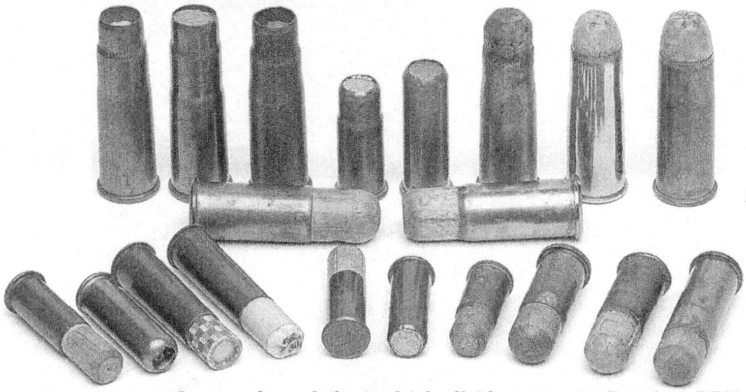

A Less Destructive Alternative

The original Buffalo Bill's Wild West (he refused to call it a "show") hit the road in 1883. Will Cody's original partner Doc Carver, a.k.a. "The Evil Spirit of the Plains," was a famous crack exhibition shooter who could hit nickels in the air with a rifle. World champion pigeon shooter Captain A.H. Bogardus demonstrated his shotgun prowess on clay pigeons. Cody, on horseback, blasted 2 ½" glass balls thrown into the air by an Indian riding 15 yards ahead.

After the first show, *the bills for broken windows and building damage downrange from the show grounds convinced Cody and Carver that shotshells should be used instead of bullets* for shooting the glass balls. They were able to persuade Winchester to make smoothbore 1873 lever-action rifles and special extra-length all-brass .44-40 cartridges containing ¼ oz. of number 7-1/2 shot for them.

Cody and ill-tempered Carver soon quarreled, split the show's property and Carver started his own competing show. Winchester now had at least two high-volume customers for their special guns and ammo, plus 50 or so one-ring circuses, most of which had exhibition shooters and the rodeos and inferior Western-style shows that were springing up to compete.

Five-foot, 110-lb. Annie Oakley and her husband Frank Butler joined Buffalo Bill's Wild West exposition in 1885 to replace Bogardus and his four sons. Annie had already developed her own idea of shooting while riding horseback when she and Frank toured with the Sells Brothers Circus in 1884. She promptly proved to the boys she

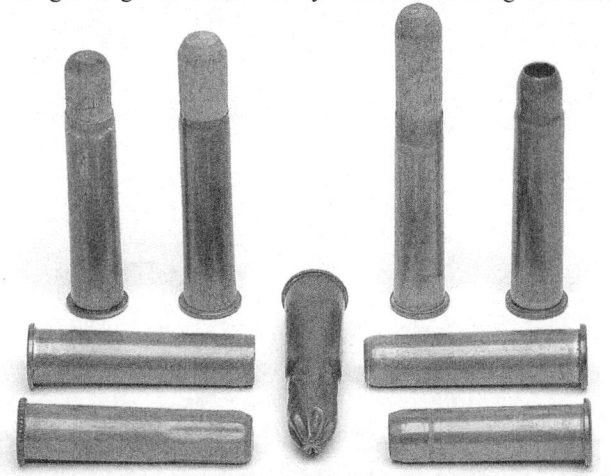

Back row, from left: Three versions of U.S. Cartridge full-length .38-40s, Winchester .32 S&W, Peters .38 Spl., UMC wood sabot .38-40, UMC and two paper-saboted .38-40s by American Cartridge Co.
Center, from left: Multi-ball Phoenix .44 Russian REM-UMC wood sabot .44 S&W Russian.
Front, from left: Remington .310 Short rimfire, .310 Long rimfire, Eley and Kynoch .310 centerfires with paper sabots, UMC .32 Short centerfire with sabot, UMC .32 Long rimfire by UMC; UMC .32 S&W, UMC .38 Short CF, American .38 Short rimfire and UMC .38 Long.

The best known of the rifle-caliber shotshells are the Army's .45-70 forager rounds, issued from the 1880s until just before World War I. Back row, from left: Three shot-filled wood bullets and bullet-shaped crimp to aid feeding. Center, from left: Egyptian .433. Front, from left: .45-70 Guard Cartridges loaded bigger shot for serious social intent.

After the UMC patent ran out, various manufacturers used hollow wood sabots for the .45-70 to hold the shot. Image: Kenneth McPheeters (McpheetersAntiqueMilitaria.com)

From left: Three versions of taper crimps used to hold the overshot cards in place, special Winchester long .44 WCF case ready to be formed into shot cartridges — REM-UMC .44-40 WCF with wood sabot, Peters full-length .38-40 and REM-UMC .32 WCF shot cartridges.

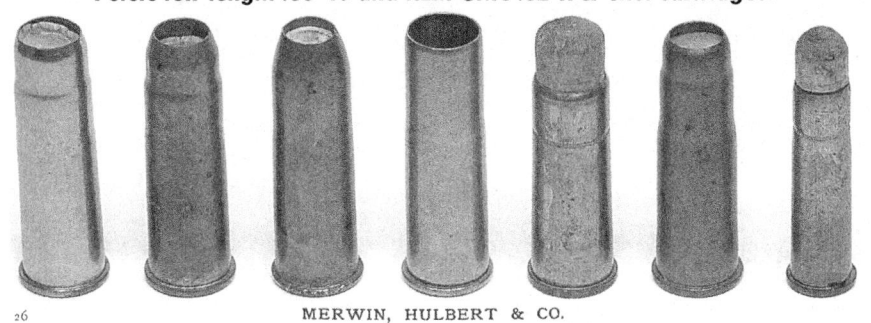

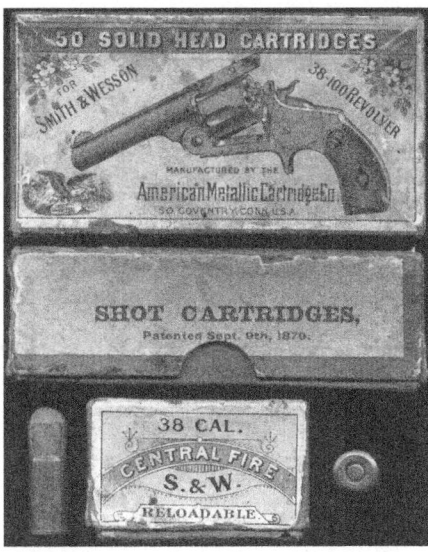

American Cartridge Company for the S&W 38-100 revolver. The paper sabot patent was granted to Henry W. Mason Sept. 9, 1879. He was involved with both American and the Phoenix Metallic Cartridge Company, as well as his own H.W. Mason cartridge company. Image: Guy Hildebrand (OldAmmo.com)

Merwin, Hulbert & Company offered private label brand American Cartridge Company rifle and revolver shot cartridges in their 1887 catalog. They were made by M, H & Co.'s subsidiary Phoenix Metallic Cartridge Company.

could easily break their balls riding sidesaddle using standard rifles and ammunition, with Frank throwing them. Her style, amazing skills and overall versatility with a pistol, rifle and shotgun quickly made her wildly popular with audiences.

Food for the Pot

Back in the real world, enlisted men's Army rations on the western frontier were notoriously bad. None could afford the prices officers paid the fort sutlers for their hauled-in canned goods. Most outposts had enlisted men's pitiful, scrawny gardens struggling for survival outside the walls.

In the early 1880s, the Army cobbled together some Springfield 20-gauge shotguns from old rifle parts and smoothbore barrels. Their intended use was for foraging small game to supplement the enlisted men's wretched rations. A special gun requiring a totally different cartridge was just more stress on an already strained supply system, however, and relatively few were made.

Shot for Springfields

Some bright light must have been impressed by the feats of the Wild West show shooters and thought that a shot cartridge for standard Springfield rifles would be the ideal solution. It was simple enough for the U.S. Army's Frankford Arsenal to produce, and much cheaper and far easier than supplying decent food. Apparently this dreamer-upper (and his superiors who approved the idea) *had no clue how quickly and how badly a rifled barrel scatters shot.*

Somewhere around the mid-1880s the Union Metallic Cartridge Company patented a hollow wooden bullet filled with birdshot, and the Frankford Arsenal loaded them in .45-70

Some bright light must have been impressed by the feats of the Wild West show shooters and thought a shot cartridge for standard Springfield rifles would be the ideal solution.

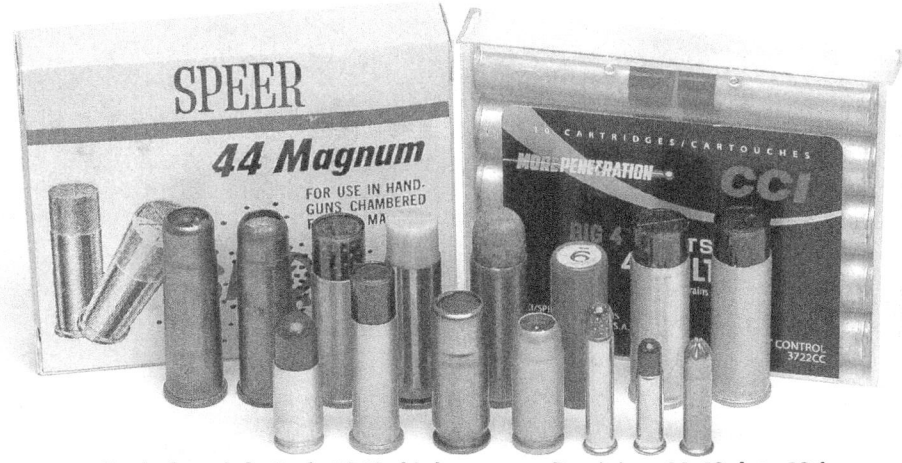

Back, from left: Early 1960s high-pressure Dominion .44-40, late 19th century Winchester .44 WCF rifle, CCI .44 Special, discontinued CCI .44 Magnum, early U.M.C. wood sabot .45 Colt, 1950s Alcan .45 Colt, CCI .45 Colts with red and blue capsules indicating #4 and #9 shot. Front, from left: CCI 9mm and .38 Special, government issue .45 ACP, CCI .40 S&W, CCI .22 WMR, CCI .22 LR, Winchester and Federal .22 LR.

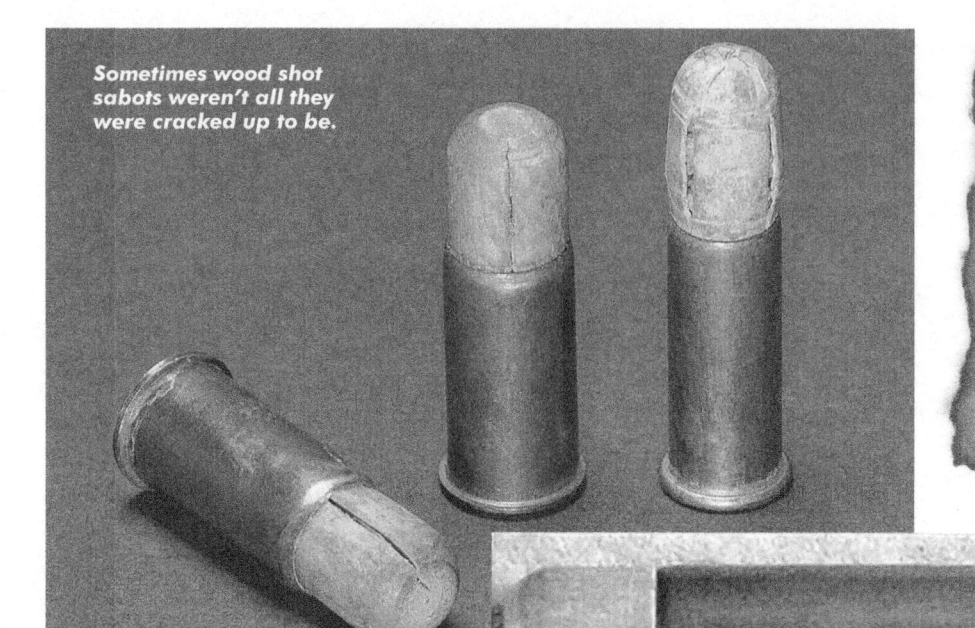

Sometimes wood shot sabots weren't all they were cracked up to be.

> The rifling of any gun barrel produces a doughnut pattern with a hole in the middle so large at 20 yards a rabbit could easily escape unscathed.

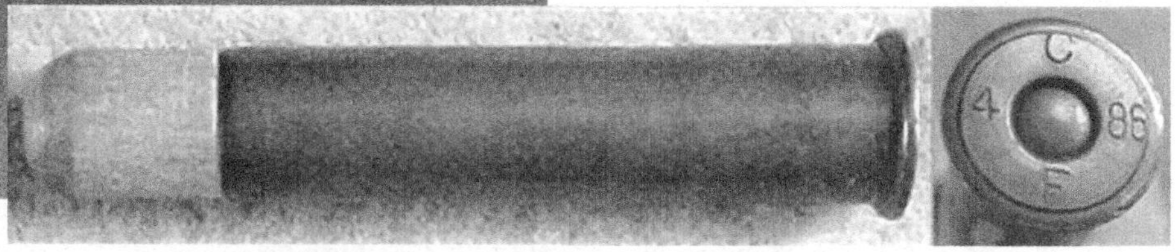

A Benet-primed .45-70 forager cartridge. The "F" in the headstamp indicates it came from the Frankford Arsenal. The "C" means it contains the 55-grain Cavalry powder charge, not the Infantry's 70-grain charge. "4" and "86" mean it was made in April 1886. Image: Kenneth McPheeters (McPheetersAntiqueMilitaria.com)

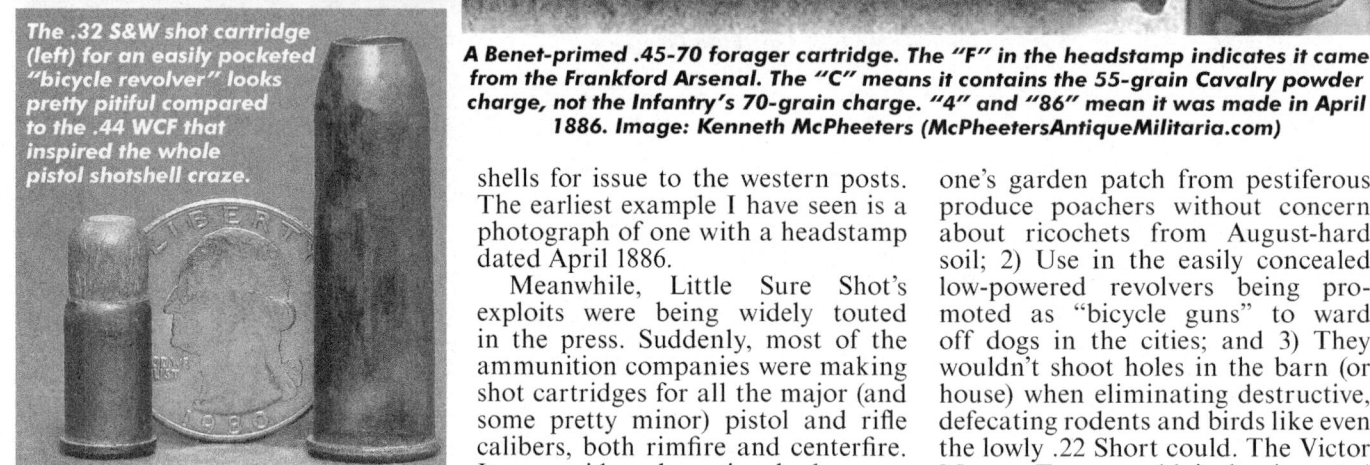

The .32 S&W shot cartridge (left) for an easily pocketed "bicycle revolver" looks pretty pitiful compared to the .44 WCF that inspired the whole pistol shotshell craze.

The CCI .45 Colt shot cartridge holds approximately ⅓ oz (146 grains) of #9 shot. A modern recreation of the old .45-70 forager cartridge holds ½ oz. (219 grains), now with no wood sabot needed and plenty of room leftover, thanks to far less bulky smokeless powder.

Clear plastic overshot wads like these on 1950-'60s Dominion .44-40 shotshells were a 1931 innovation by Peters.

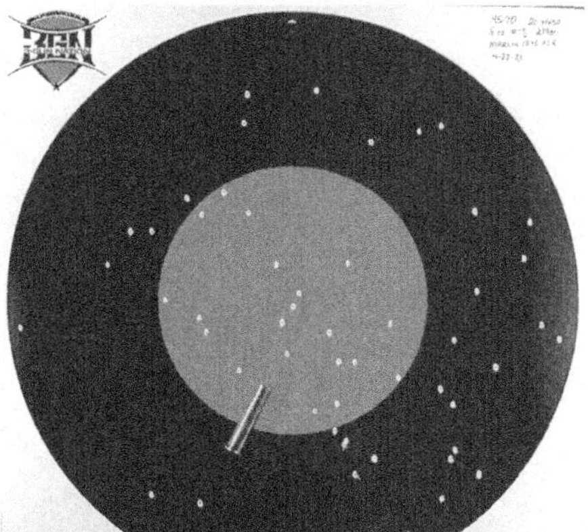

A modern .45-70 shot cartridge containing ½ oz. of #7-1/2 shot fired from 1:20" twist 24" Marlin at 20 yards. The old cavalry Trapdoor Springfields had a 22" barrel with a 1:22" twist rate. Of 174 pellets, 35 hit the 17" black ring, and only 20 hit the 8" red ring.

shells for issue to the western posts. The earliest example I have seen is a photograph of one with a headstamp dated April 1886.

Meanwhile, Little Sure Shot's exploits were being widely touted in the press. Suddenly, most of the ammunition companies were making shot cartridges for all the major (and some pretty minor) pistol and rifle calibers, both rimfire and centerfire. It was an idea whose time had come.

The logic seems to have run along three main themes: 1) Unless your nearest neighbor was at least a mile away, they were safer to use to protect one's garden patch from pestiferous produce poachers without concern about ricochets from August-hard soil; 2) Use in the easily concealed low-powered revolvers being promoted as "bicycle guns" to ward off dogs in the cities; and 3) They wouldn't shoot holes in the barn (or house) when eliminating destructive, defecating rodents and birds like even the lowly .22 Short could. The Victor Mouse Trap wouldn't be invented until 1898.

During the 1898 Spanish-American War in Cuba and the Philippines, field rations weren't any better. Frankford was busy manufacturing cartridges for the new bolt-action .30 Army (.30-40 Krag) and was no longer making .45-70 ammunition for the Army. Instead, Winchester, U.S. Cartridge Co. and UMC received contracts to make both ball and forager ammo to feed the old single-shot Springfields still in service.

Performance?

So how well did the shot cartridge idea work? The modern-day version of those forager cartridges would be shooting .410 shotgun shells in a single-shot .45-70. A bit of internet research echoes what J.G. Kirk wrote in 1936: Regardless of caliber, the rifling of any gun barrel produces a doughnut pattern with a hole in the middle so large at 20 yards a rabbit could easily escape unscathed. It's why reduced-power .45-70 reloads using old-fashioned 146-grain round balls were much preferred for small game. (For more information see my article "Collar Buttons for the .45-70 Gentleman" in the 2021 *GUNS Magazine Old West Special Edition*.)

As Kirk concluded in Phil Sharpe's 1937 book, *Complete Guide to Handloading*, "Accordingly, the ammunition makers abandoned these [shot] loads and today they are rarely found."

However, shot cartridges with far more serious social intent were the grandfathers of today's .410 self-defense shells — the .45-70 "Guard Cartridges" made by Peters, UMC and Winchester. These suckers were loaded with multiple balls of various sizes for the specific intent of using them on people. Not only in jails and prisons on those attempting unauthorized egress but also on those with less than honorable intent during clandestine visits to prohibited places where a wild 405-grain lead slug might be too hazardous to the workers and equipment. Think powder factories, ammunition plants, armories and other defense-industry facilities. *There was even a special version for Gatling guns for unruly mobs.*

Epilogue

The demise of the pistol and rifle shotshell cartridge craze can be seen in the pages of Remington-UMC catalogs. On the eve of WWI, their 1918–1919 catalog listed six rimfire cartridges from .22 through .41 caliber, and 19 centerfire metallic pistol and rifle shot cartridges. After the war, the 1923 catalog was down to three rimfire cartridges and nine centerfires. Just prior to WWII, the 1941 catalog offered .22 and .32 rimfires and just two centerfires, both in .44. After the war, all that was left was the .22 LR.

The idea never completely went away, though. Alcan made some in the 1950s and Dominion in Canada was still making .44-40s in the late 1960s. CCI currently offers pistol cartridges in several calibers with shot-filled plastic capsules, as well as the capsules to make your own for up-close snake and small-rodent control. My opinion is the .45 Colt is the best candidate for this. I was unaware of Kirk's opinion written in the 1930s (when smoothbore handguns were still legal) that the .45 Colt case made the best revolver shot cartridges and were highly effective small-game loads out to 20 yards. In spite of rifled barrels nowadays, the classic best is still hard to beat, eh?

Special thanks to Joe St. Charles, (seller OldWestCartridges on Gunbroker.com), Guy Hildebrand, (OldAmmo.com) and Kenneth L. McPheeters (McPheetersAntiqueMilitaria.com) for furthering my education by generously sharing their knowledge with me, and for selling me duplicate cartridges from their collections to use for this article.

A face full or three of birdshot quickly delivered from one's bicycle gun like this H&R 1909 Bicycle Revolver or the short-barreled S&W Safety Hammerless would discourage most dogs and miscreants.

H. & R. "Bicycle Hammerless" Revolver.

Description. 32 Caliber. 5 Shot. 2 Inch Barrel. Weight 12 Ounces. C. F. S. & W. Cartridge. Finish- Nickel or Blue.

This revolver is small of frame, compact, effective, reliable and safe. Has independent cylinder stop and automatic shell ejecting device. Cocks without catch or drag, and as the name indicates, has no hammer to catch in the clothing when hurriedly withdrawn.

GUNS OLD WEST SPECIAL EDITION 2022 AD INDEX

American Gunsmithing Institute	35
American Handgunner Subscription	35
FMG Special Editions	3, 97, 123
Bond Arms	23
Dixie Gun Works	55
GUNS Magazine Subscription	75
Low-Pro Products	6
Mernickle Custom Holsters	3
Northern Precision Custom Bullets	59
Prolix Lubricant	84
Redding Reloading Equipment	6
Skinner Sights LLC	131
Slickbald Customs	17
Taylor's & Company	2
Turnbull Restoration	7
Uberti-USA	2
Volkmann Precision Inc.	29

John Taffin
FAVORITES:
Replica Single Action Sixguns

This pair of stainless steel Cimarron .45 Model Ps have been fitted with Buffalo Brothers faux ivory grips.

Choosing favorites is not always easy. Sometimes I can pick one favorite while other times it will be several. With that in mind we herein look at "Taffin's Top Replica Single Action Sixguns." Please note they are replicas, not clones — the latter is a biological term and until we can get steel sixguns to reproduce themselves it's the wrong terminology.

The early copies of the Colt Single Action revolvers were somewhat lacking in authenticity. In fact, all those early "Single Actions" were fitted with brass grip frames such as had originally only been found on cap-and-ball revolvers. The original Colt Model of 1873 was always fitted with a steel grip frame. With the coming of Cowboy Action Shooting and also the diligent work of several importers, both the authenticity and quality of replica sixguns and leverguns have improved tremendously. Actions are much smoother and finishes look more authentic, instead of the very poor quality case coloring found in the 1970s. Dimensions and shape are also held very closely to what they were in the 1870s. Most importantly, grip frames on Single Action Army replicas are now steel.

Excellent Work

Today's Single Action Army replicas are so well finished one has to look carefully to make sure they are actually foreign "Colts" and not domestic versions. I am particularly fond of the 7 ½" copies when chambered in .45 Colt, .44-40, .38-40 and .32-20 which were the top four chamberings of the original Single Actions. However, in this piece I'll be looking at other replica Single Actions. Before the 1873 Peacemaker arrived, Colt offered both Richards and Richards-Mason Cartridge Conversions on their 1860 Army percussion revolvers by fitting new cylinders and loading gates. These were followed by the 1871-72 Open Top. All of these revolvers were topless, that is there was no top strap. All of these are now, or have been, available as replicas and they make a most interesting shooting connection with the past. Because of their construction definitely use standard loads only!

Two of my favorite replica Single Actions are a mismatched pair somewhat out of the ordinary. These Ultimate Single Actions are from American Western Arms (AWA) and deviate from the norm in they are fitted with octagon barrels, one in 7 ½" and the other 10". They have also been tuned by master single-action sixgunsmith Jim Martin, who also fitted them with one-piece mesquite grips. To add icing to the cake these .44-40 sixguns are also fitted with .44 Special cylinders, allowing a lot of room for experimentation. With either cylinder, both of these sixguns are excellent shooters.

In the movie *Tombstone* Kurt Russell, as Wyatt Earp, uses a 10" Buntline Special with a special medallion on the right grip frame. This sixgun was provided by Cimarron Firearms and

Replicas of the 1875 are available in blue or nickel plating; these are by EMF and Navy Arms, respectively.

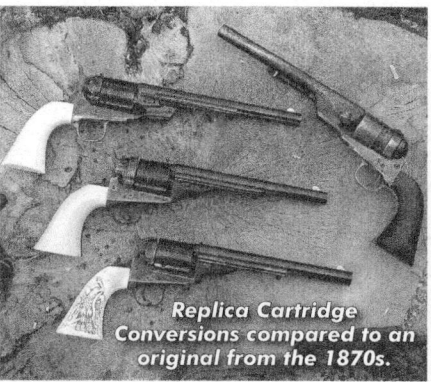

Replica Cartridge Conversions compared to an original from the 1870s.

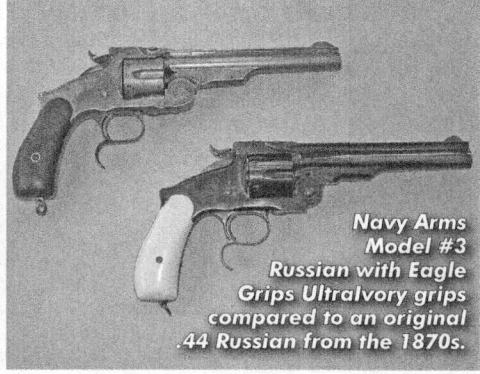

Navy Arms Model #3 Russian with Eagle Grips Ultralvory grips compared to an original .44 Russian from the 1870s.

since the movie has been available to shooters. For me the 10" balances much better and handles much easier than the 12" Colt Buntline Special. It also shoots exceptionally well. In fact, I have probably experienced at least 100 replica sixguns in the past 35 years or so, and I have yet to find one that doesn't shoot well. This speaks very well of the Italian firearms industry.

Stainless

Most importers are now offering stainless steel Single Action Army replicas, however it was Cimarron Firearms that led the way. Why stainless steel in a traditional single action? As an outdoor finish it's pretty hard to beat stainless steel. Also I like to shoot black powder loads, and although cleanup is not as tedious as some would have us believe, it still requires more care than when using smokeless powder loads. Stainless steel is not only easier to clean, it also makes it easier to see the places that remain to be cleaned.

Cimarron is importing Uberti-manufactured stainless steel Model Ps in .45 Colt in the three standard barrel lengths of 4 ¾", 5 ½" and 7 ½". I have been shooting a pair of 7 ½" .45s for nearly 10 years now. My almost perennial complaint about all replicas is the grade of wood used in the stocks. The grips are just about perfect as to shape and size and they are well fitted to the frame, however the color and finish is just not quite right.

For my pair of 7 ½" stainless steel Cimarrons I selected antique faux ivory stocks from Buffalo Brothers. One is fitted with stocks with a Longhorn steer skull on both sides, while a double Mexican Eagle decorates both panels of the other. The combination of polished stainless steel and antique ivory is most pleasing to the eye and the carving on the grips provides a comfortable non-slip surface for the hands.

S&W Arrives

More than two decades ago Navy Arms gave us the first Smith & Wesson replica, with the Schofield Model. These Top-Breaks hearken to 1875 when the originals were chambered in .45 S&W, a shorter cartridge than the .45 Colt. Today's versions are mostly chambered in .45 Colt, however .45 S&W/Schofield ammunition is available from Black Hills, and Starline offers brass to allow more authentic shooting of this excellent sixgun. My pair is fitted with Buffalo Brothers grips.

The Schofield was the beginning S&W replica. Next came the New Model Russian chambered in, what else, but the historic and magnificent .44 Russian. The Navy Arms New Model Russian — or Model 3 Russian — is a faithful copy of the original, finished overall in a deep blue-black finish set off with a case-colored hammer, trigger guard and locking latch. Factory stocks are smooth European walnut, however while quite comfortable do not add anything to the appearance of this fine replica sixgun. This was however quite easily corrected with a pair of Eagle's UltraIvory grips which, when combined with the dark finish of the .44 Russian, provides an appearance which is quite striking.

All original .44 Russian brass is of the folded head, or balloon style originally used with black powder. I believe the manufacture of this brass stopped either just prior to or shortly after World War II. Now 60-plus years later, Starline offers solid head .44 Russian brass for ammunition companies as well as reloaders. Black Hills was the first to offer modern .44 Russian ammunition, with a 210-grain load clocking right at 750 fps.

Changes

Cartridge-firing, big-bore sixguns arrived shortly after the end of the Civil War. First came the Smith & Wesson American Model #3 in 1870. Colt followed with the 1871-72 Open-Top and then the Single Action Army in 1873. Remington followed with the Model 1875 two years later, with a large contract of 10,000 pieces for the Egyptian government. The 7 ½" 1st Model 1875s were chambered in .44 Remington, however it was joined by both the .45 Colt and .44-40 in 1878 and both of the latter are available today in replica form.

The Remington Single Action Model 1875 looks much like a Colt but there are differences. The grip frame of the Remington is part of the main frame, resulting in a more solid and possibly stronger sixgun. The trigger guard is brass, separate from the main frame, and it does not form part of the front grip strap as on the Colt. The Remington achieves its unique appearance from a web under the barrel running from the end of ejector housing to the front of the frame, and the cylinder pin also runs all the way to the end of the ejector tube.

Navy Arms was the first to offer the 1875 replica and I acquired a pair of 7 ½" nickel-plated versions more than a quarter-century back. These were chambered in .45 Colt and .44-40. I had both of them fitted with rifle-style front sights with a gold bead and used the latter for spotlighting jack rabbits when it was still possible to get a permit to hunt our southern desert.

In later years I have added a third .45 Colt 7 ½" Remington 1875 from EMF, another excellent shooting sixgun which has been fitted with Texas Star checkered faux ivory grips from Buffalo Brothers. We not only have replica 1875 Remingtons available but we also can enjoy shooting the 1890s version which has a more streamlined web under the barrel. A pair of these in .45 Colt with 5 ¾" barrels and Buffalo Brothers antique-looking, faux ivory grips, complete with age cracks, are most attractive and good shooting pair of single actions.

Enjoy today's excellent classic sixgun copies and don't let the fact they're not "real" stop you. They're very real — and any Old West cowboy would have been proud to own one.

The first S&W Single Action replica was the Schofield Model, here fitted with Buffalo Brothers grips (left). Replica Single Actions fitted with 1860 Army grip frames: USPFA .44 Special in Tombstone Leather holster flanked by a Cimarron original finish .44-40 and a second USPFA chambered in .45 Colt (below).

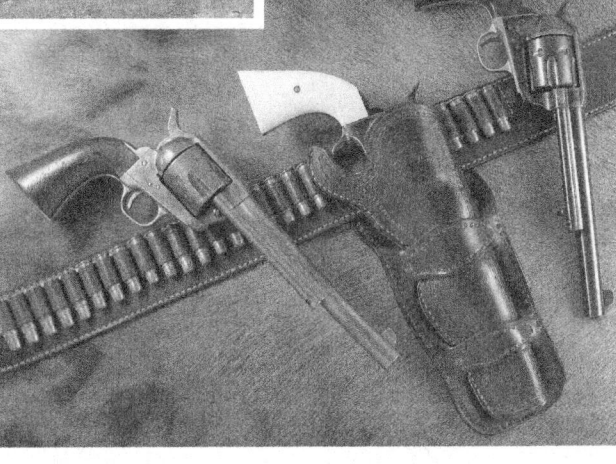

The Complete Collection Of GUNCRANK DIARIES

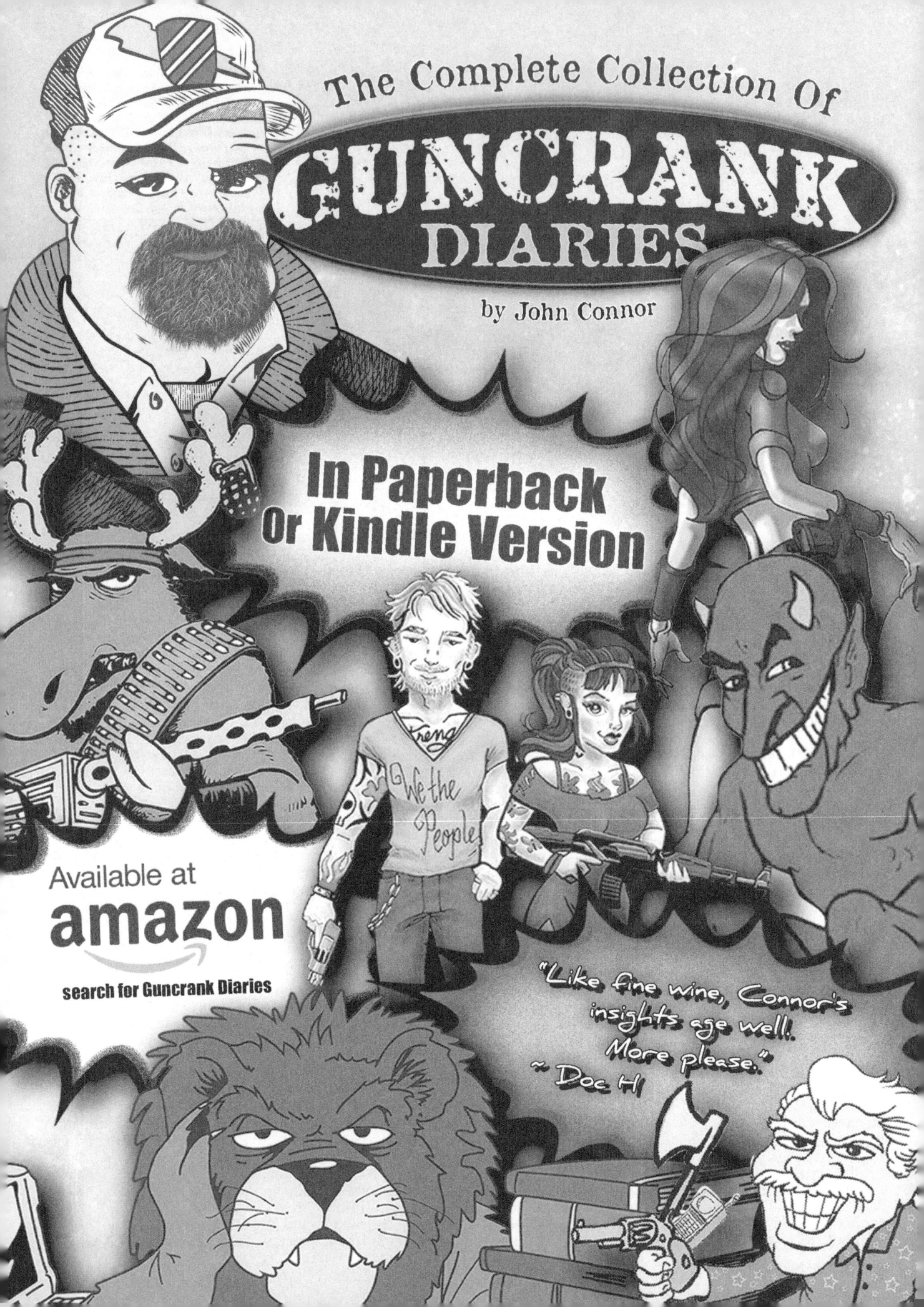

by John Connor

In Paperback Or Kindle Version

Available at
amazon
search for Guncrank Diaries

"Like fine wine, Connor's insights age well. More please."
~ Doc H

Skinner® Sights LLC

THE SKINNER HTF GARMENT BAG

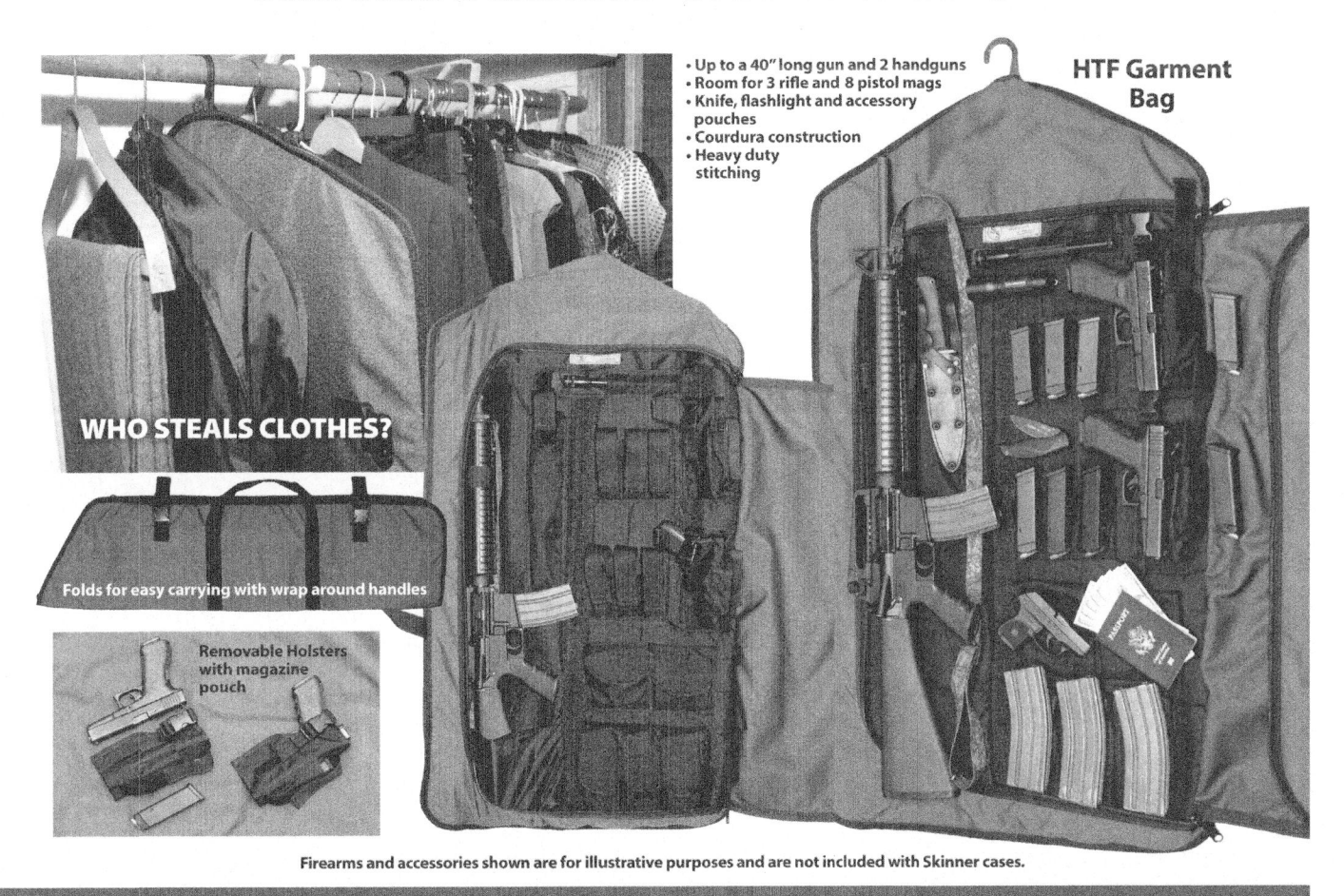

- Up to a 40" long gun and 2 handguns
- Room for 3 rifle and 8 pistol mags
- Knife, flashlight and accessory pouches
- Courdura construction
- Heavy duty stitching

HTF Garment Bag

WHO STEALS CLOTHES?

Folds for easy carrying with wrap around handles

Removable Holsters with magazine pouch

Firearms and accessories shown are for illustrative purposes and are not included with Skinner cases.

THE SKINNER® SIGHTS "HTF" BAG ALLOWS YOUR FIREPOWER TO BE "CONCEALED IN PLAIN SIGHT" YET READY IN CASE OF AN EMERGENCY.

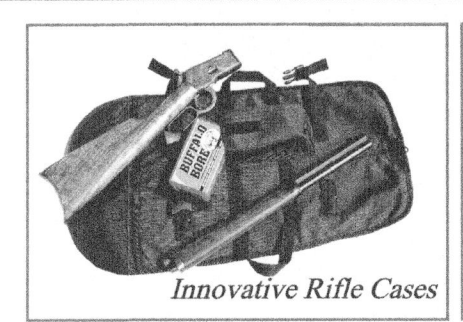

Innovative Rifle Cases

PEEP SIGHTS FOR RIFLES

SKINNER SIGHTS ™

BIG BOY "EXPRESS"

www.skinnersights.com

MACHINED FROM SOLID BARSTOCK

MADE IN U.S.A PRODUCT

PLEASE SEE OUR WEBSITE FOR MORE INFORMATION
WWW.SKINNERSIGHTS.COM
406-745-4570 • P.O. Box 1810, St. Ignatius, MT 59865

Printed in Great Britain
by Amazon